MW00786821

THE PINBALL COMPENDIUM
1930s-1960s
MICHAEL SHALHOUB
Schiffer Publishing Ltd
4880 Lower Valley Road, Atglen, PA 19310 USA

DEDICATION

There are a few people I would like to dedicate this book to.

My good friend Lindsay Morgan who sadly lost the fight with cancer on February 16, 2001 at the age of thirty-six. Lindsay loved his toys and pinballs but his biggest love of all was his lovely wife Robyn; Dana, age nine; and the little champ Jenson, age five.

Pinball historian, Richard Bueschel, a man I never met but who has encouraged me in so many ways. Sadly passed away on April 18, 1998.

To my heroes, the designers and artists who have captivated millions with their creative and inspirational work. They were the backbone in the success of this industry.

To my family, my wife Anne for her support and encouragement; my four beautiful children, Anthony, Ashley, Cameron, Andrew, whom I have been away from while spending hours writing. I promise to make it up to you.

Shortly before this book was published, the terrible events of September 11, 2001 took place in America. I would also like to dedicate this book to all the innocent victims and their families. We will forever remember them in our prayers. God bless America.

Library of Congress Control Number: 2001096990

Designed by John P. Cheek
Cover design by Bruce M. Waters
Type set in Lithograph/Korinna BT

ISBN: 0-7643-1527-7
Printed in China
1 2 3 4

Published by Schiffer Publishing Ltd.
4880 Lower Valley Road
Atglen, PA 19310
Phone: (610) 593-1777; Fax: (610) 593-2002
E-mail: Schifferbk@aol.com
Please visit our web site catalog at
www.schifferbooks.com
We are always looking for people to write books on new and related subjects. If you have an idea for a book, please contact us at the above address.

This book may be purchased from the publisher.
Include $3.95 for shipping.
Please try your bookstore first.
You may write for a free catalog.

In Europe, Schiffer books are distributed by
Bushwood Books
6 Marksbury Avenue
Kew Gardens
Surrey TW9 4JF England
Phone: 44 (0) 20 8392 8585
Fax: 44 (0) 20 8392 9876
E-mail: Bushwd@aol.com
Free postage in the UK. Europe: air mail at cost.

CONTENTS

ACKNOWLEDGMENTS

I would like to thank the following people who have contributed their time in creating this book.

Alvin Gottlieb and Gary Stern, who have been so inspirational and helpful.

The great designers who have shared their stories and given me priceless photos: Ed Cebula, Norm Clark, Harvey Heiss, Joe Kaminkow, Greg Kmiec, Steve Kordek, Ed Krynski, Pat Lawler, Wendell McAdams, Wayne Neyens, Barry Oursler, John Osborne, Mark Ritchie, Steve Ritchie, Adolf Seitz, Roger Sharpe, and John Tredeau.

The great artists who have shared there stories with me: Dave Christensen, Paul Faris, Greg Freres, Margaret Hudson, Jerry Kelley, Kevin O'Connor, and John Youssi.

Historian and pinball collector Russ Jensen, who has supplied information and photos for the book. Thanks for your inspiration, Russ.

Photography: Gary Brettell, Joshua Tunks, and I took the majority of the photos in the book.

Pinball collectors: I appreciate Alan Tate and Jason Douglas letting me photograph their machines. Thanks for your time and effort, as all these machines were stacked to the ceiling.

Computer whiz: Michael Bowden – I couldn't have compiled the book without him.

People who have contributed their stories, photos and time in this book: Shay Assad, Bob Borden, Paul Brisbane, Rob Carruthers, Ron Coover, BJ Cunningham, Gene Cunningham, Jason Douglas, John Edwards, Steve Engel, Lee Feldwick, Tim Ferrante, Peter Frasciello, Barry Gooding, Alvin Gottlieb, Jeff Grummel, Gordon Hasse, Mark Jackson, Russ Jensen, Troy Meredith, Del Reiss, Jim Schelberg, Herb Silver, Chris Soulidis, Gary Stern, Bruce Thompson, Ron Tyler, Gordon Williams, Robert Young, and Steve Young.

Special note: I had originally planned for one book on pinballs, but due to the amount of pictures and text my publisher and I decided to split it in two (this book will cover the 1930s to the 1960s and the second book will cover the 1970s to the present). While writing the book, I contacted many people who have done tremendous work in the industry. They gave me their time and shared stories about themselves. Many had extremely busy schedules but all sent photos and stories to me. I regret not being able to share all of their stories in this book, but those not included here will hopefully be in the next volume. All of these wonderful people have helped me so much; they have encouraged me and given me support. I cannot thank them enough for what they have done for me.

INTRODUCTION

First, a little about myself: I am thirty-nine years old and married to my lovely wife, Anne. I have four children: Anthony, twelve; Ashley, ten; Cameron, seven; and Andrew, six, who wants to be a pinball master when he grows up. I have lived in Sydney, Australia all my life and have always loved pinballs.

At the early age of six my fascination with the silverball had already begun. I can still remember playing a woodrail pinball called *KEWPIE DOLL* made in 1960. I have always been a collector of football cards, cars, soldiers, and stamps. I always wanted to have the most. My father (God bless him) had a fast food store that was next door to an engineering firm where I would obtain my ball bearings and make billycarts. I had over ten carts at a time. When I started collecting pinballs, I had a burning desire to have a huge collection. In 1985, I purchased two pinball machines: a 1969 Target Pool and a 1972 Wild Life. What started as a bit of fun ended up as a serious business, as there are now over four hundred machines in my collection. God only knows if I lived in the States how many machines I would own.

The famous Luna Park in Sydney, which opened in October 1935. The origins lie in America, as Coney Island, New York, was the home of the amusement park.

Sydneysiders enjoying a day at Luna Park.

My beautiful family: me, Anthony, Anne, Ashley, Cameron, Andrew, and Brandy the Jack Russell.

I remember asking my father if I could store machines in his garage for a couple of weeks. Well, that was over ten years ago and he still can't get his car in there. As a kid growing up I would go to the local hangout instead of going to church on Sunday mornings and play a 1972 Williams Spanish Eyes. I would win games and sell them off.

Growing up, I would play games in milk bars, poolrooms, laundromats, snooker rooms, and amusement centers. In Australia today, the pinballs have disappeared and you would be lucky to even find one in an amusement center. My favorite pinball parlors where I spent a lot of my time were "Big Top," located in George St., Sydney; Crystal palace, located next to Town Hall station; and the unforgettable "Coney Island" at Luna Park. I have a passion more for the electromechanical games and the way they play – I prefer the artwork and love the sound of the bell and chimes.

I asked my father to store a few machines – he is still waiting to get the car in the garage.

My love for the pinball machine led me to set up my business, "Pinball Master Sales and Service," repairing and selling machines from the 1930s to 2000. In November 2000 I decided I couldn't keep up with the demand of pinball repairs and sales. I was spending less time working on and restoring my favorite games, so I sold part of my business to the Pinball Warehouse.

In the years of being in business, I have made a lot of friends and have seen some great collections of pinballs and novelty games. A very good friend of mine, Alan Tate, is setting up a pinball museum on the Gold Coast, Queensland, Australia. A majority of the machines shown in this book will be in the museum. This will be the first of its kind in Australia, as people can come see and play these rare games.

Alan Tate and me. It won't be long and the first pinball museum will be built in Australia.

I have made a lot of friends in the States. I am the madman down under who buys machines without looking at them. I have bought machines from the West Coast to the East Coast of America. I attended the Chicago Coin Show last November (2000) and had the time of my life, looking at machines I had only seen in books. Prior to going to the States, I had purchased a few machines and was having some delivered to the show so I could then load them onto a container. As people were walking past the trucks and vans they would see old machines in the back and would inquire, "Are those machines for sale?" The owner would reply that they were sold and when the inquirers asked who had bought them they were told "Michael from Australia." I loved Chicago and found the people very kind and friendly, even though they thought my accent was a little strange. I would like to thank Paul Sides, my good friend from Memphis who was with me in Chicago and helped me load the container. The funny thing is that we both had hernia operations – Paul in January and me in February – and it was hard work loading the container. My thanks to JJ for helping out as well.

While writing this book I kept thinking of the late Richard Bueschel and his great work. It then dawned on me to contact another great historian and pinball collector, Russ Jensen. What followed were the greatest moments in my life, as through Russ I was able to make contact with some of the greatest designers in the pinball industry. These great men contributed so much to this book. A few of them are Wayne Neyens, Harvey Heiss, Ed Krynski, Steve Kordek, Norm Clark, Wendell McAdams, Ed Cebula, Joe Kaminkow, Greg Kmiec, Steve Ritchie, Mark Ritchie, Pat Lawlor, Adolph Seitz, Barry Oursler, Ed Cebula, and John Osborne. I cannot express in words what I felt inside as I was speaking to them. I kept reminding them that it was both an honor and a privilege to talk to them. These men have designed games that millions of people around the world have enjoyed.

The first person I spoke with was Wayne Neyens; it will be a moment in my life that I will never forget. I couldn't believe I had made contact with this great designer. I told him about the book and asked if he would like to be part of it. He was happy to help me and I thank him for that. While speaking with Wayne, I mentioned that I knew my history on pinball machines; he then asked if I was up to a couple of trivia questions. I replied yes, so he first asked "What year was Niagara released?" I told him 1951 and described the game. The next question was when Oklahoma was released. I replied 1961 and told him I loved the two roto-targets on the machine. I think he was impressed with me and that put me on top of the world and gave me a huge confidence boost. The games designed by these men will be around for a very long time.

Another idea came to me – I decided to ask fellow collectors to take photos of themselves and share stories of how they got started. The day after I spoke to Wayne Neyens, I was talking to my friend Shay Assad, who has a great collection of machines as well, and was telling him about my phone conversation with Wayne. I mentioned that if I could meet anyone in the world I would choose him. Shay replied, "Mike, you've lost the plot."

Another great person I spoke with was Alvin Gottlieb, who has been involved with pinball machines all his life. I asked him to do a little tribute to his father, the founder of the Gottlieb company. It was also a pleasure talking with Gary Stern, who I rung in the middle of an important meeting. I cannot express my joy in speaking to him. I asked him to do a tribute to his father as well, another pioneer in the industry. I have contacted other great designers and artists and their stories will be found throughout the book. I have a great passion for these machines and I feel they should be documented from the beginning till now.

There are many others who share a passion for these machines. One is Rob Berk, who started the "Pinball Expos" first held in Chicago in 1985 and now held annually. I asked him what the inspiration was behind the Expos and he replied, "I wanted to honor my heroes." That he did with four of the greatest designers attending the first show: Steve Kordek, Wayne Neyens, Harvey Heiss, and Norm Clark. This was the first time at any convention that this had happened. I would like to congratulate you Rob, as you have inspired many people around the world including me.

For many years the idea of putting out a book on pinballs has crossed my mind. Now I have finally done it. I hope you enjoy the book.

God Bless,
Michael Shalhoub

Photographer Joshua Tunks.

Photographer Gary Brettell.

It was hard work getting the machines ready – thank God the photos turned out.

MY WIFE'S THOUGHTS

Hi, my name is Anne and I have been married to my husband for fourteen years. Michael asked me to write a small section of what I thought of his hobby. I would like to start by saying I am very proud of him writing this book – he has spent many hours locked in a room writing and planning.

When I met him he had some pinballs at his father' s house; as soon as we got married and moved in together so did the machines. I don't know how many wives, girlfriends, or partners can relate to this but the machines had to stay in his games room or garage – a few times he would sweeten me up and I would let a couple drift into the lounge but only for a few days.

I remember him buying a pinball machine called Nags. He told me he paid a $100 for it, but personally I wouldn't have paid $10 as it was a mess. A friend of Michael's, Jason Douglas, was over one day dropping off some machines and commented that this machine Nags was a gem. I asked him how much the machine had cost Michael. He told me he had paid $1000 for it and that it was a great buy. When Michael arrived home I nearly killed him.

On his thirtieth birthday I held a surprise birthday party for him. At the time, a favorite machine of his was Diamond Lill, so I ordered a cake for him in the shape of a pinball called Diamond Lill. He loved it and didn't want to cut it.

I played pinballs growing up and loved them too. The one game I particularly enjoyed was Joker Poker and Michael had one in the games room. We would have a pinball challenge every night. That was before the kids came along. Sometimes it was boring playing with him, as the ball would never leave the playfield and all I would do is watch him play. I remember one evening we went to the movies and they had pinballs and video games there. Well, he had to have a quick game. The machine was Indiana Jones and with one coin he played and played that machine, winning free games. I had to drag him away from it as the movie was about to start.

Our youngest son, Andrew, wants to be like his dad and when anyone asks him what do you want to be when you grow up he replies "a pinball master." Michael has given him tools and lets him tinker on machines that are going to get stripped. Michael recently sold his work van and my son was devastated, as this was going to be his car when he grew up.

My favorite modern game is Lethal Weapon 3. I must admit I love the movies as well. My husband has recently contacted some designers of pinballs from the early days. That's all he talks about; he rings them every day and every morning checks his e-mails as he gets around twenty per day.

Michael loves his pinballs and is always giving advice over the phone, which never stops ringing. I remember one night at Bible Study a question was asked as to what enjoyment you have in your life today. He answered that his enjoyment was his family and his work. This surprised a few people – one person couldn't believe that his work gave him enjoyment. My husband is very enthusiastic about his work and when it comes to pinballs he is a little boy enjoying a passion that he truly loves. I missed him last year when he went to Chicago and he has been asked to also attend this year's pinball Expo. I wish I could be there with him but it is difficult with our four young children. I am very proud of you, Michael.

—Anne Shalhoub

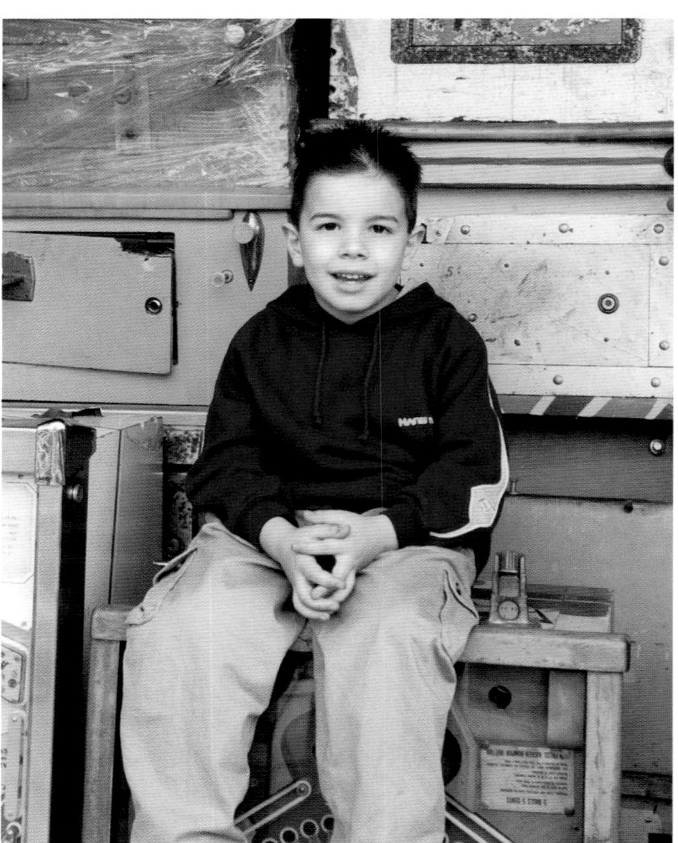

This is my baby, who wants to follow in his dad's footprints and become a "Pinball Master."

CONDITION AND PRICING OF PINBALL MACHINES

In the past, people have valued pinball machines from class one (excellent condition) to class five (poor condition). Today, a class five machine can be restored to be a class one game. We have Herb Silver at Fabulous Fantasies, Steve Engel at Mayfair Amusement, Gordon Williams and Lee Feldwick at Pinball Rescue reproducing pinball backglasses, playfield mylars and plastics. Steve Young at Pinball Resource is reproducing pinball parts that bring pinballs back to life.

I have had machines professionally restored by repainting the cabinet, rechroming the metal parts, replacing the backglass with a reproduction, and fully shopping it out. The end result is a pinball looking like it did the day it was manufactured. It's not cheap but it is well worth it, as the outcome is a class one machine. Bob Borden, at Bordens Amusements in the Unites States, also specializes in pinball restoration. All his restored machines are in the class one range.

The values of the pinball machines in this book are for class one. There may be a few that are not in this class yet, but when restored they will be. Every day around the world, there are people reliving their childhood and buying pinballs. Once the bug hits, they start collecting and feel that they own a part of history. There is no turning back.

Surprisingly, most of the machines today are in the home market; gone are the days when pinballs were located in all amusement centers, laundromats, and shopping centers. In arcades today there are high tech video games and redemption machines. My two young children only want to play the games with ticket awards. I spend $20 to receive a toy worth .50 cents. It is a shame that pinballs are not in circulation like they were decades ago. Gary Stern at Stern Pinball is still producing these games today. He is the last man standing and understands the business better than anyone on this planet. Good luck to Gary and the team, let's hope he can revive this pastime that has survived for so long.

The Internet has generated a great interest in these machines, as it has brought the world together. If you are new to the game of pinballs or haven't discovered them yet, turn on your computer and type in http://www.mrpinball.com. Daina Pettit maintains one of the most popular pinball sites on the Internet.

What is a machine worth? It is worth what someone is willing to pay for it. I see these games as reflecting the past. They capture a part of American history that has influenced millions and millions around the world. Eventually, all machines will be purchased by collectors and there will be none left to buy, so owning these machines today is a great investment.

CHAPTER ONE
THE 1930S

The pinball machines we enjoy today are the result of creative and technical progression since the turn of the century. Modern day machines evolved from a simple table game called Bagatelle, which surfaced in the 1700s. Somewhere between billiards and pinball, the popular parlor game entertained the nineteenth century's wealthy. Early machines were for private entertainment and were originally handmade from wood and metal mechanical devices. The first commercially produced Bagatelle was *LOG CABIN*, manufactured by the Caille Brothers in 1901. The early arcades gave the coin-operated amusement industry its launch. Originally found in travelling carnivals, the games arcade soon became a permanent fixture. The promise of fun and family entertainment all for a penny gave rise to the early "Penny Arcades," which derived their name from the single penny dropped into the slot.

Pinball pioneer David Gottlieb began commercially producing "grip testers" called *HUSKY GRIP GAUGE* and thus D.Gottlieb & Co. was formed in 1927. The company was located at 4318 West Chicago Avenue in Chicago. In 1931, Gottlieb purchased the rights to manufacture and distribute bingo type games from the Bingo Novelty Company. In December 1931, the company released *BAFFLE BALL*, which became Gottleib's first mass produced pinball game. Not only did it escape the costly royalties tied to bingo, it became the first ever commercially successful, coin-operated game. It blitzed its early rivals and transformed D. Gottleib & Co. into the first financially successful pinball production company. Its popularity with both players and operators turned this fad into a financially viable industry.

With over fifty thousand orders, Gottleib was unable to keep up with the market's demand. This saw Raymond T. Maloney, a partner with his Lion Manufacturing Company employed as a distributor for *BAFFLE BALL*, enter the pinball scene. Ray Maloney, being a young, innovative businessman like Gottlieb, recognized the pinball machine's potential. With the added bonus of his company's distribution experience and contacts throughout the States, he seized his opportunity in March of 1932 with the new game *BALLYHOO*. Maloney's own design, *BALLYHOO* produced some fifty thousand machines. Like *BAFFLE BALL*, it was an instant success. Having taken the game's name from an early thirties magazine, Maloney went on to call his company Bally, reflecting the machine's popularity. Bally was located at 304-16 West Erie Street in Chicago.

The competition between the two companies continued with the introduction of a special hole on the playfield that would double the score. Gottlieb called it baffle hole and Bally called it the bally hole. This further fueled the feud between Gottlieb and Bally as Dave Gottlieb felt betrayed and his game copied.

Hot on their heels, in 1932, the French released *LE DIAMANT* and the Germans released *TURA BALL*, both very similar to Gottlieb's *BAFFLE BALL* and Bally's *BALLYHOO*.

Tura Ball. *Alan Tate collection.* $700.

By now pinball machines had evolved to small countertop models that could be placed anywhere. Whilst the early manufacturers operated business from their backyards, the popularity and increased demand for these games saw the establishment of factories mass producing this product. The Mills Novelty Company produced pinballs and played an important role in their development. Herbert S. Mills and his sons owned the company, which was located at 4100 Fullerton Avenue in Chicago. One of the first pinballs they produced was *MILLS OFFICIAL*, released in July 1932. This was a countertop game and measured 24" in length and 12-1/2" in width. The player received ten balls for a penny.

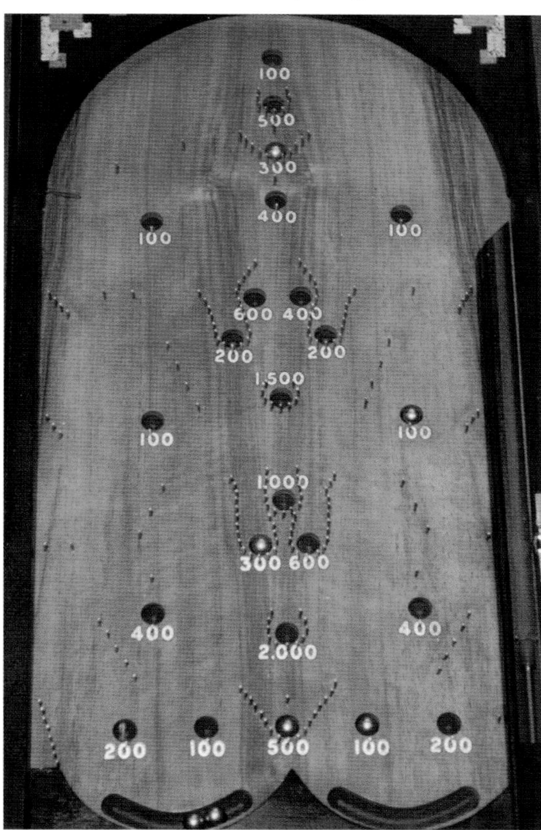

Mills Official. *Paul Brisbane collection.* $700.

There were other types of amusement machines already on the market but it is said that "pinball machines hit the Americans faster than the depression did." The pinball's outstanding popularity caused other major amusement companies to diversify into manufacturing pinballs as well. For example, Mills and Rockola Manufacturing (located at 617-31 Jackson Blvd. in Chicago) both started manufacturing pinball machines as well as jukeboxes. The Exhibit Supply Company, also known for its novelty games, commenced producing them as well. Today, Rockola still makes jukeboxes. Mills' first pinball machine was released in February 1932 and their last one, *OWL*, was released in December 1942. Their early game *OFFICIAL PIN TABLE*, from July 1932, used smaller balls and featured a gold ball that would double its score. It caught the attention of people who couldn' t resist putting in their coins! With no mechanical scoring developed yet, the player would add up his or her own points. Cash or prizes like cigars were awarded when certain scores were reached.

The market soon became flooded to satisfy the tremendous demand for these machines – there were over one hundred new companies producing these games. The majority have disappeared and are no longer heard of, such as The A.B.C Machine Company, which only released two machines, *BELL SKILL* and *JOCKEY CLUB*, both in 1932. Another company, Barok, also released only two machines: *ROLLET* in December 1931 and *HOOEY BALL* in February 1932. Lynwood Mfg. Co. produced its only one, *ROLLING A GATE*, that same month.

Due to this extensive flooding of the market and therefore believing that *FIVE STAR FINAL* (released in May 1932) would be his last game, David Gottlieb set out to make it different. This game introduced a double field arrangement with the ball travelling in a figure eight before entering the field of play. It was a huge hit for Gottlieb. The original was a countertop model known as *FIVE STAR JUNIOR*. This was followed by the *FIVE STAR SENIOR*, which was larger and had legs. Rival company Bally copied this game as well, releasing *SCREWY* one month later. The resulting huge demand, particularly

Five Star Final. *Alan Tate collection.* $750.

from Europe, prompted Gottlieb to establish a new factory in Winnipeg called the Canadian Gottlieb Company, initially producing *FIVE STAR* and *CLOVERLEAF* in October. The two machines pictured here were both bought from a collector in Winnipeg, Canada and are two of my favorite early games. David Gottlieb was a pioneer of the pinball game's creation and early development. He was not afraid to take risks and his company dominated the pinball market for decades.

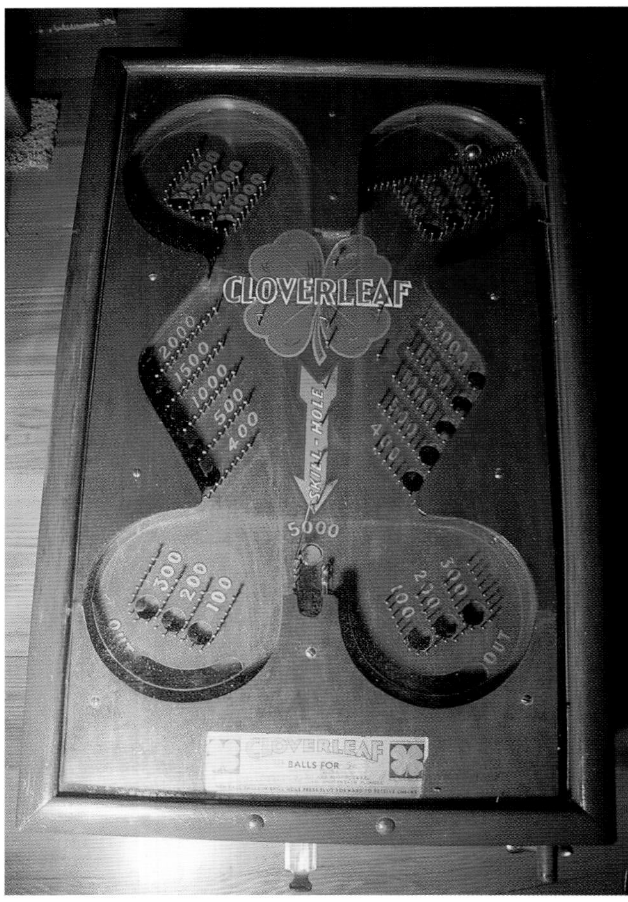

Cloverleaf. *Alan Tate collection.* $800.

As new games came on the market a new industry emerged, that of the pinball operator. The operator would put a machine on location, splitting the profits with the owner of the venue –usually fifty/fifty. As novelty faded and earnings decreased, the operator would rotate games from other locations. The operator bought his machines from distributors who were established all over the country. Soon there were distributors and operators all over the world enjoying what the Americans had. Today machines from this period are highly collectible, symbolizing true American history.

Machines of this era consisted of a cabinet into which a coin was inserted, enabling the player to push the coin mechanism forward, which released the balls to the ball lift position. The player would then fire the balls onto the playfield, where there were holes surrounded by pins, each hole attracting a different score. At the end of the game the players would tally up their score. Most of the machines from 1932 were very basic.

A major change happened to the industry in August 1933, when the release of Rockola's *JIGSAW* was the first to emphasize artwork. This game celebrated the World's Fair held in San Francisco. The bottom of the playfield featured a jigsaw puzzle. As balls landed in the appropriate holes, a piece of the puzzle would flip over, revealing the picture and awarding a different score. This machine is considered amongst collectors as the ultimate classic pinball of the 1930s and would be the highlight of any collection today.

Jigsaw. *Alan Tate collection.* $2000.

Bally Manufacturing released the first automatic payout pinball machine, *ROCKET*, in September 1933. It was designed by Herman Seiden. Being the first to pay out cash meant players were now competing for money. Prior to this, pinball machines had been classed as novelty games but now some became gambling machines.

It was the pinball machine *CONTACT*, released by Pacific Manufacturing in April 1934, that saw the first use of electricity. A dry cell battery supplied it. Designed by Harry Williams, this machine was made in California. Another innovation present in the design of this game was the use of the bell. Players were now able to see the ball ejected from a special hole, ringing a bell as it sprang back onto the playfield, making this machine an instant success. This caused Harry Williams to move to Chicago, the pinball capital of the world. Here, his first major work in the industry was to become chief engineer at Rockola in 1935. He then moved to Bally in 1937. Another Williams invention was the pedestal tilt, first appearing on Bally's *SIGNAL*. It was during his employment at Bally that Williams met Lyn Durant. Together they left Bally and went to the Exhibit Supply Company.

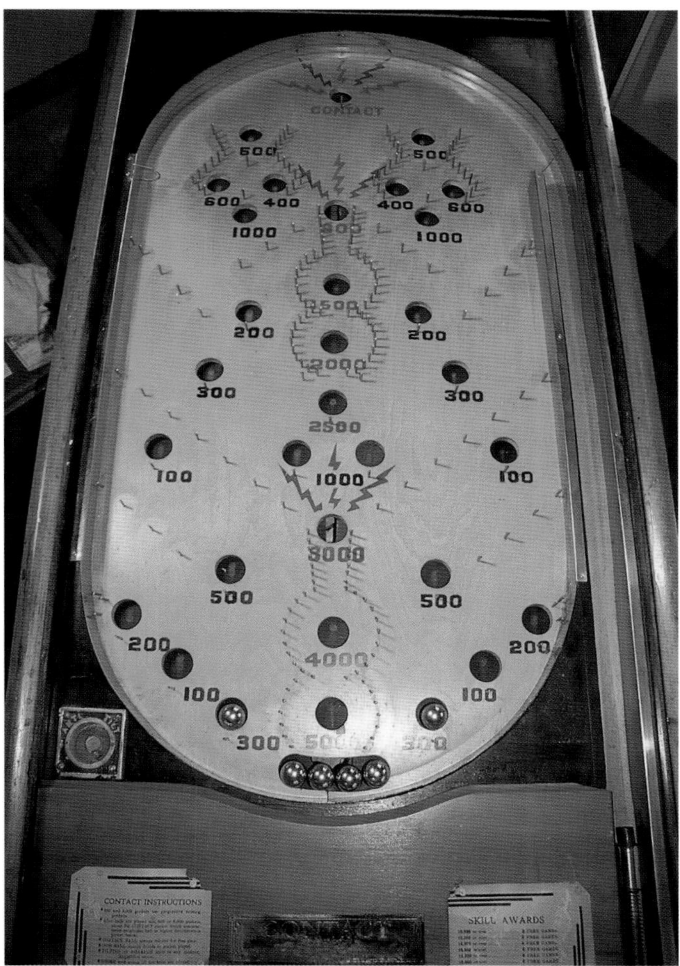

Contact. *Alan Tate collection.* $800.

Another company producing pinball machines in this period was Western Equipment & Supply Company. They produced their first machine, called *FUTURITY*, in May 1934 and their last, called *FEED BAG*, in July 1938. The company was owned and run by Jimmy Johnson, who had a big influence on the industry. He once told the *Coin Machine Journal* "I don't feel I had done anything particularly worthy of note except that I either had

Jimmy Johnson, founder of Western Equipment. *Courtesy Wayne Neyens.*

the ability or good fortune to select good numbers and more especially to select good men with which to build an organization." In January 1935, the company released *PUT 'N' TAKE*, which was a very successful game. Jimmy hung the mantle of recognition around the shoulders of his chief engineer, Eric Bjornander. He presented him with a round trip ticket to his native Sweden in recognition of his ability as an engineer and loyalty as an employee. This is an example of the generosity of Jimmy Johnson, who had a big heart. A few of the employees at the company would in years to come have a great creative input in the pinball industry. Such men were Lyn Durant, Harry Mabs, and Wayne Neyens.

Rockola's next machine was *WORLD SERIES*, released in May 1934. Truly an exceptional machine for its time, it featured a mechanical disk that would advance the ball onto a baseball diamond on the playfield. The machine was advertised before it came onto the market. Due to the nature of this industry's competition, *WORLD SERIES* was soon copied by The Genco Company who renamed it *OFFICIAL BASEBALL*. Genco was actually able to release their version one month before

Rockola's original *WORLD SERIES* hit the market. They even copied Rockola's advertising. This resulted in Rockola suing Genco, eventually winning the case. Rockola's *TOTALITE* was released in August 1937. The rollovers are set at an angle, challenging the player's skill to score points.

World Series. *Alan Tate collection.* $1800.

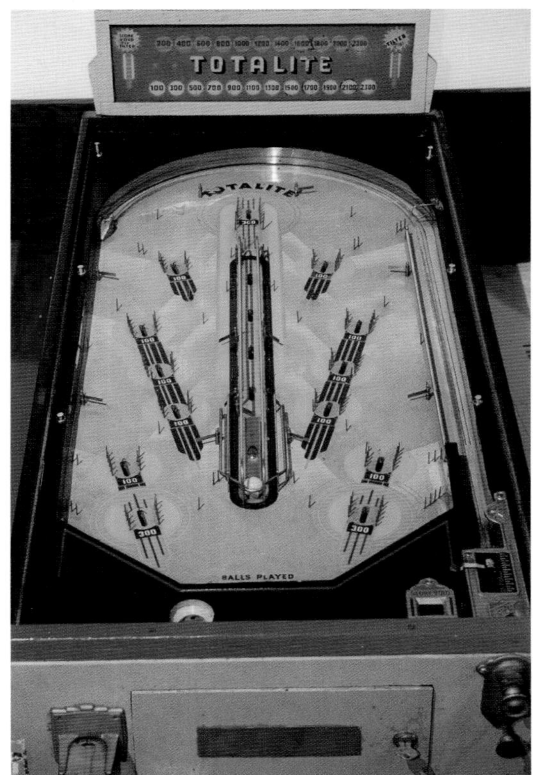

Totalite. *Jason Douglas collection.* $800.

In early 1934, the Exhibit Supply Company had been contracted to make *CONTACT* for Pacific Amusement Manufacturing. As the royalties being paid to Harry Williams were low, he renamed his game *LIGHTNING*, which became Exhibit Supply Company's first pinball machine in June 1934. The game was similar to *CONTACT*. Notice the red on the top of the playfield, which made the game stand out. The company released *GOLDEN GATE* in August.

Lightning. *Author's collection.* $800.

Another dominant contender in the 1930s was Stoner Manufacturing, started in 1933 by Marvin Stoner and his two sons, Ted and Harry. Their first game was *AMBASSADOR*, released in February. The following year in July they released *SUPER 8*, truly a classic game. The chipping of the glass balls used in *SUPER 8* became a problem and they were soon replaced by steel ones. Players then quickly caught onto the idea of using a magnet to manipulate the steel balls into the highest scoring holes. The manufacturers overcame this by changing the balls to nickel-plated bronze.

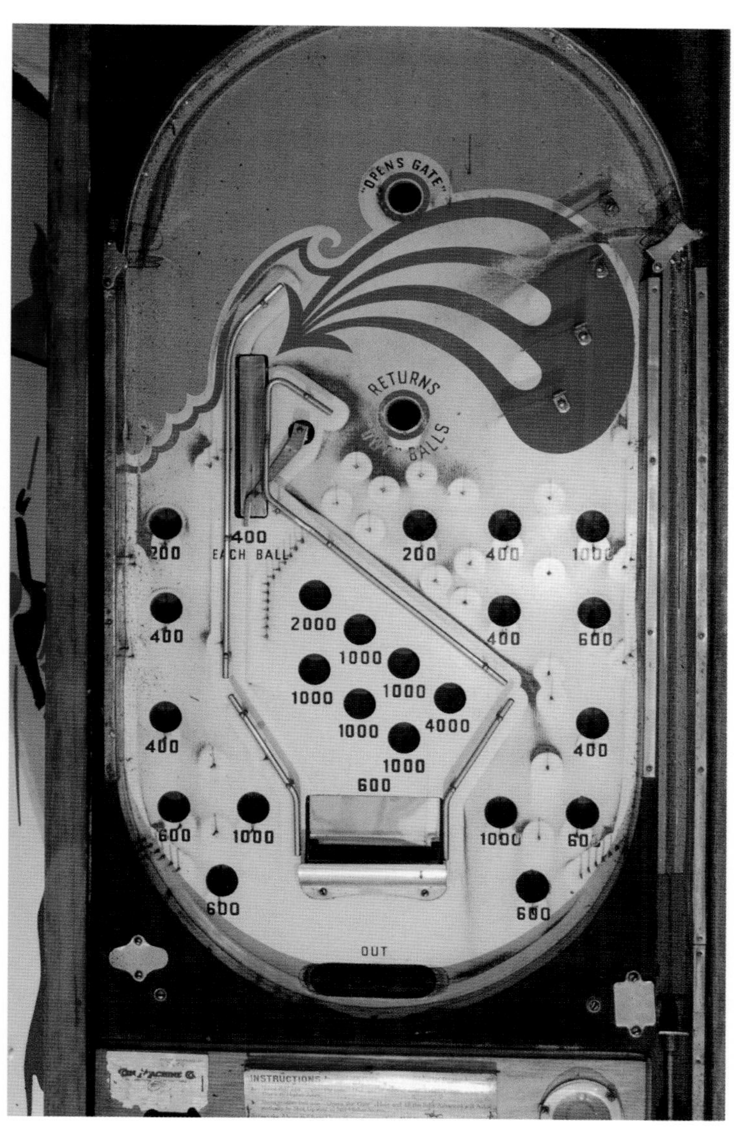

Golden Gate. *Jason Douglas collection*. $800.

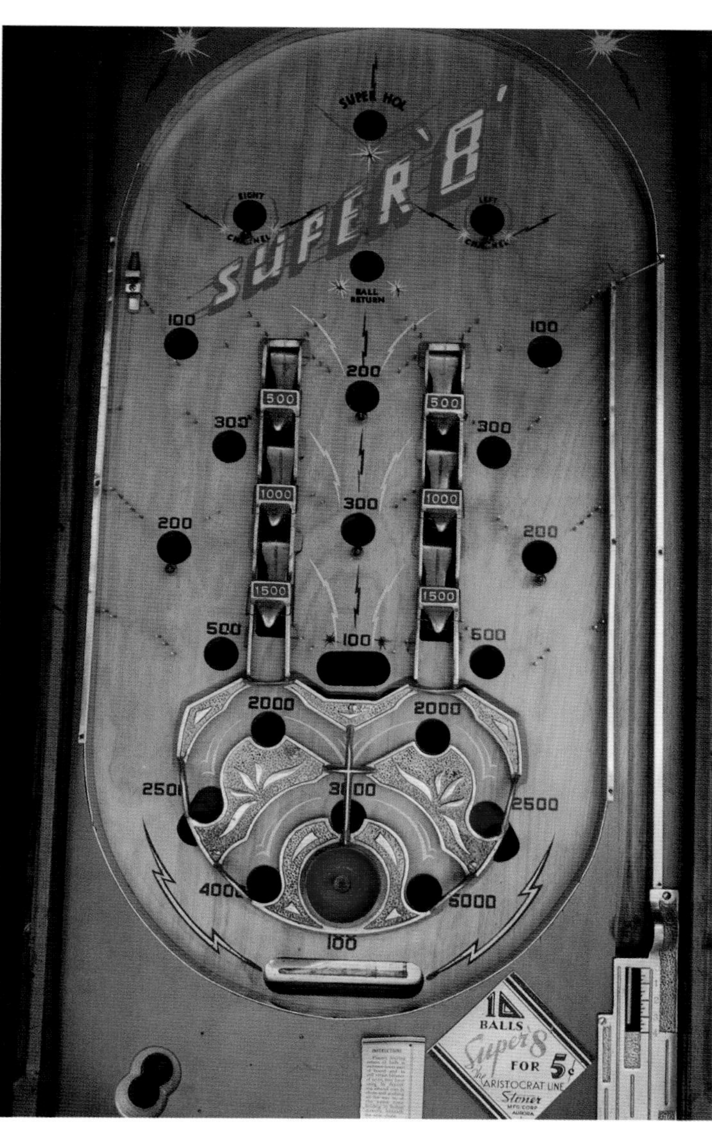

Super 8. *Author's collection*. $900.

The founder of Bally, Ray Maloney, never saw himself as a games designer. Having a team of tremendous designers working for the company saw Bally release some unforgettable games. One of these was *FLEET*, released in June 1934. It had a kicking cannon that shot out balls into the action hole at the top of the machine, where they would advance to the next cannon. When all seven cannons were loaded the excitement started, as they would all fire out balls at once. This resulted in seven balls simultaneously in play, causing the machine to be a great success for Bally. They released a smaller version in August 1934 called *FLEET JUNIOR*.

Pinballs placed on counters caused a problem for the owner of the location, as players often gathered around the machine, but the introduction of legs solved this problem. Now these machines could be placed in a corner, out of the way of general customers. This saw the machines grow in size; an example is seen on Gottlieb's *CYCLONE* of February 1935. In April 1937, Genco released one of the last countertops, called *RUNNING WILD*, which was ideal in smaller locations.

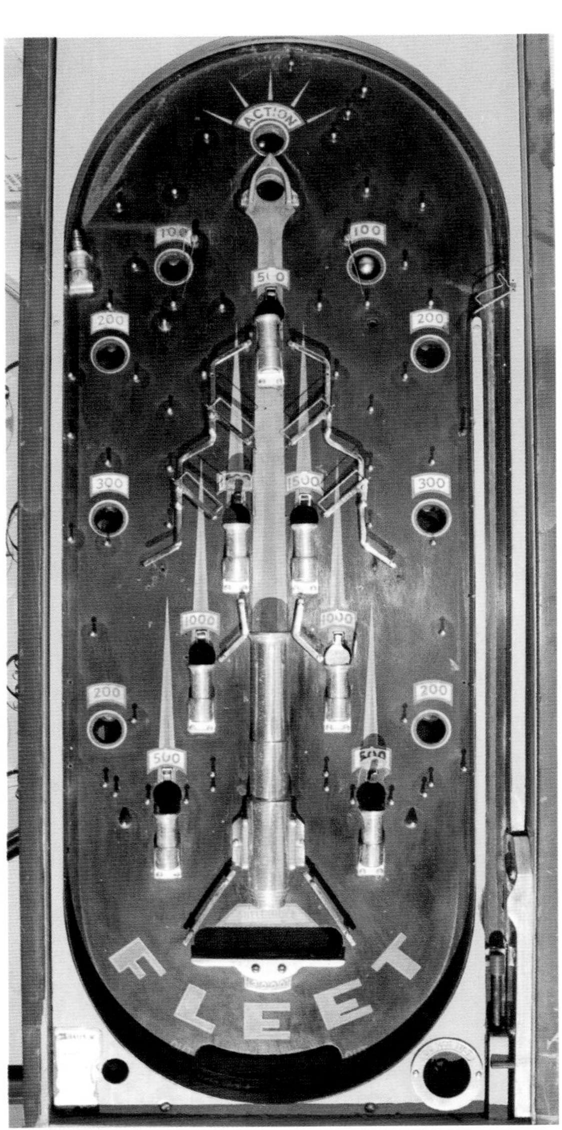

Fleet. *Jason Douglas collection*. $750.

Cyclone. *Author's collection*. $800.

Running Wild. *Paul Brisbane collection.* $950.

The backglass was introduced to attract players, first appearing on Genco's *CRISS CROSS A-LITE*, released in February 1935. The introduction of electricity to pinballs enabled the Chicago Coin Company to innovate the use of lights on the playfield with the release of *BEAM LITE* in March 1935.

Bally was currently focused on both the novelty aspects of the game and payout games. Gottlieb produced a few payout games in the 1930s but returned to novelty games. Bally was dominating the market with payout pinballs; a popular game with players was *BALLY BONUS*, released in February 1936. Had Gottlieb pursued the same gambling path as Bally, I feel the pinball industry would have had a disastrous end. As it was, the Gottlieb company was setting the standards during this period and did so well into the seventies.

Stoner released *TURF CHAMP* in January 1936. This horse racing theme payout was very popular with players. The player would first select his horse, then deposit the coin. The machine randomly selected the odds, shown on the upper left of the playfield. Getting the ball in the selected horse slot awarded the player coins in the tray, in front of the cabinet.

Payout version of Bally Classic. *Author's collection.* $1000.

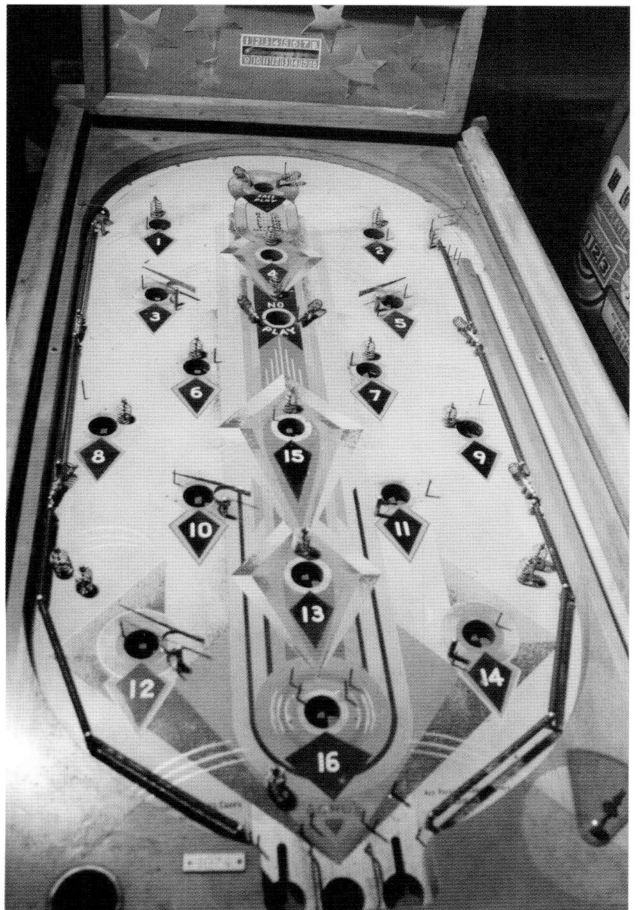

Turf Champ. *Author's collection.* $1500.

Bally released *ROUNDUP* in July 1936. This was a one ball payout machine that flashed two red lights at the bottom of the playfield when you inserted a coin. If either light remained lit, the mystery pocket paid out special tokens. This machine also featured a coin escalator that enabled the operator to see if any slugs were deposited into the machine. Up to twenty coins could be seen before entering the cash box. The artwork on *ROUNDUP* was particularly eye-catching. Bally had a lot of success with one-ball machines, dominating the field in this particular area. The company released *CLASSIC*, another payout machine, in August 1937. The unique feature on this game was the stainless steel playfield and the mirrored backglass.

Classic. *Jason Douglas collection.* $1000.

Roundup. *Alan Tate collection.* $1000.

Bumper. *Jason Douglas collection.* $1200.

A revolution began when Bally released *BUMPER* in December 1936. The first machine to use a bumper, it also featured a backboard totaliser. Every time the bumper was hit, a projection device would project the score onto the center of the backglass. The score would advance on the backglass as each bumper was hit. This new feature was an instant success for the company. Bally released *SKIPPER* in February 1937, a payout version of *BUMPER*. The playfield and cabinet on both machines were identical. The difference was that the backglass of *SKIPPER* had the score offset to the right; on the left was the free game window (which would increase as you reached scores, set by the operators). At the end of the game the player had the choice of either playing off the free games or pushing a button at the bottom of the cabinet, releasing coins into the swing out cup.

Skipper. *Jason Douglas collection.* $1200.

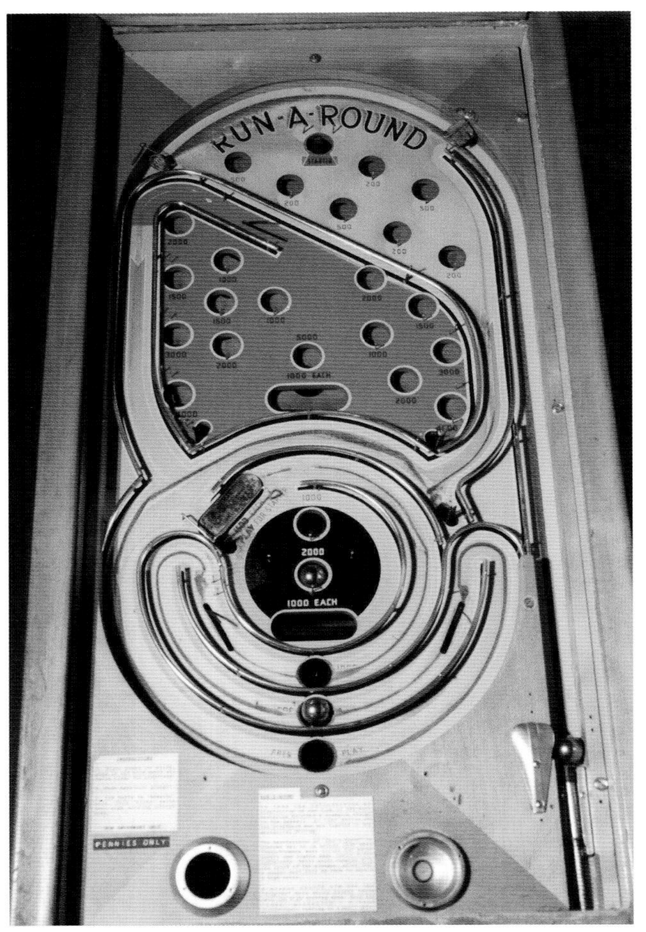

Run-a-Round. *Alan Tate collection.* $900.

Lightning. *Alan Tate collection.* $1300.

A game I could find no history on was *RUN-A-ROUND*. I asked historian Russ Jensen if he could identify this game, but to my disappointment he to couldn' t find any record of it. It is my opinion that *RUN-A-ROUND* was manufactured in the mid 1930s.

The Mills Novelty Company was also a major slot machine maker; their machines today are sought after by collectors worldwide. The majority of their machines in this period were payouts. They released *FLASHER* in November 1937. A slot machine in a pinball body, the mechanism for this game was cleverly put into the cabinet. The playfield glass is mirrored and looks like a large slot machine. The company continued making pinballs until *OWL*, their last in December 1942.

Exhibit Supply released *LIGHTNING* in August 1938. It had no bumpers or holes on the playfield but relied instead on magnets under the playfield that would bounce the ball around. *LIGHTNING* had a half size backglass with progressive scoring on it. Another feature was a roll over button on the bottom center of the playfield that would score 1000 points, ringing a bell inside the machine.

Champion. *Alan Tate collection.* $1200.

Backglasses were now becoming a common feature on pinball machines. Backglass artwork played the important role of attracting and inciting players – most being men in this era – to deposit their coins. By 1939, the backglass had doubled in size to accommodate bigger and better designs. One of the most impressive backglasses of the period was that on *CHAMPION*. Released by Bally in August 1939, it featured backglass animation. The two girls on the left and right tower would progress towards the water as scores were made.

Stoner released *CHUBBIE* in November 1938 and *SNOOKS* in May 1939. Both these games had the feature that as you got the numbers out on the playfield, the corresponding number would light on the backglass. Another feature was the "return out ball:" when the

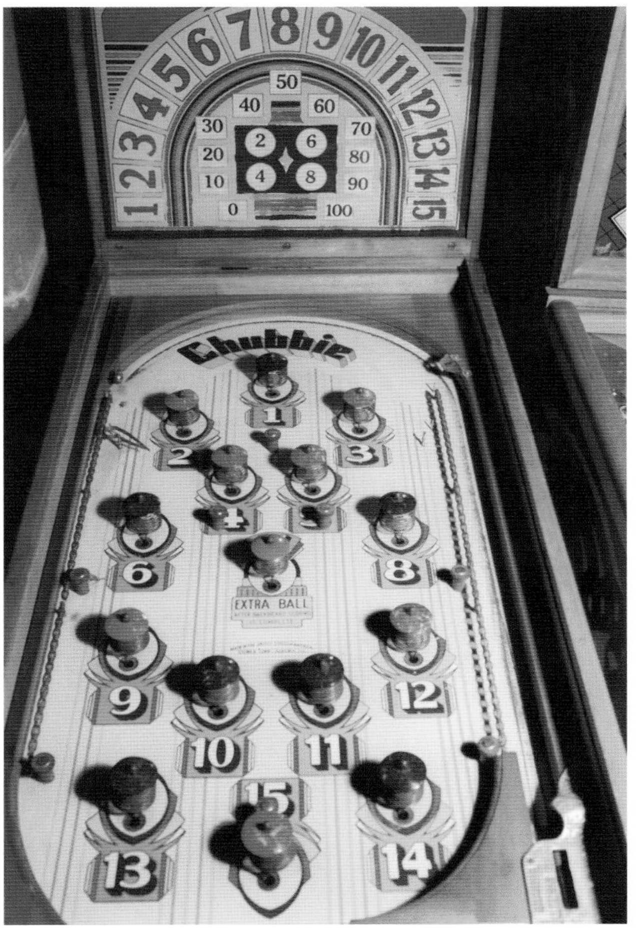

Chubbie. *Alan Tate collection.* $1000.

bumper was lit and then hit by the ball, the player received a free ball. The aim on both games was to complete the sequence 1-15.

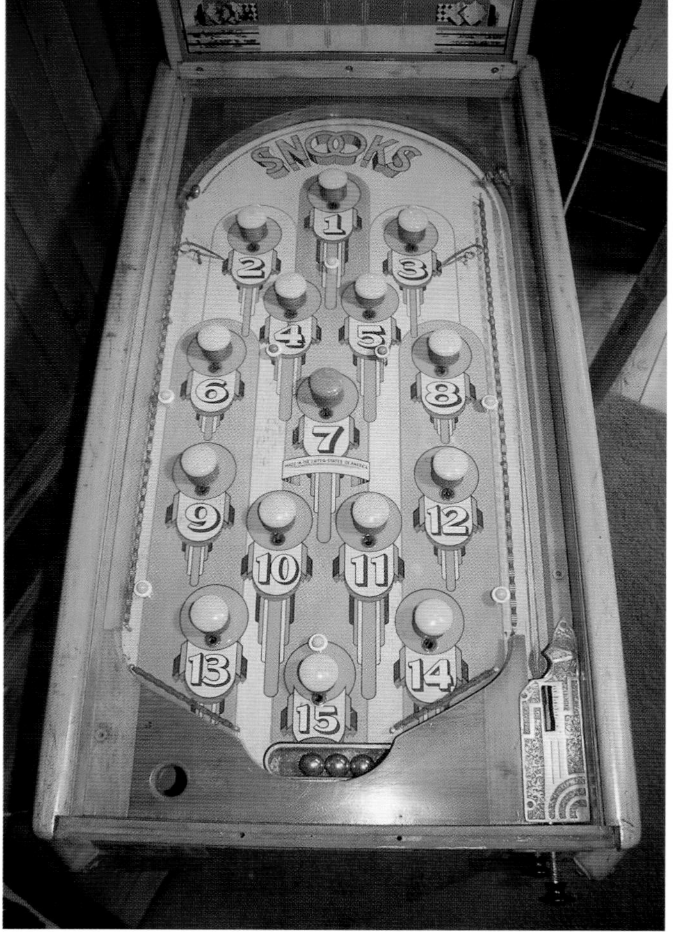

Snooks. *Alan Tate collection.* $1000.

Fleet. *Author's collection.* $1200.

The famous Penny Arcade in Luna Park, Sydney, Australia.

By the end of the 1930s pinballs had come a long way from the simple countertop machines seen in the early days. The introduction of electricity allowed solenoids to be used in machines. Also, the introduction of legs, backglass scoring, bumpers, magnets, payout machines, and even animation on the backglass, all created in this early era, set the standards for future pinball development. On Bally's *FLEET* we see the strength of the American Navy and Air Force. This was a reflection of the times, and the players loved it.

Can you believe it? There are two Bally Bumper pinball machines on either side of a Bally Paramount (1936).

Ray Maloney being presented with the Bally Trophy. *Courtesy Wayne Neyens*.

CHAPTER TWO
THE 1940S

By the 1940s, pinballs had taken on a similar shape to the ones we see today – a backbox bolted to the cabinet with a backglass displaying a fantasy of glowing lights. At the start of this era, the manufacturers were limited in the playfield arrangements, as only a few pinball features were available. As the 1940s progressed, however, so did the advancement of the pinball machine. Sound effects, for example, were introduced on machines and this gimmick played an important role in drawing people's attention to the game.

A few years ago, machines from this era didn't generate as much interest as games from later eras. Today, however, things have changed and these machines are appreciated and in demand by collectors. The bumpers used in these early games are called dead bumpers, as they were purely used to score points. They were usually constructed from a round illuminated plastic assembly and, unlike the bumpers used today, they had no electromechanical action.

In 1939, World War II had started in Europe. America had not yet entered the war and manufacturers were busy making games while materials were still available. All games were now operated from standard electrical outlets; the battery operated games were converted by installing a transformer. This made the games more reliable, as the batteries would often go flat and have to be replaced.

PRE-FLIPPER GAMES

A good sports theme game always attracts attention and reflects the American popular culture. An unusual game released by Genco in February 1940 was called *LUCKY STRIKE* and was based on the popular game, Ten Pin bowling. In *LUCKY STRIKE*, the pins on the playfield are lit at the beginning of the game. Once they are struck by the ball, the lights go out and the corresponding pin lights up on the backglass.

Lucky Strike. *Author's collection.* $1200.

All American. *Author's collection*. $1500.

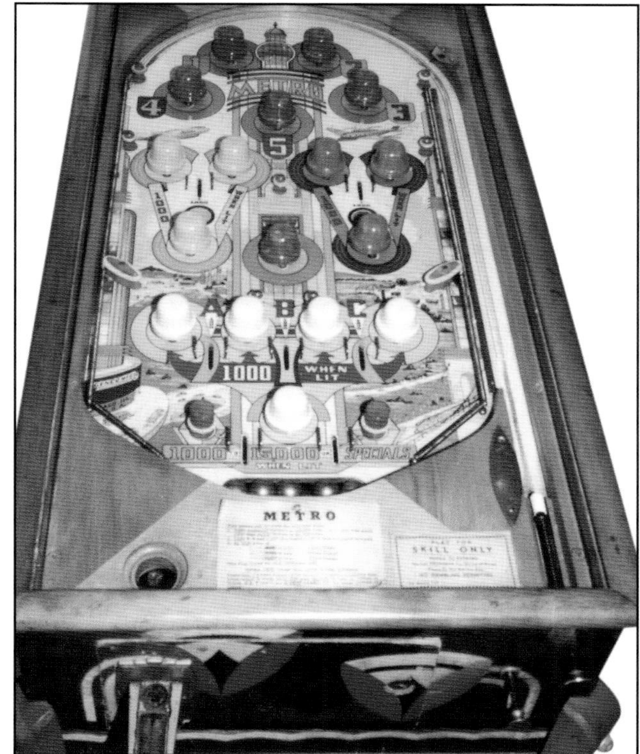

Metro. *Russ Jensen collection*. $1000.

Chicago Coin Machine Manufacturing Company, better known as Chicago Coin, started producing pinballs in the early 1930s. Sam Wolberg and Sam Gensberg had formed the company. The first game they produced was *BLACKSTONE*, released in July 1933. *ALL AMERICAN* was released in October 1940 and is one of my favorites, as the theme appeals to me. As you know, from early childhood I have always loved pinballs, so the words "All American" capture my dreams.

METRO, released by Genco in 1940, features artwork by Roy Parker, who captures a city of the future on the backglass.

Slugger. *Alan Tate collection.* $1300.

The company also released *SLUGGER* in 1941, based on one of America's favorite sports, baseball, and a collectible game today. This game gave you five balls for a nickel. There is action on the backglass and a playfield loaded with features. The company had moved itself into a position of being a major player in the manufacturing of pinball machines.

Another manufacturer of pinballs in the 1930s and 1940s was the J. H. Keeney Company, Inc; Jack Keeney formed the company in 1934. *TWIN SIX*, released in July 1941, is an early example of machines beginning

Twin Six. *Jason Douglas collection.* $800.

to use what is standard on all games today, the rollover lane. The rollovers on the upper and lower section of the playfield spot the indicated numbers. Chicago Coin released *SNAPPY* in May 1941 with a very colorful backglass. Pinball production soon stopped due to the war in Europe. America at this stage was not involved in the war, and the demand for pinballs was at its peak.

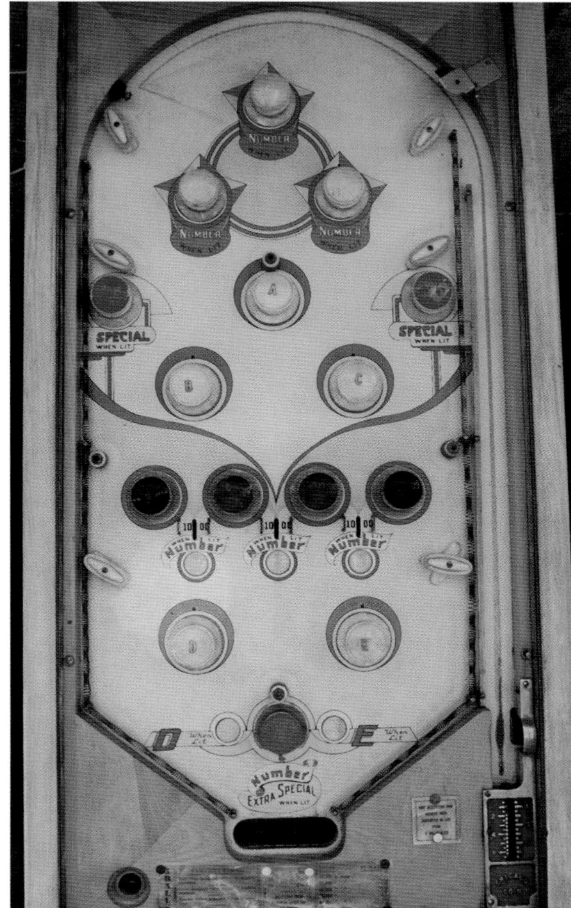

Snappy. *Author's collection.* $900.

Knockout. *Author's collection.* $1000.

The Exhibit Supply Company released *KNOCKOUT* in October 1941. In the center of the backglass, the boxer is down for the count. The player, by completing the sequence 1-10, lights up special. One month before America entered the war on December 7, 1941, the Exhibit Supply Company released *BIG PARADE*. On the backglass are military soldiers in a marching parade; the artwork was done by George Molentin. This game, designed by Lyn Durant and Harry Williams, was a hit with players and operators. The machine was later converted to *RIVIERA* in 1945. The machine pictured here is all original and is one of my most prized machines.

Big Parade. *Author's collection*. $1000.

Riviera. *Author's collection*. $1000.

War related themes used by manufacturers were very popular with players before, during, and after the war. Another favorite of mine is *FOUR ACES*, released by the Genco manufacturing company in May 1942. The artwork on the backglass is very captivating, showing fighter planes flying over New York City with the Statue of Liberty in the background. The name "Four Aces" is embedded on the American eagle. This machine today symbolizes the true patriotism of the American people during World War II.

Four Aces. *Alan Tate collection.* $1500.

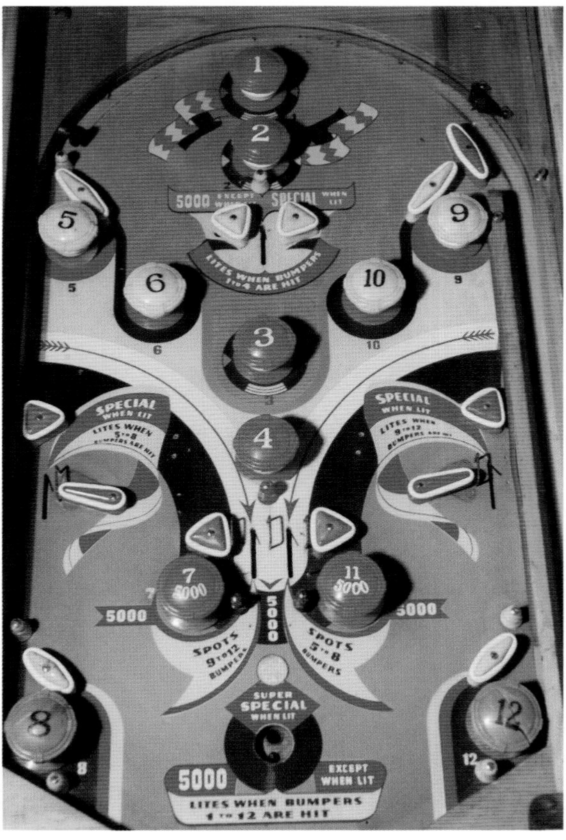

Arizona. *Alan Tate collection.* $1000.

During World War II, pinball production was discontinued as the resources were needed for the war; the only games produced were conversions of pre-war ones. The major pinball companies ceased manufacturing pinball machines and were making items such as ammunition and parachutes. During the war, the desire to play pinball was stimulated with machines located at army bases and training camps. Machines were sent all over the world for the troops to play. They even were taken to locations in the South Pacific – imagine the natives of these islands watching the G.I's playing pinball machines.

Once America entered the war, new games were no longer being manufactured in Chicago. The pre-war games were being played now all over the world, even in Europe and Asia, and with constant play began to show signs of wear and tear. Lyn Durant and Harry Williams, both formerly with Exhibit Supply Company, formed the United Manufacturing Company during the war. They had a goal, which was to revamp pinballs with rebuilt and redesigned games. Their first game, *MIDWAY*, was released in August 1942. It was a World War II conversion of an Exhibit supply game called *ZOMBIE*. The second game released by United Manufacturing was *SUN VALLEY* and their third game was *ARIZONA*, released in February 1943. The *ARIZONA* pictured originally didn't have flippers; they were added later.

Surf Queens. *Alan Tate collection.* $1500.

As soon as World War II ended in August 1945, there was a big demand for games in America and around the world. America had won the war and the people were celebrating; the economy was booming. An important development in pinballs was the introduction of plastic products on pinball machines – these were inexpensive and were used on rollover buttons and pop bumpers. Charlie Caestaker, who founded the firm American Molded Products Co. in late 1939, invented these. He invented the first pop bumper, which differed from the dead bumper. It had a vertically looped spring wrapped around its body and a solenoid beneath the playfield. When the bumper was hit, the top of the bumper would push down, making the spring expand and pushing the ball away.

Bally released *VICTORY SPECIAL*, a horse race game, in August 1945. Gottlieb's first post war game was *STAGE DOOR CANTEEN*, released in November 1945. This machine was designed by Harry Mabs and the artwork was by Roy Parker. These two would be responsible for some of the greatest pinball innovation and artwork ever produced. United's first post war game was *SOUTH SEAS*, released in November 1945.

After the war, Lyn Durant had a disagreement with Harry Williams. Harry sold his share of the company to Lyn Durant and then launched his own company, Williams Manufacturing Co. The first pinball released by Williams was *LAURA* in November 1945. Bally's first pinball machine produced after World War II was *SURF QUEENS*. Released in January 1946, the machine has a very attractive backglass. Looking at the playfield, you would think there were four flippers on the machine; these with other posts were used to deflect the ball around the playfield. The flipper shape was there, but at this stage wasn't utilized.

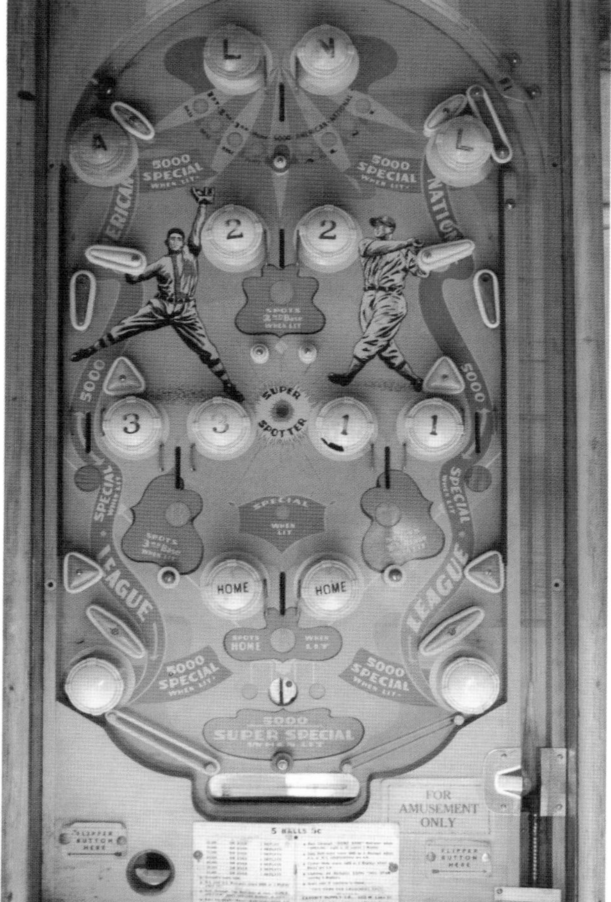

Fast Ball. *Jason Douglas collection*. $1400.

The games in this period were identical to machines made prior to the war. Exhibit Supply Company released *FAST BALL* in July 1946. This machine had it all; "the war was over now let's play ball." It was in this period that we start seeing backglasses being highly imaginative, which added greatly to the appeal of the machine. A problem that the Exhibit Supply Company had in this period was that its two main designers, Lyn Durant and Harry Williams, had left and started separate companies that were now in competition with them.

Kilroy. *Author's collection*. $1400.

In the late 1940s, Bally was the only manufacturer of payout pinballs. They released *BALLY ENTRY* in December 1946, which was a payout machine. *SPECIAL ENTRY* was released the same month, the difference being that this machine gave replays instead of coins. This didn't stop the operators from giving coins out for the free games that had accumulated, however. These machines are quite large and awkward to handle.

Chicago Coin released *KILROY* in January 1947. It was designed by Jerry Koci and the artwork was by Roy Parker. The scoring starts at 10,000 on the backglass and you can score up to 200,000. Players loved the new design and eventually machines would score up to 900,000 points. In the same month, United Manufacturing released *RIO*, which had a very interesting playfield. By lighting R.I.O, you would score 10,000 points and extra special is given when the numbers one to twelve are completed. If you were able to attain both these features you would receive super special.

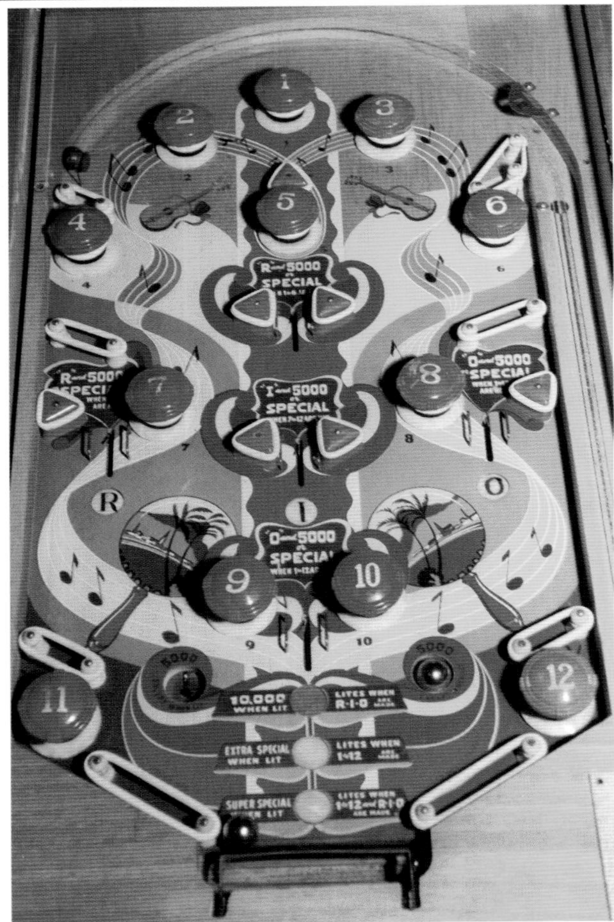

Rio. *Alan Tate collection.* $1200.

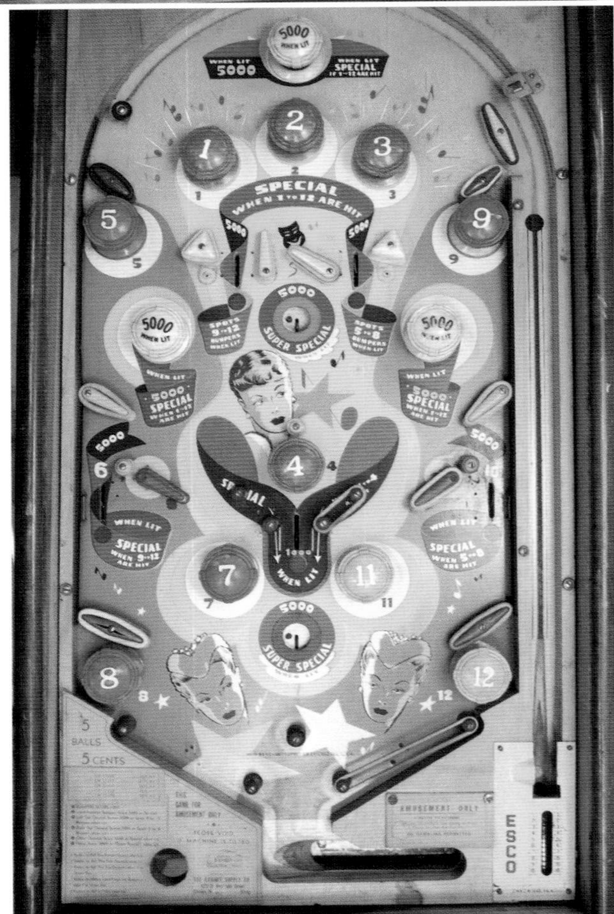

Vanities. *Jason Douglas collection.* $1200.

The Exhibit Novelty Company released *VANITIES* in February 1947. It had two kickout coils on the playfield. The object was to light the numbers one to twelve on the backglass, which was done by going through the rollovers or by hitting the corresponding bumper.

Rocket. *Jason Douglas collection*. $1200.

Bally released *ROCKET* in April 1947 with a space related theme. This sparked an interest among the American people, as the space age was just about to dawn. Chicago Coin released *PLAYBOY* in May 1947. The artwork was by Roy Parker and on the backglass we see five beautiful women dressing daringly for the times. On this machine the maximum score the player could obtain was 399,000. On Chicago Coin's next machine, *GOLD BALL*, released in August 1947, the maximum attainable score was 999,000. Artwork was by Roy Parker.

Playboy. *Author's collection*. $1400.

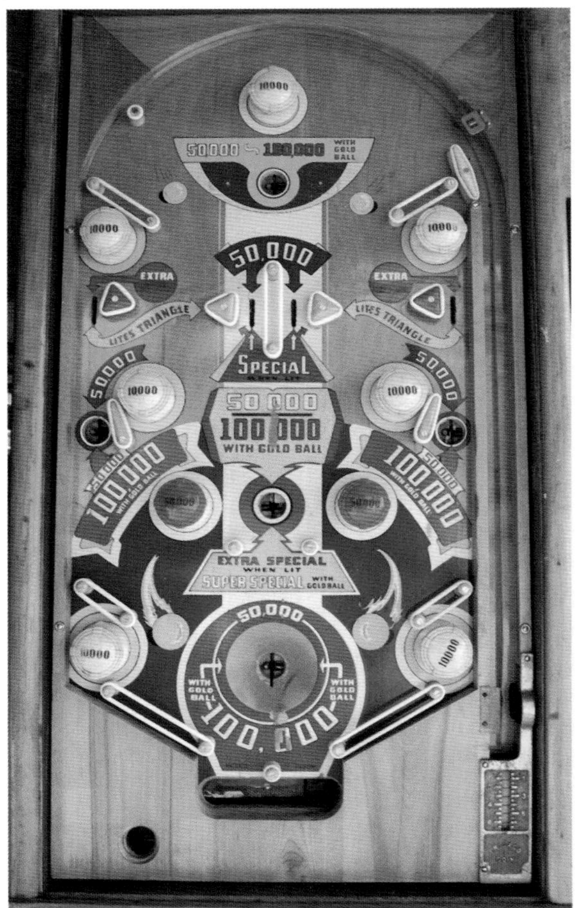

Gold Ball. *Author's collection*. $1200.

In July 1946, Gottlieb released *SUPERLINER*, designed by Harry Mabs and artwork by Roy Parker. Prior to the war, Gottlieb had been the leading producer of pinball games. The whole industry was waiting for new Gottlieb games and they were never disappointed. Gottlieb promoted his games with the statement "There is no substitute for quality."

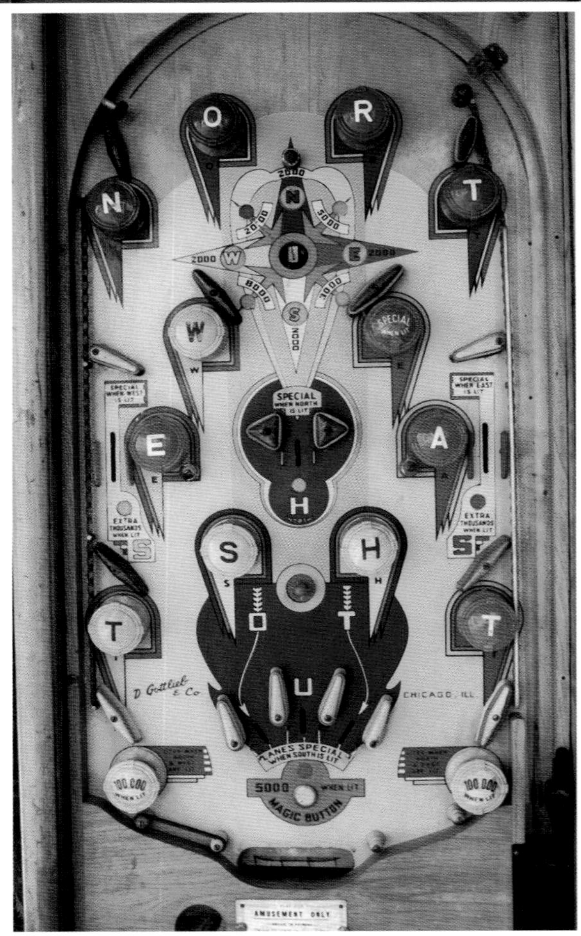

Superliner. *Author's collection*. $1200.

Lucky Star. *Author's collection*. $1200.

Artwork was now playing a vital role in pinballs: it was the backglass that captivated the players' imaginations and lured them to deposit a coin and have a game. The two people who pioneered pinball artwork were Roy Parker and George Molentin. Roy Parker worked for a firm called "Advertising Posters" in the 1940s and this company did the majority of the artwork on backglasses and playfields. After seeing his work, David Gottlieb wanted Roy to do all the artwork on his company' s games. George Molentin, on the other hand, met Harry Williams when he was working at Exhibit Supply and United Manufacturing. George Molentin's artwork impressed Harry Williams and, like Roy Parker, he could also draw women. In the early Williams backglasses, a woman would be in the center as the main attraction. The artwork by Parker and Molentin was both delightful and creative.

Gottlieb released *LUCKY STAR* in May 1947, one of the last machines manufactured without flippers.

THE INTRODUCTION OF "FLIPPERS"

When Gottlieb released *HUMPTY DUMPTY* in October 1947, the pinball game would never be the same again. On *HUMPTY DUMPTY* we see the introduction of flippers. The game now is not one of chance but one of skill. The person who invented this was Harry Mabs, who was the chief designer at Gottlieb. David Gottlieb was not afraid to experiment with new ideas, which is why Gottlieb was responsible for introducing many new features in pinball, the most important being the flipper. *HUMPTY DUMPTY* was the first in a series of pinballs whose artwork themes were based on fairy tales and nursery rhymes. Collectors today refer to these machines as from the "Fairy Tale Series." Gottlieb produced 6,500 of the *HUMPTY DUMPTY* machines, which was model number one. *LADY ROBIN HOOD*, released on January 31, 1948, had a production run of 6000 and was model number two. *CINDERELLA*, released in March 1948, had a production run of 4000 and was model number three. *JACK 'N JILL*, released in April 1948, had a production run of 2000 and was model number four. *OLDE KING COLE*, released in May 1948, had a production of 1500 and was model number five. *ALI BABA*, released in June 1948, had a production run of 1700 and was model number six. The last machine in this series was *ALICE IN WONDERLAND*, released in August 1948 with a production run of 1000. It is a rarity to have the complete set of this series. Currently, I am helping Alan Tate with the set-up of the first pinball museum on the Gold Coast Australia and the "Fairy Tale Series" will be one of the highlights of the exhibit.

Part of the Gottlieb team. Standing, left to right: Doc Garbark, Alvin Gottlieb, Bob Smith, Wayne Neyens, Frank Underhill, Abe Waxler, and Bill Wanzel. Seated, left to right: Harry Mabs, Tony Gerard, Joe Conners. *Courtesy of Wayne Neyens.*

I asked Wayne Neyens if the name Humpty Dumpty was originally known as Flipper:

> *Dave Gottlieb changed many of the names; that is why, when the games were passing through the engineering room, they always had a number assigned to them. The name had no meaning till the final artwork was done. A good example would be Humpty Dumpty. The original artwork was done using the name "Flipper." At the last minute Dave changed the name and theme and a feature was added (A, B, C, D feature).*
>
> *When we at Gottlieb – I don't know about the other companies – designed a game, the artist never saw the game till we told him what we wanted. We would give him drawings and he worked from them. Sometimes the artists never saw the game till it was produced.*
>
> —*Wayne Neyens*

These games all had six flippers, three on either side of the playfield. One coil would have to drive three flippers, making them weak, but at least players could control the ball. When a player activated the flipper button on the cabi-

Above & right: Humpty Dumpty. *Alan Tate collection.* $2500.

Lady Robin Hood. *Alan Tate collection.* $2000.

net, this would activate the flippers. If the player hit the button on the left side, the left side flippers would be activated. If he hit the button on the right sie, the right side flippers would be activated. This was not the case on early Williams, Genco, Exhibit, and Bally machines. They had dual action flippers, meaning the left or right flipper would activate both flippers, therefore making the flippers slow and weak. The machines that had single action flippers gave the players better ball control and were more powerful.

Cinderella. *Alan Tate collection.* $2000.

Jack 'N Jill. *Alan Tate collection.* $2000

Olde King Cole. *Alan Tate collection.* $2000.

Ali Baba. *Alan Tate collection.* $2000.

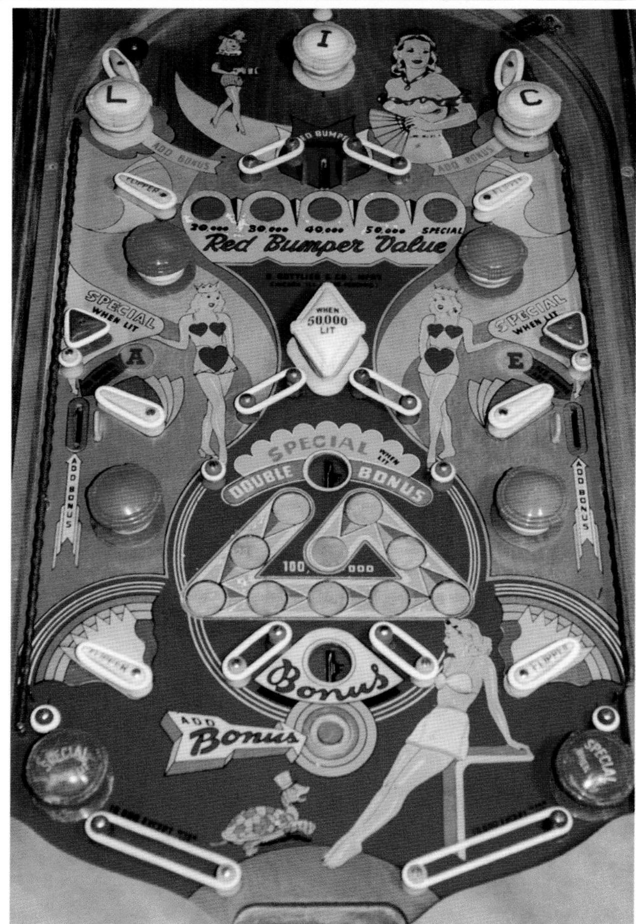

Alice in Wonderland. *Alan Tate collection.* $2000.

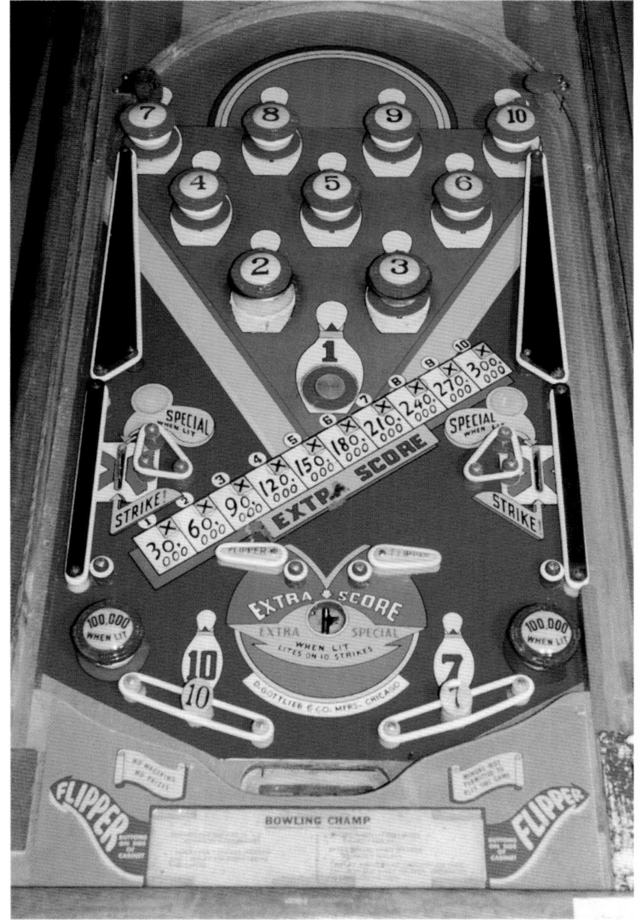

Bowling Champ. *Alan Tate collection*. $1500.

Sharpshooter. *Alan Tate collection*. $1500.

College Daze. *Author's collection*. $1800.

After the "Fairy tale Series," Gottlieb's next game was *BARNACLE BILL*, a machine with four flippers. Gottlieb released *BOWLING CHAMP* in February 1949 and *DOUBLE SHUFFLE* in June 1949; they had substantial success with their bowling theme machines as these were favored with players. The flippers were still reversed but unlike most of the other manufacturers the flipper action was dual controlled. Another advantage the player had was being able to hold the flipper up, giving them better ball control. Gottlieb released *SHARPSHOOTER* in May 1949, with artwork on the backglass by Roy Parker. Parker was responsible for all of Gottlieb's artwork in this period. Gottlieb released *COLLEGE DAZE* in August 1949, which was Wayne Neyens's first attempt at designing a pinball and an instant hit with players. Prior to this machine, Harry Mabs was designing all of Gottlieb's games.

One of the greatest designers in the pinball industry is Wayne Neyens, whom I have had the pleasure of speaking with over the phone. Wayne was born on July 29, 1918 in Mason City, Iowa. He designed many classic pinballs in the "Golden Era" and all are collectible today. I have rung him on numerous occasions and he has kindly helped me with putting this book together. The first time I spoke with him I had to pinch myself to make sure I wasn't dreaming. I kept reminding him that it was an honor and a privilege to speak to with him. I asked him to share with me his story:

The master designer, Wayne Neyens, at the Gottlieb factory. *Courtesy of Wayne Neyens.*

My employment in the coin machine industry began on February 11, 1936, on a part time basis, with a company called Western Equipment & Supply Co. They were located at 925 West North Ave. Chicago, Illinois. The owner of the company was Jimmy Johnson, who had a big influence on the industry at the time. Jimmy was a graduate of the University of Nebraska, where he was a lineman on the football team. While at Western we built a game called Aksarben, Nebraska spelled backward, of which he was very proud.

In early 1936, the industry was in the throes of converting from battery operated Pin Games over to what we called, at the time, Battery Eliminators or Power Packs. These were nothing but transformers with Rectifiers. All games operated on D.C at the time, A.C. came much later. A lot of factory conversions were going on at this time. During the summer of 1936, I did a lot of converting.

Jimmy was very lucky to be in the right business at the right time with the best employees. Most of the people he had working with him at the time I started with him went on to other companies in responsible positions. As a good example I was hired as a part time draftsman to help a young engineer by the name of Lyn Durant. Lyn later went on to become the owner of United Manufacturing Co. and was very successful with Shuffle Alleys, Pin Games and later on he built Bingo Games. Working along with Lyn Durant was another well known man who later designed the Flipper, Harry Mabs. Other well known men at Western at this time were the Chief Engineer Eric Bjornander, Harry Kozel, Emil Goodman, Don Anderson, Claud Hutchinson, Gus Erickson and Herb Breitenstein, not to be confused with his brother who was a well known engineer at Bally. With all this talent, which left Jimmy Johnson one by one, Western Equipment & Supply Co. was in constant financial difficulties.

I was hired as a part time draftsman to help Lyn Durant develop a solenoid operated payout unit. This job was short lived and by June 1936 I found myself doing odd jobs all over the factory, and now working full time. Freeplay games were just beginning to catch on at this time and Jimmy, true to his luck or skill, held the patent on the Freeplay Coin Chute. The Freeplay unit it self was of a very poor design and gave no end of trouble. We were buying step switches from a company called G.M. Laboratories at the time and I took one of these step switches and by using a coil and lever was able to modify the step switch into a very workable Freeplay unit. This eventually became the standard of the industry, and was my first try at designing anything. I signed away all rights to this unit to G.M. Laboratories on October 5, 1937 for $50.00, which at the time was a lot of money. I don't know if a patent was ever issued or applied for. It was this all round experience which enabled me to hang on, with two other men, Emil Goodman and Don Anderson, when Western went into bankruptcy (1938). The three of us designed games, built the games, packed them, and loaded them on trucks.

It was during this period of time that I gained the experience that stood me in good stead later on at Gottlieb. We developed a game that became very popular called Western Base Ball and because of this game Jimmy was able to get back on his feet financially (1939).

On August 31, 1939 I could see no future for me at Western, so like so many before me I quit the company. I quit shortly after noon and that same afternoon I started work at D. Gottlieb & Co. It was a toss up whether to apply for a job at Gottlieb, Chicago Coin, or Genco; they were all located within a few blocks of each other. I opted for Gottlieb, only because my good friend Harry Mabs was by this time their designer. I was hired the same afternoon I quit Western, so on that particular day I worked at both companies, Western in the morning and Gottlieb in the afternoon.

My first job at Gottlieb was in the factory testing play boards; this position lasted about a month. I was then moved into the engineering room as a helper to Robert Smith, the chief engineer, and to Harry Mabs the designer. This was the big break that I needed. I was Harry's helper the day he invented the Flipper (1947) and was the second person to hit a ball with a Flipper. This association with Harry gave me free time to occasionally work on my own, so I decided to design my own game, and over a period of several months was able to build my first game, later to be known as College Daze. This put me in direct competition with my good friend Harry Mabs. This, along with many other reasons too numerous to mention, caused Harry Mabs to leave Gottlieb and go over to Williams Mfg. as their designer, where he was very successful for many years. The leaving of Harry left me responsible for designing all the games, so from 1950 through 1964 I was the only designer at Gottlieb.

Perhaps my single most important design was the four player game concept, as it is known today; that game was called Super Jumbo (1954) and eventually became the standard game of the industry. The original concept is still the standard game today. I also designed the so-called Add-A-Ball (non-replay) under direction of Alvin Gottlieb, who conceived the idea of a non-replay type of game. I hold the patent on the bumper contact as used to this day; it replaced the carbon ring and stem that had been used by companies in the industry. The Roto-Target was also a unit that was quite popular and used in many games in the fifties.

On November 1, 1963 I was promoted to Chief Engineer in charge of all engineering and design functions. Edward Krynski was hired soon after to do the designing and most games from this time on were his. Although I did not do any further designing I was responsible for and participated in all design decisions. On May 19, 1971 I was promoted to Director of Engineering and Product Development. I was subsequently promoted to Vice President of Engineering, which title I held until my retirement from active involvement on August 1, 1980. I remained with D. Gottlieb & Co. as a consultant until August 1, 1983, after which time I officially retired from the company after forty-four years of service. Counting the three and a half years at Western Equipment & Supply Company, I spent a total of forty-seven and a half years in the Coin Machine Industry.

—Wayne Neyens

Sally. *Author's collection.* $1500.

Another major pinball manufacturer was the Chicago Coin Manufacturing Company. Their first flipper game was *BERMUDA*, released in November 1947. They were the first manufacturers to fit flippers on their games after Gottlieb introduced them on *HUMPTY DUMPTY*. Chicago Coin released *CATALINA* in January 1948; this was their second game with flippers. Next they released *TRINIDAD* in March 1948, with a similar playfield to that on *CATALINA*. The main difference was the use of only two flippers, giving them more power.

Jeri Koci was the chief designer at Chicago Coin. He believed he had invented the flipper before Harry Mabs at Gottlieb. He was working on a baseball game and came up with the idea of putting the swinging bat on a pinball game, but the hierarchy at the company was not interested.

One of my favorite Chicago Coin games was *SALLY*, released in October 1948. It was games like this that inspired me to write this book. I can't get enough of these machines – it doesn't matter how many I have, the lure is there and I keep wanting to buy them. Note that the side flippers on earlier games are placed at the bottom of the playfield and the huge gap between them allows the ball to be lost easily.

Chicago Coin released *SUPER HOCKEY* in April 1949; on the playfield layout you would feel as if you were playing hockey against the machine.

Super Hockey. *Alan Tate collection.* $1300.

At the United Manufacturing Company, Lyn Durant resisted flippers more than anyone else in the industry. He once told pinball designer Wayne Neyens that "I will never put flippers on pinball machines." United released *SINGAPORE*, which was a non-flipper game, in December 1947. Although this machine had no flippers it was still successful for the company. In February 1948 they released *TROPICANA*. The concept on these games was to light up the name "Singapore" or "Tropicana" in the backglass; when this was achieved special would be lit. When the last letter on the playfield was hit, a bell would be heard in the machine. The next game United released was *WISCONSIN*. It was released in April 1948 and was their first flipper game – Lyn finally gave in and included flippers on his machines.

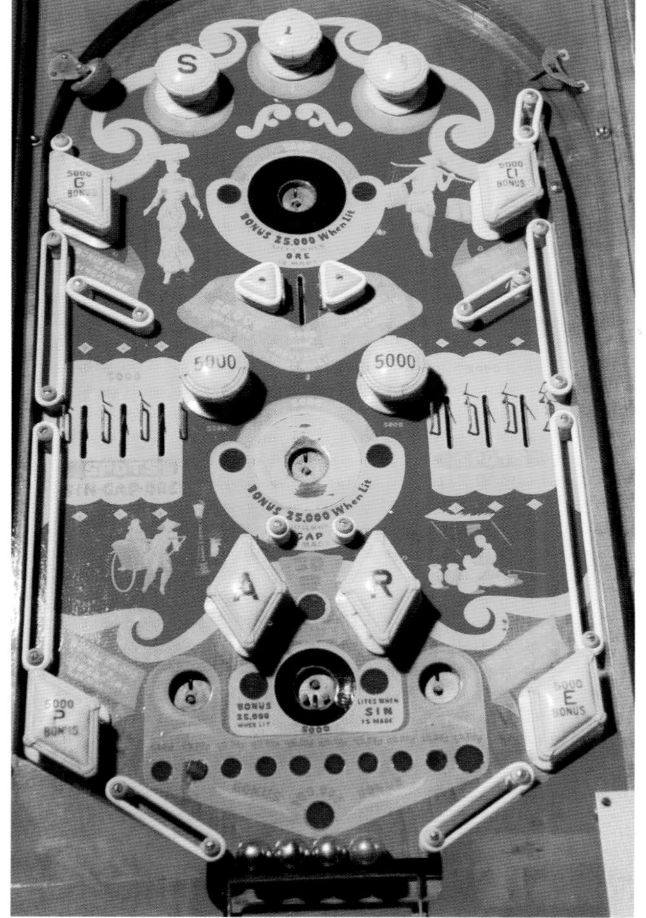

Singapore. *Alan Tate collection.* $1200.

Tropicana. *Alan Tate collection.* $1200.

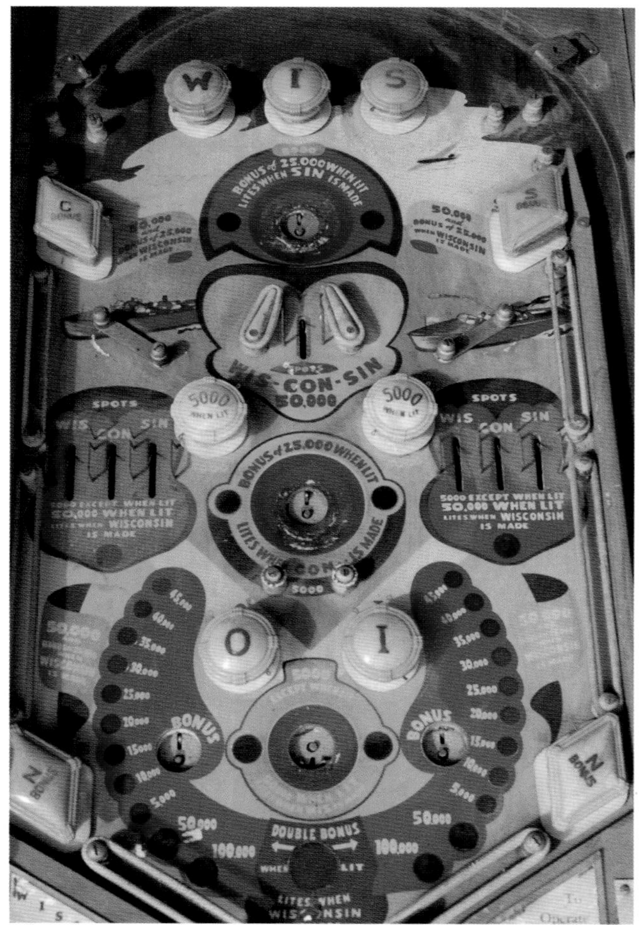

Wisconsin. *Author's collection*. $1500.

The standard plastic flipper was used by all the manufacturers except United. Their flipper consisted of a metal plate with two short metal posts; a rubber ring would stretch over them and when the flipper was activated it was the rubber ring that hit the ball. On the playfield of *WISCONSIN* the actual flippers are situated just above the center of the playfield, one on either side. Other manufacturers used flippers in the shape of the two seen in the center of the playfield. On this game, however, the two in the center were only used to rebound the ball.

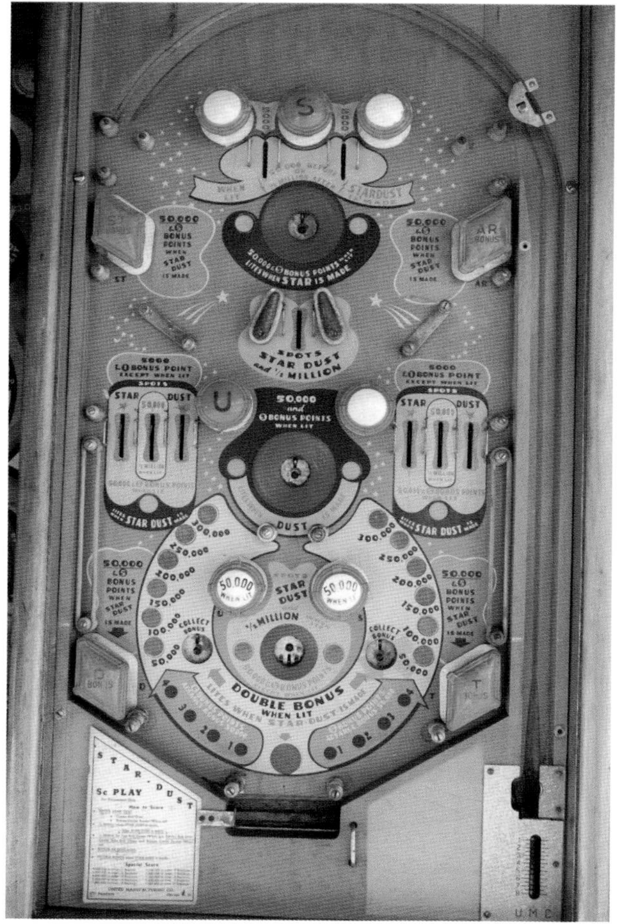

Stardust. *Author's collection*. $1200.

United went on to make *STARDUST* and *CARIBBEAN* in May of 1948, *RONDEEVOO* in June, *PARADISE* in August, *BLUE SKIES* in November, and *SERENADE* in December. They produced only a few more pinballs; a few examples of those produced the following year are *SHOWBOAT* in January, *RAMONA* in February, and *AQUACADE* in May. The last pinball machine United produced was *RED SHOES*, released in November 1950. The company concentrated more on their arcade games, particularly their Ball and Shuffle Alleys.

The introduction of flippers made the non-flipper games obsolete. There were companies that offered kits to non-flipper games to upgrade them to a flipper machine; this can be seen on United's 1943 *ARIZONA*, shown previously (see page 31).

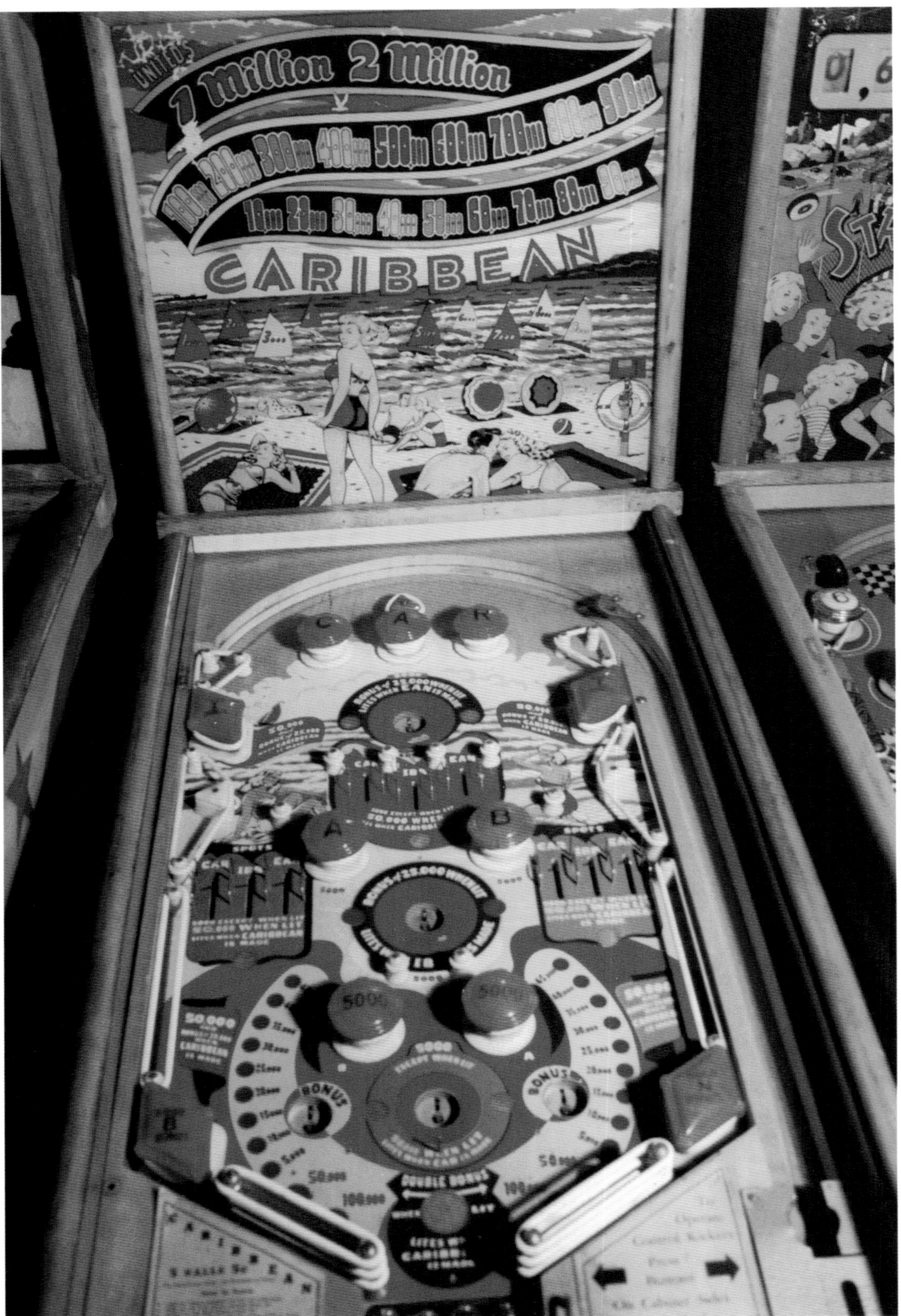

Caribbean. *Alan Tate collection.* $1200.

Rondeevoo. *Jason Douglas collection.* $1200.

Paradise. *Jason Douglas collection.* $1200.

Blue Skies. *Author's collection*. $1200.

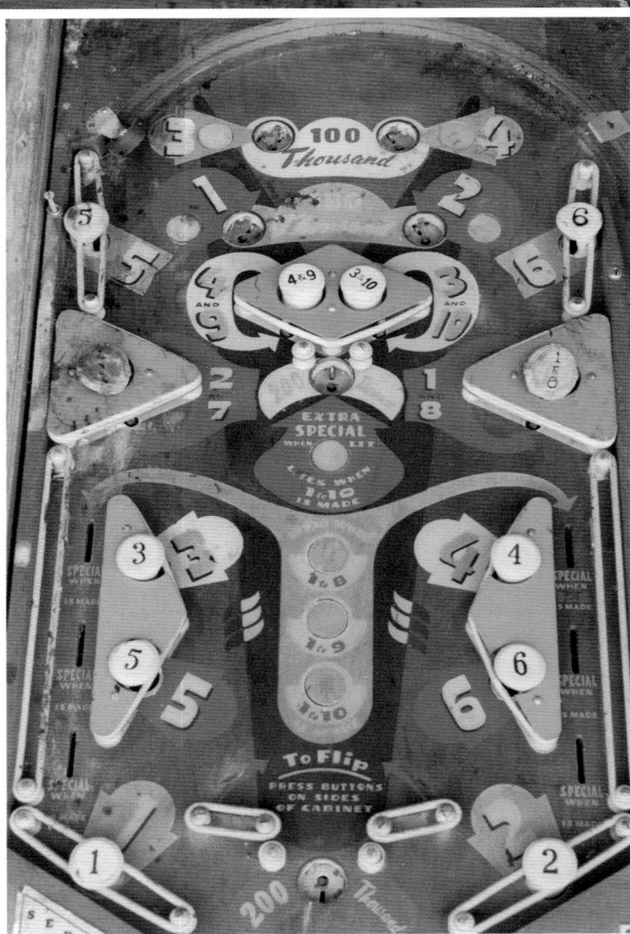

Serenade. *Author's collection*. $1200.

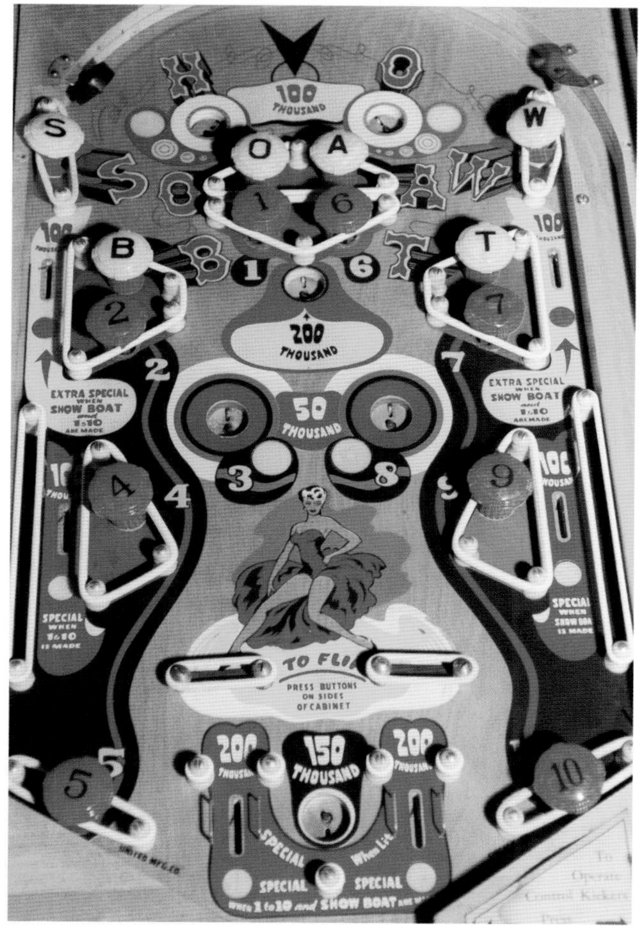

Showboat. *Alan Tate collection.* $1200.

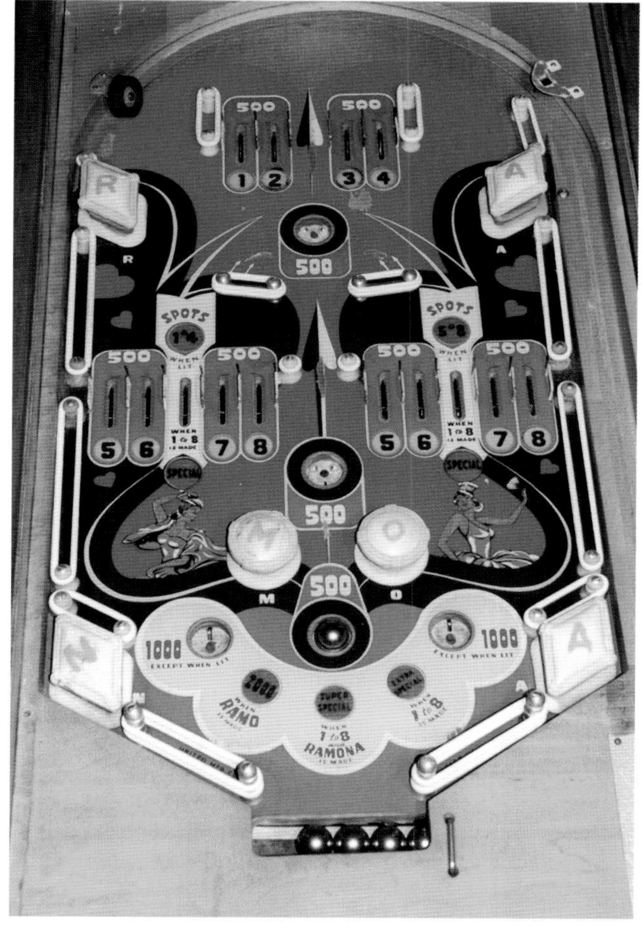

Ramona. *Alan Tate collection.* $1200.

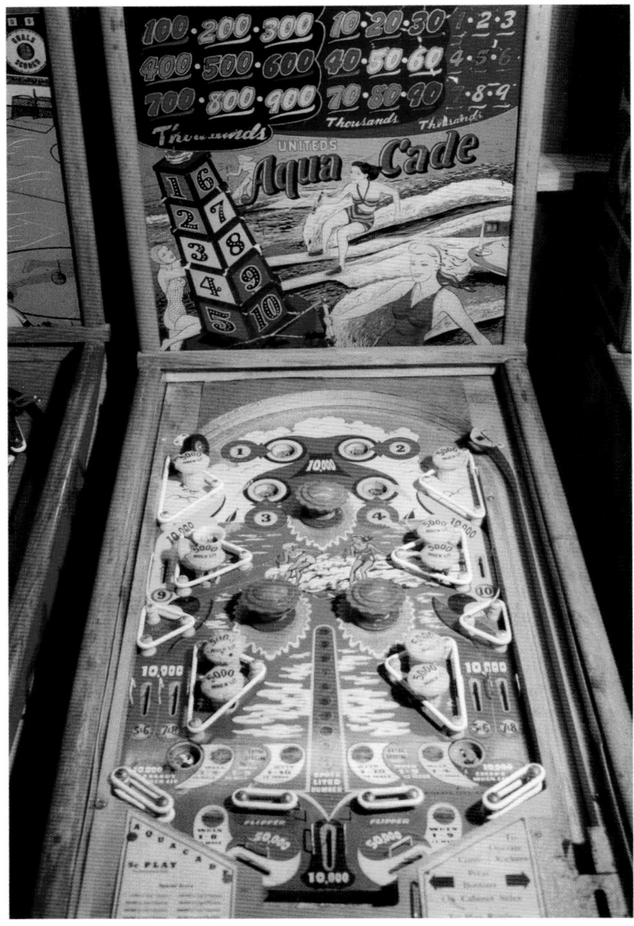

Aquacade. *Author's collection.* $1200.

Genco Manufacturing released their first flipper game, *TRIPLE ACTION*, in January 1948. It was designed by Steve Kordek, who had joined Genco in 1937 as an assistant to the other designer at the company, Harvey Heiss. Unlike all other flipper games, this one by Genco was the first to use two flippers at the bottom of the playfield. Eventually all the other manufactures followed this trend, as this was the most practical place to put them. This machine had dual action flippers; hitting either flipper button would activate both flippers. Also on this machine, when the flipper button was pressed the flippers would be energized then would drop back down; this was called a single flip operation. This was not the case at Gottlieb, as their flippers worked like the ones today: when a player kept the flipper button closed, the flipper would remain energized.

PUDDIN' HEAD was released in November 1948, with no bumpers on the playfield. This was a hit with players and the design of the playfield ensured plenty of action. On *ONE-TWO-THREE*, released in December, bumpers were put back on the playfield, replacing the bouncing rubbers that were on machines like *PUDDIN' HEAD* and *SCREWBALL*. In March 1949, Genco released *BLACK GOLD* and in October they released *RIP SNORTER*. Both were designed by Harvey Heiss. On *RIP SNORTER*, the Goofy character appears and the playfield had seven kickout holes (known as saucers), which were in a vertical line in the center of the playfield.

The flippers used on pinballs in this period were pointed towards the outside edge of the playfield; the term used today for this is "the reverse flippers." It was not till the early 1950s that the flippers were positioned like the ones we see today, pointed towards the center of the playfield.

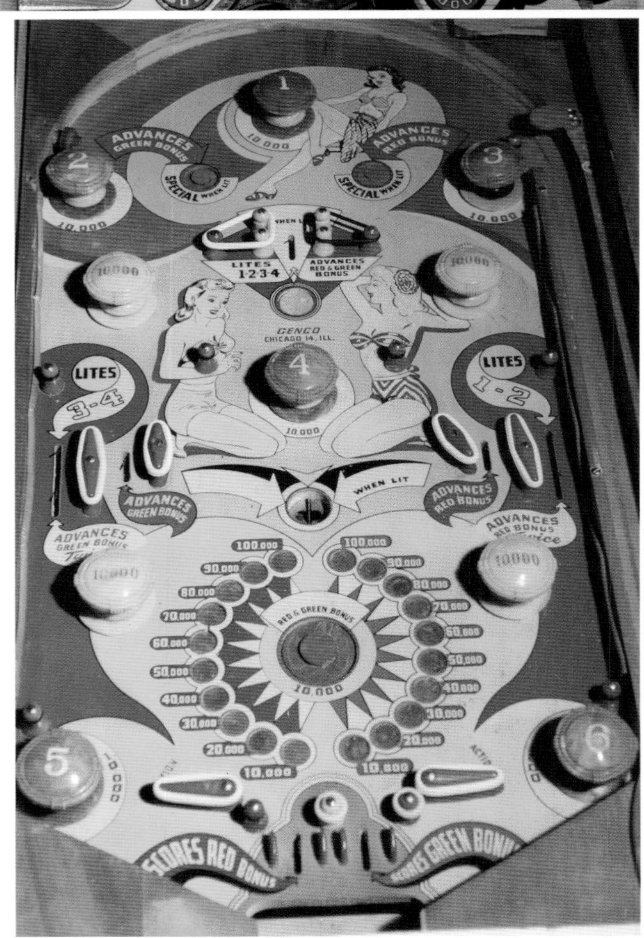

Triple Action. *Alan Tate collection.* $2500.

Puddin' Head. *Alan Tate collection.* $1500.

Black Gold. *Alan Tate collection.* $1400.

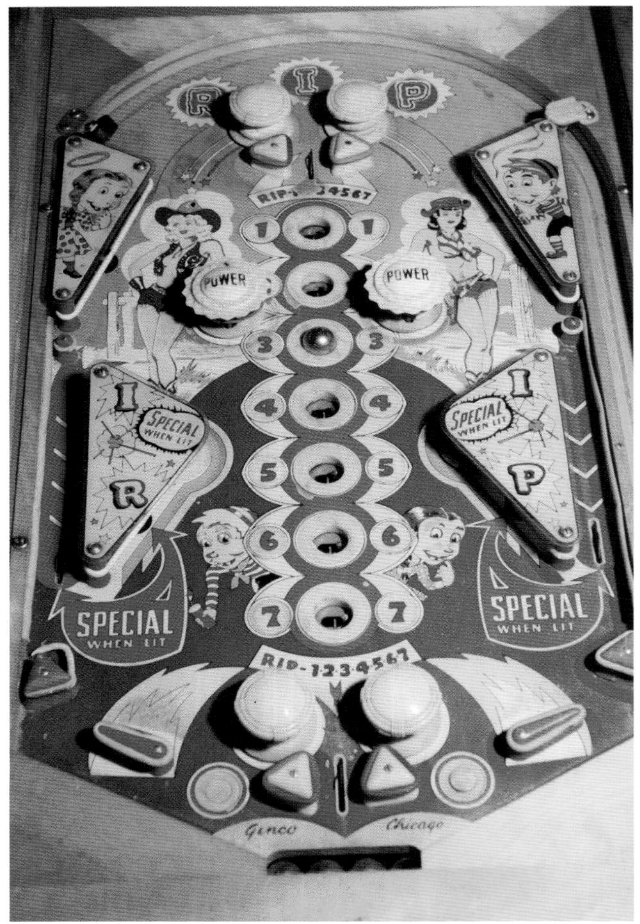

Rip Snorter. *Alan Tate collection*. $1500.

Steve Kordek needs no introduction to pinball machine enthusiasts – he is a true legend who gave me so much information while I was writing this book. Steve, who officially retired on November 30, 2000, is often referred to as the Patriarch of Pinball. He still goes to the Williams plant an average of once a week, compiling memorabilia from the industry that he so much loves. He has created some great innovations in pinball design; for example, he designed the first pinball to have two flippers at the bottom of the playfield, the first pinball to incorporate the moving target seen on *HOLLYWOOD* 1961, and the first pinball to use the drop target, *VAGABOND* 1962, amongst others. Steve was honored to be given the Lifetime Achievement Award by the Amusement and Music Operators Association in March 2001. I have asked him to share his story with me.

I was born on December 26, 1911, the eldest of ten children. When I graduated from high school in 1930 I attended another school called Coyne Electric, which is where I got a background in electrical circuitry. I wanted to go to college but couldn't, as my family needed help. It was the Depression at the time and my family would never go on relief. So I decided to get a job to help them out. At the time I found odd jobs that paid 10 cents an hour, but it wasn't enough. I had no alternative but to join the Civilian Conservation Corps. After I completed my commitment there I was transferred to the Department of Agriculture. I worked there for three years as a dispatcher of forest firefighters. I used to take care of forest fires; this time of my life was exciting and fun.

Steve Kordek, attending a picnic after graduating in 1930. Steve is in front of the windshield. The car is a Pierce Arrow, used as a flower car for funerals. *Courtesy Steve Kordek*.

Steve Kordek (on the left) working as a firefighter one year prior to starting work at Genco. *Courtesy Steve Kordek.*

of the production line; and Ed Berninger, an electrical engineer. I worked at Bally for eighteen months working on different types of gun games. I was approached by Sam Stern and was offered a job at Williams Electronics.

Harry Mabs was the designer there and was getting on in age. I remember telling Bill about the offer from Williams and that I wanted to accept it; he told me to go ahead but I couldn't take the three guys I had brought over with me from Genco. They had established themselves so well he didn't want to let them go. I was hired at Williams as a designer and commenced working there in February 1960. At the time Harry Mabs was working there designing games; by the end of the year Harry had retired to Florida, where he passed away. The first game I worked on at the company was a gun game called Space Glider in 1960. At Williams, I returned to designing pinball machines and became their sole designer. The first pinball that I designed was Bobo, released in 1961, and the last was Pokerino, released in 1979. In the years 1976-1986 I was hiring, training, and leading the new generation of pinball designers. Also in 1976 Williams hired Michael Stroll to lead the firm into the solid-state era. He brought in the electrical engineers that produced the new generation of Williams's games. I loved working in the industry; I have been associated with some of the most creative people and have been blessed to be part of it.

—Steve Kordek

In the winter of 1936 I left and went back to Chicago as I missed my family. For months I looked for a job there. I used to go to church every morning and pray that I would find a job. Nothing came up, then one morning in April of 1937 I was walking down a street in Chicago and it started pounding with rain. To avoid getting drenched I ducked into an entrance to a building and shut the door behind me. Little did I realize at the time I had walked into the Genco Plant, a manufacturer of pinball machines. I remember a woman opening the reception window and asking me if I was looking for a job. Because of my decent electrical background they hired me on the spot. The company was owned by three brothers named Gensberg. Although I had never seen a pinball machine I was put on the production line.

I began to use my training in circuitry to help with troubleshooting on the production line. Soon after, I was moved to the engineering department. I started working with the sole designer at the company, Harvey Heiss, who became my mentor. We built up a friendship that is still strong today. Our first joint effort was Stop and Go, which the company released in November 1938. I learned all about designing and playfield layout from Harvey. In 1947 I designed the first machine to use only two flippers, Triple Action. I would say this is the machine I am most proud of. Harvey Heiss left the company in 1955 and moved to Florida. I eventually left the company after twenty-six years, as the company closed its doors in 1958. I went and saw my good friend Bill O'Donnell at Bally and I, along with my three good friends who also worked at Genco, was hired there. The others were Harry Thompson, mechanical engineer; John Merczac, who was in charge

Steve Kordek in his office at the Williams factory. *Courtesy Steve Kordek.*

Exhibit Supply had lost ground after the war by not producing a full line of new equipment. They released *TREASURE CHEST* in December 1947 and their first flipper game was *BUILD UP*, released in January 1948. Exhibit was concentrating more on building arcade games and only released a few more pinballs. *PLAYTIME* was released in August 1949 and in October they released *SHANTYTOWN*. This machine had a flipper in the center that would flip in both directions – a very clever device. Exhibit continued to produce only a few more games, their last being *OASIS*, released in October 1950.

Treasure Chest. *Alan Tate collection.* $1200.

Shantytown. *Alan Tate collection.* $2000.

Bally Manufacturing Company released *MELODY* in November 1947; this was their first flipper game. *BALLERINA* was released in February 1948 with an identical playfield to that of *MELODY*. The company only produced a few more flipper games, concentrating more on payouts. Their last flipper game in the 1940s was *CARNIVAL*, which was released in June 1948. Bally was still producing Horse Race games; they released *GOLD CUP* in February 1948, which gave players replays. The payout version of this game was *CLUB TROPHY*, released at the same time. The following year, 1949, four of Bally's six games were horserace gambling games – the company was moving away from pinballs and concentrating more on gambling style machines. One machine that was not a gambling machine in 1949 was *HOT RODS*, which came out in March. This is a very rare game and used wooden balls instead of steel ones.

Melody. *Alan Tate collection*. $2000.

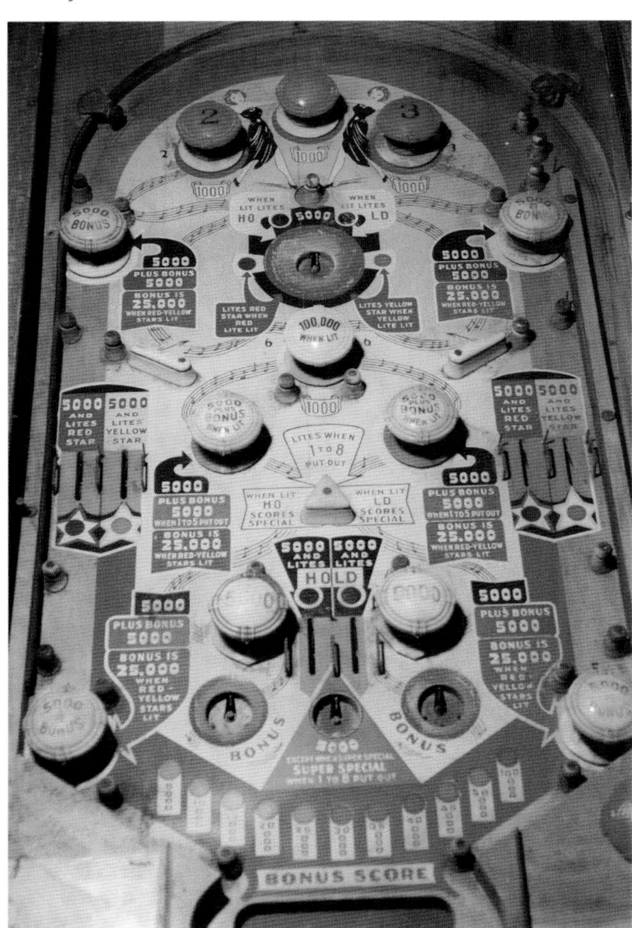

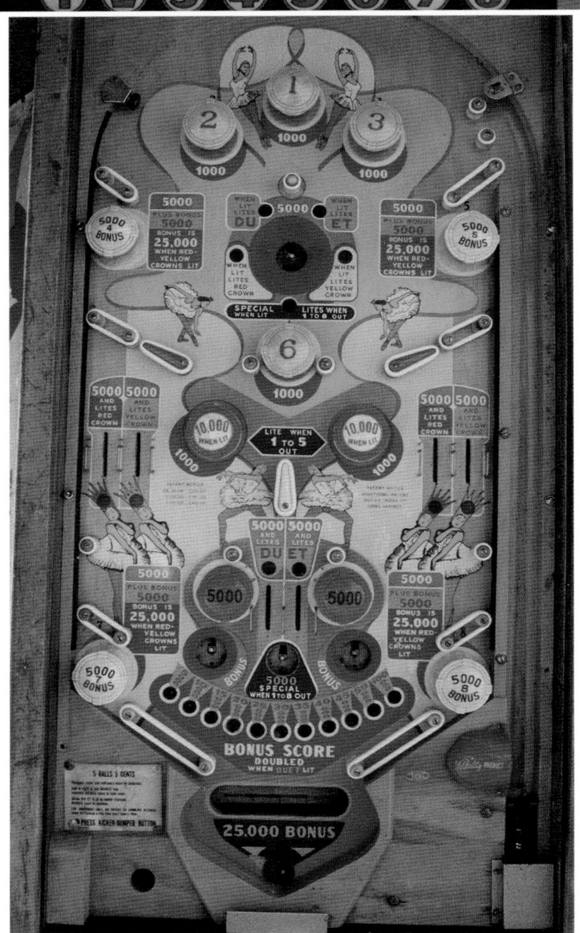

Ballerina. *Author's collection*. $1600.

Carnival. *Jason Douglas collection*. $1600.

Hot Rods. *Alan Tate collection*. $1700.

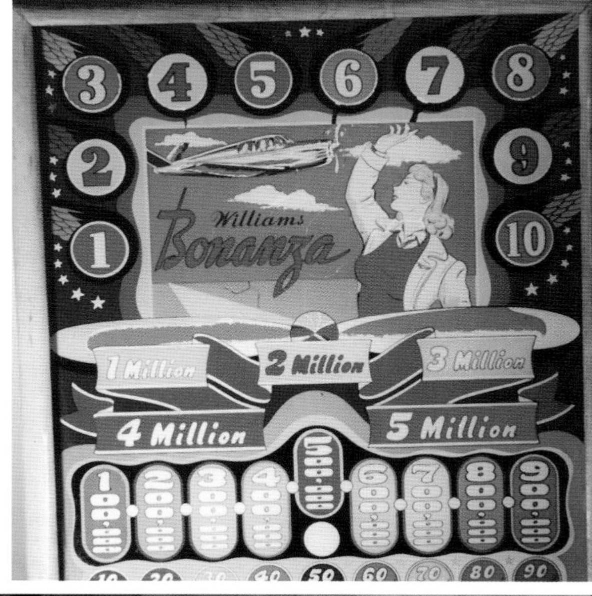

Williams released *BONANZA*, their last non-flipper machine, in November 1947. The next game manufactured by this company was *SUNNY;* it was their first flipper game and was released in December 1947. Williams released *TENNESSEE* in February 1948 and, like the Gottlieb "Fairy Tale Series," it had six flippers in the same arrangement as the Gottlieb games. No other manufacturer copied this format. In 1947, Sam Stern had become part owner of Williams Manufacturing. *GIZMO*, released in August 1948, was designed by both Harry Williams and Sam Stern and the artwork was by George Molentin. The following month, Williams released *SPEEDWAY*, another classic game.

A major change to the bumper was to take place on the company's *SARATOGA*, released in October 1948. Williams first used the power bumper on this machine (it was referred to as the powered bumper). When the ball hit the bumper it would be propelled away. The bumper had a metal ring built around it and was connected to a solenoid by two rods. The ball would first trigger the bumper skirt, then when contact was made a relay was activated and the solenoid pulsed, pushing the ring down towards the ball. This all happened at lightning speed, thus adding to the challenges of playing pinballs. This new design would revolutionize bumpers and the design is still used in modern pinballs today.

In February 1949, Williams released *ST LOUIS*, one of a series of machines named after cities in America. These games were all advertised as having "Original Power Bumpers." The company released *DE ICER* in November 1949 and this was the last game for Williams in the 1940s. It had reverse flippers, which, unlike those at Gottlieb, still worked together.

Bonanza. *Alan Tate collection.* $1200.

Tennessee. *Alan Tate collection.* $2000.

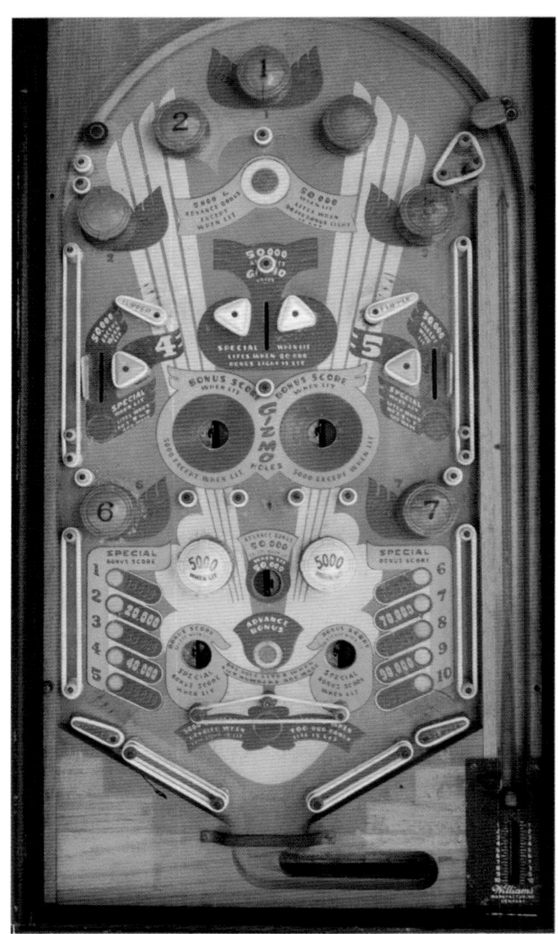

Gizmo. *Author's collection.* $1500.

Speedway. *Alan Tate collection.* $1600.

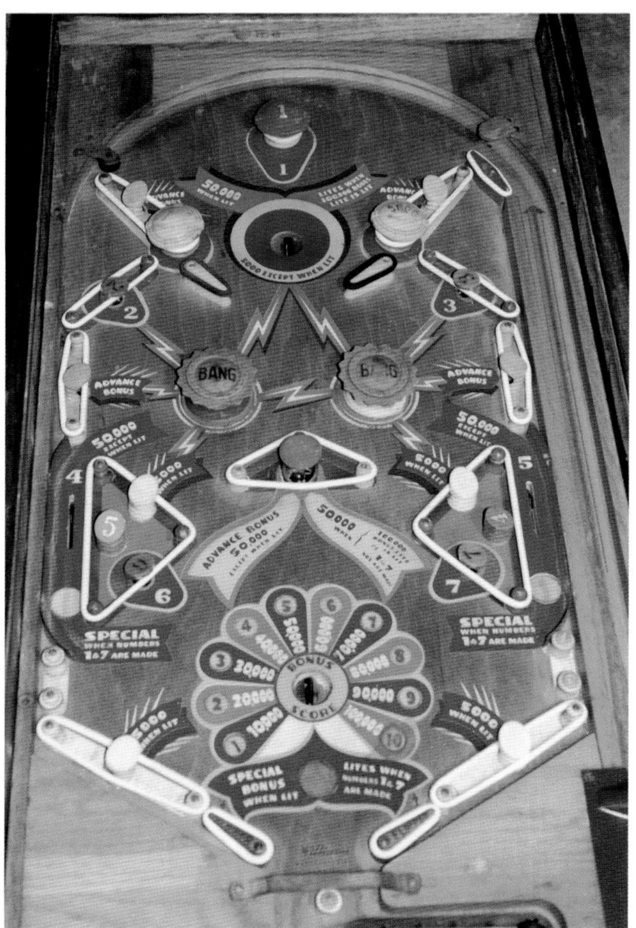

Saratoga. *Author's collection.* $1500.

St Louis. *Jason Douglas collection*. $1500.

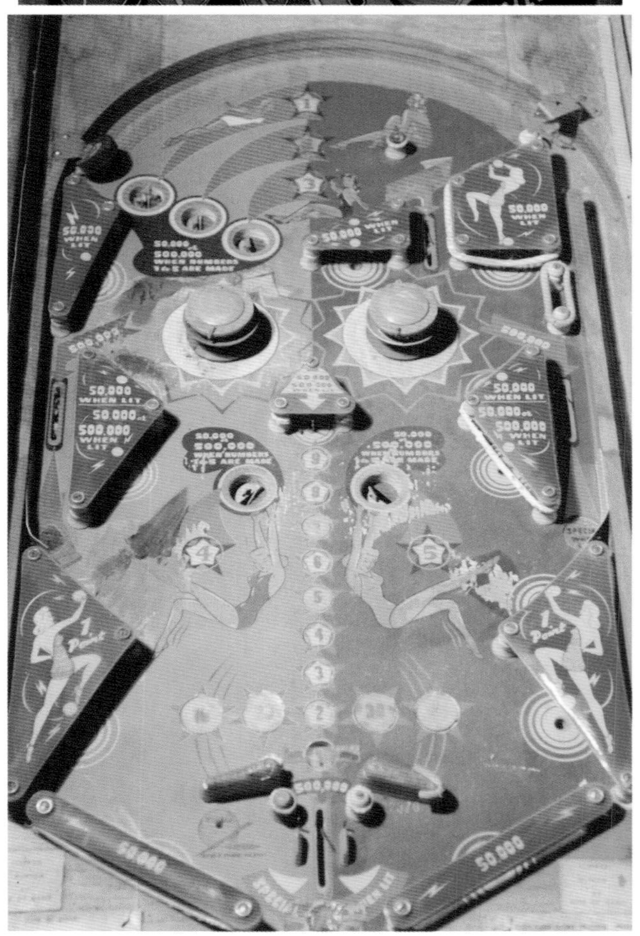

De-Icer. *Author's collection*. $1500.

Nate Schneller Inc. was one of the companies doing conversions of earlier games at this time. They released *MADAM BUTTERFLY* in April 1949. This machine was originally a United *SINGAPORE*; with the upgrade, it had two flippers pointed towards the upper half of the playfield. All pre-flipper games had become obsolete since the birth of the flipper. Companies like Nate Schneller offered operators upgrade kits that converted these pre-flipper games into flipper games.

The Universal Company was a subsidiary of United Manufacturing. They released *PHOTO FINISH*, a multiple coin horse race machine, in July 1949. This is a very rare game and even featured the A-B-C-D scoring bumpers.

Madam Butterfly. *Paul Brisbane collection.* $2000.

By the end of the 1940s, both Gottlieb and Williams remained in constant pinball production. The flipper and the power bumper had both been introduced. The games now offered players a real challenge and test of their skills. With the flipper, a player now controlled the ball and the game was not one of chance but one of skill. The machines produced towards the end of the 1940s exemplified the type of imaginative and innovative concepts that gave rise to the machines made in the following decade – the 1950s. These machines today are referred to as having been produced in the "Golden Age of Pinball."

Photo Finish. *Alan Tate collection.* $1500.

CHAPTER THREE
THE 1950S

In this period, the artists were busy turning out backglasses. They would have been on a tight schedule, sometimes having to sketch, do the artwork, and then have the machine screen-printed all in less than a month.

In the 1950s, there were new innovations to the pinball machine. We see the introduction of the gobble hole, score reels, multi-player games, and roto-targets. This was an American form of entertainment that had challenged, captivated, and inspired millions all around the world and continues to do so even today. D. Gottlieb & Co. dominated pinball in this era, followed by Williams.

There were many classic pinballs produced in this decade. I have pictured a few of the classics and have put them in date order in order to show readers the progress of the pinball from the early 1950s to the late 1950s.

1950

In 1950, Bally only manufactured horserace games; they had stopped producing pinball machines. *TURF KING* was released in April 1950 and featured five buttons on the top of the cabinet. Unlike previous games, this was a new concept, enabling the player to make different selections in the game.

Genco released *SOUTH PACIFIC,* with very enchanting artwork, in February. This machine was designed by Harvey Heiss and had ten kickout saucers in a diagonal row on the playfield. Completion of the sequence would light up the specials on the playfield. Genco also released *HARVEST TIME* in September, another classic game with an American Indian theme.

D. Gottlieb & Co. released *JUST 21* in January. This was a first – a pinball with two flippers facing towards the center of the playfield. This is the flipper format face on machines today. Harry Mabs designed the machine and we see the introduction of the turret shooter. Unlike other pinballs (which used a plunger to fire the ball onto the playfield), the player in this case, by activating the flipper button, would shoot the ball from the center of the playfield. The turret shooter would rotate from the left side of the playfield to the right, so that the player could aim at where the ball would be shot.

Turf King. *Author's collection.* $1500.

South Pacific. *Author's collection*. $1700.

Harvest Time. *Alan Tate collection*. $1500.

Gottlieb released *SELECT-A-CARD* in April. This machine featured select-a-card-play: there is a selector knob on the front of the cabinet and the player can choose any one of four cards on which to score; the player shoots to hit the numbered targets on top of the playfield and on the numbered bumpers on the playfield. The aim of the game is to get all the cards out; replays depend on how many balls were played to complete the card. The fewer the balls, the greater the number of replays. *SELECT-A-CARD* also used the turret shooter. This innovation was short lived as the novelty wore off. The last machine to use this feature in the 1950s was *BANK-A-BALL*. The playfields on machines with the turret shooter were open, and the drain between the flippers made it difficult for players to keep the ball in play.

Gottlieb released *DOUBLE FEATURE* in December 1950. This machine was designed by Wayne Neyens and was the first machine to use the kicking rubber; when the ball hits the rubber it kicks it around the playfield. In their flyer for this machine, Gottlieb stated "New Cyclonic Ball action with Whizzing-Whirling-Lightning speed sweeps Gottlieb's Double Feature."

Just 21. *Alan Tate collection.* $2000.

Select a Card. *Alan Tate collection.* $2000.

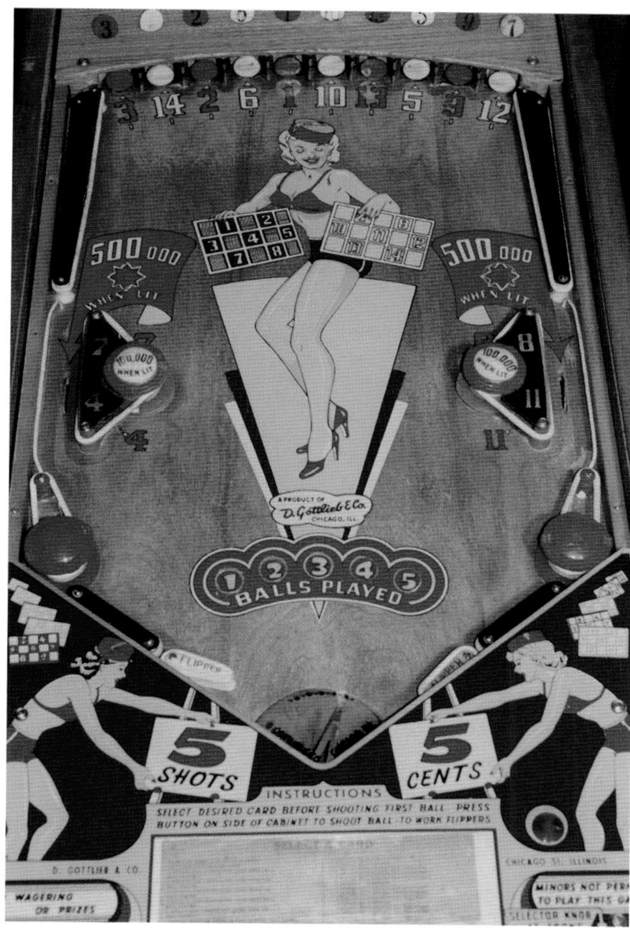

Select a Card. *Alan Tate collection.* $2000.

Harry Mabs designed *KNOCKOUT* in December; today this machine would be the most prized in anyone's collection. The playfield had a miniature boxing ring and two manikins would fight as certain features were hit with the ball. The combination of the two designers Harry Mabs and Wayne Neyens, along with artist Roy Parker, saw D. Gottlieb & Co. dominate the pinball industry during this period.

Williams released *DREAMY* in February. The player, by completing the sequence 1-5, lights up the special on the two side rollovers. Harry Williams designed this pinball and the artwork was by George Molentin. George Molentin captured the player's attention with his artwork – another example can be seen on *GEORGIA*, released in July. *PINKY* was released in September, with a new playfield layout unlike other machines in this period. It was asymmetrical, meaning the left side of the playfield was different from the right side.

Knockout. *Stan Muraski collection. Photo courtesy Russ Jensen.* $4000.

Dreamy. *Author's collection.* $1400.

Georgia. *Alan Tate collection.* $1400.

1951

When one-ball machines became illegal in this period, we saw the birth of the bingo machine; another name for this machine was the "in line machine." This machine usually had twenty-five holes on the playfield; the objective was to line up three, four, or five balls in a row to corresponding numbers on the backglass. The first Bally bingo was *BRIGHT LIGHTS*, released in April. At the start of the game, inserting more coins would increase your odds. These machines didn't pay out coins, rather they would register your winnings on a credit meter that could register up to 999 credits. The operator would then reimburse your winnings. By hitting a switch (usually under the machine) or by turning it off, the credits would be reset to 000. *BROADWAY*, an early example of these games, was released in June. The man responsible for these machines was designer/engineer Donald E. Hooker, who had started working for the company in the 1930s. Although the machines looked similar, they all offered different features. Bally dominated the bingo market; its only challenge came from United Manufacturing. Another manufacturer of bingo type games was Universal, a subsidiary of United Manufacturing. They released *FIVE STAR* in May. This machine had a large console floor cabinet and an unusual playfield. You could play up to five cards of bingo on this machine: one coin would allow you to play one card, and every other coin deposited would give you another card.

United released *COUNTY FAIR* in September 1951. This machine had six animated horses in the backglass; it looked like a pinball but had no flippers. Another machine by United was *LEADER*. It was released in October and also had a large console floor cabinet.

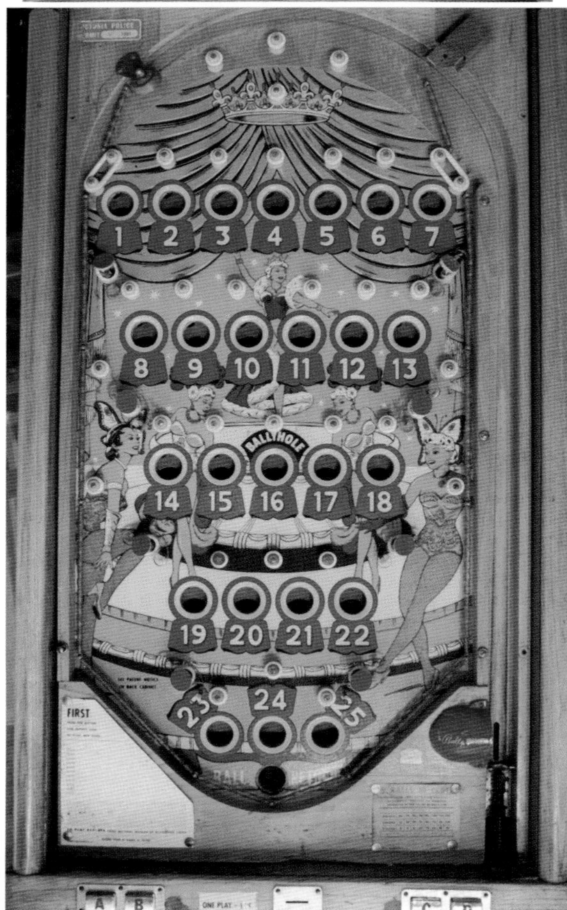

Broadway. *Jason Douglas collection*. $1200.

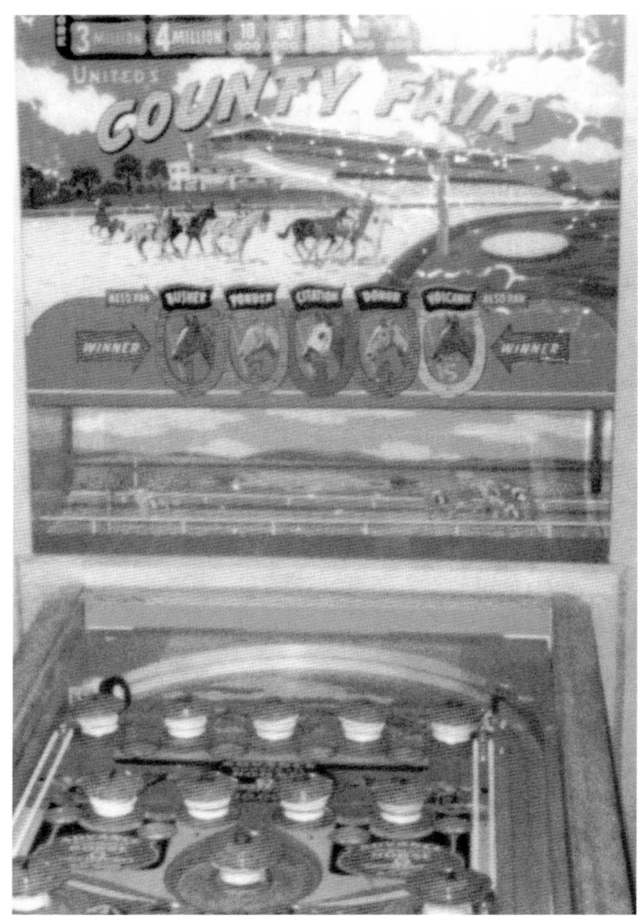

County Fair. *Richard Conger collection. Photo courtesy Russ Jensen*. $2500.

Just a small story I would like to share at this point ... Because of the rarity of old machines down here in Australia, the only way to see them, play them, and enjoy them is to import them. There is a lot of risk involved, especially for me, being so far away. Nonetheless, I have purchased machines from all over the States. In the beginning, I was so naive I thought machines could be shipped from one side of the country to the next for around $100 a machine; I later found out that the average price for moving games is $250. In mid 1999, there was a County Fair pinball for sale in South Dakota for $900. I had to have it, so I sent off the payment. To get this machine to Chicago cost me another $300; by now I had purchased enough machines to fill a container. I remember the container arriving – I was like a child with his first toy. I started unloading the container and it had some real goodies in it, but the machine I was most anxious to see was County Fair. When I got towards the back of the container, I saw it. As I started moving the machine, however, my heart sank and I felt like crying, as the only backglass to break in the whole container was County Fair. I couldn't believe it. I have tried for over a year to locate another one and had given up hope. However, a friend of mine named Gordon Williams, who has just set up a company called "Pinball Rescue," is going to re-screen it for me. You can check out his web site at www.pinballrescue.com.

Here I am with my County Fair. What's even sadder is that before it broke, the backglass was a 10/10.

It was in this period that we see the introduction of animated backglasses. Williams Manufacturing were responsible for the most collectible horseracing theme pinballs. It started with *HAYBURNERS* in June, a machine designed by Harry Williams and Sam Stern. This machine had six bumpers on it numbered one to six; hitting the bumper would move the horse whose

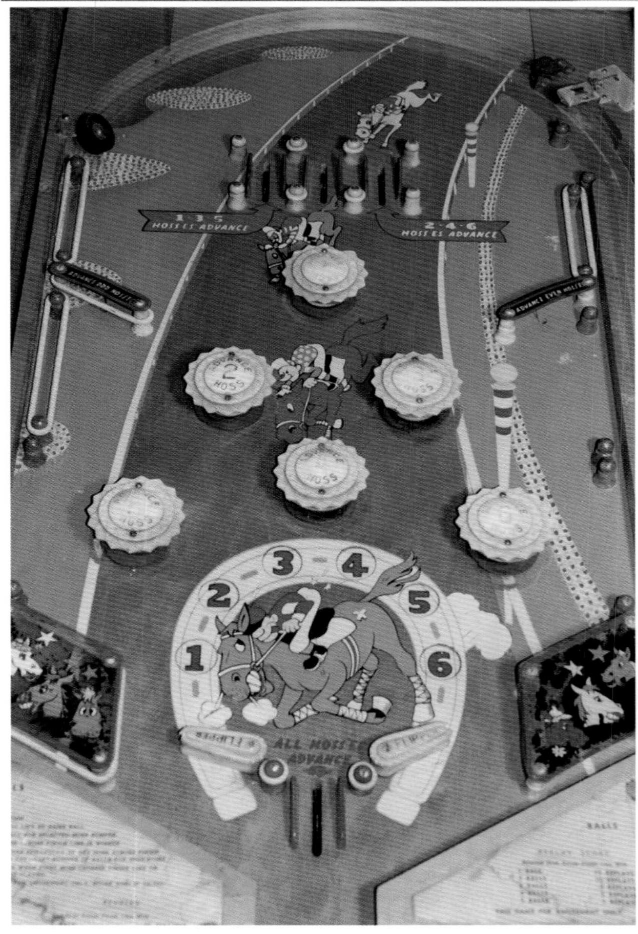

Hayburners. *Alan Tate collection.* $2500.

number was on the bumper. If you ran your designated horse home it would give you free plays, and the operator could set the machine to vary the number of replays. For example, if you raced your horse home on the first ball you would get 20 credits; on the second ball, 15 credits; on the third ball, 10 credits; on the fourth ball, 5 credits; and on the fifth ball, 2 credits. The flippers were still reversed and either flipper button would operate both flippers. In August, Williams Manufacturing released *JALOPY*, which was identical to *HAYBURNERS* but with different artwork: instead of horses racing on the backglass there were cars. *HORSESHOES*, released in December, was designed by Harry Williams and the artwork was by George Molentin. On these early games, when the ball was lost it would sit at the bottom of the playfield. When all five balls had been lost, the flippers still worked as these machines couldn' t recognize how many balls had been played.

Jalopy. *Alan Tate collection.* $2500.

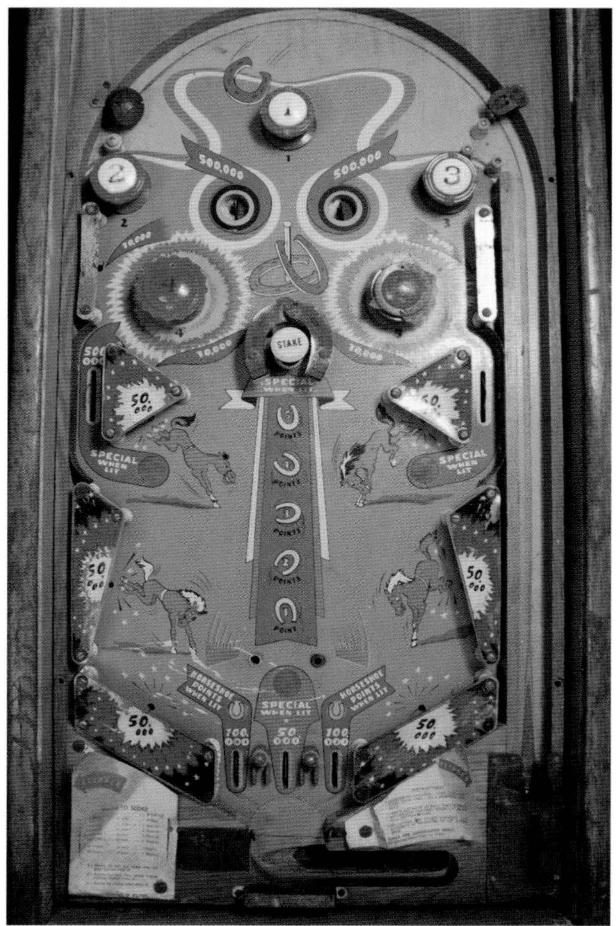

Horseshoes. *Jason Douglas collection.* $1600.

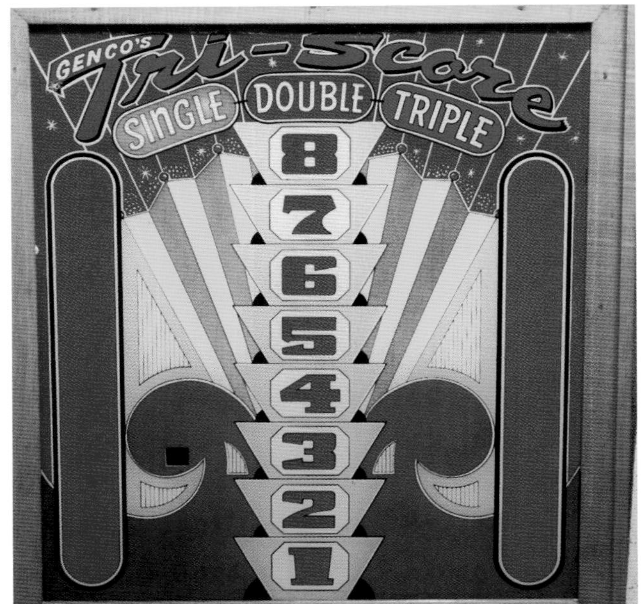

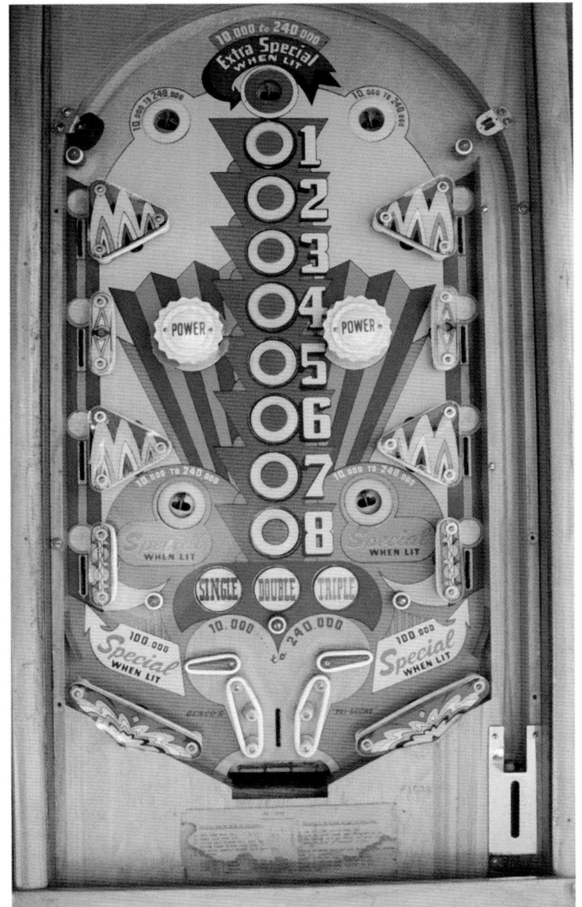

Tri-Score. *Author's collection*. $1500.

TRI–SCORE was released by Genco in February. The one thing this machine lacked was artwork. By completing the sequence 1-8 on the playfield the player would light up the special. *DOUBLE ACTION*, featuring an elevator in the backbox, was released in December. The elevator would start when the ball lands in the "Double Action Hole;" as soon as it scores in the backbox the ball is ejected back onto the playfield.

Double Action. *Author's collection*. $1800.

I have always been fascinated with Genco pinballs. I love the games and it was an honor to talk with one of their great designers, Harvey Heiss, with whom I made contact while writing this book. Harvey is the oldest living designer today. When I spoke to him he commented that he has had a wonderful life and has always enjoyed everything he did. Harvey was born on the 12th of February, 1908 and grew up in Chicago. He was one of the greatest designers of the pinball game, designing many classics while working at Genco Manufacturing. Prior to starting work at Genco, Harvey worked at the Widenmiller Co. at the age of eighteen in 1926.

The Widenmiller Co. was supplying Genco Manufacturing with parts for their games and Harvey worked in the Foundry and Die section. He was approached by David Gensberg, owner of the Genco factory, to instruct employees on how to use dyes in the fabrication of their products. Harvey would work after hours at the factory. The company was making gum ball machines and Harvey was doing the servicing during this time; being the creator that he was, he designed his own gumball machine.

Harvey Heiss is in the rear left of the Genco machine shop. *Courtesy Steve Kordek.*

At Genco his assignment was designing counter games and then pin games, which were his specialty. Harvey designed the first pinball to use steel vice glass balls. *SILVER CUP*, released in 1933, had a "score totalizer" and was the first pin game to use castings, an idea stemming from Harvey's foundry background.

On a roll-down game called *ADVANCE ROLL* that he designed, the playfield had a bingo hole layout. On this game, Harvey designed a solenoid-powered bar that would push the ball back up the playfield; it was energized by a player pushing a button if the ball missed all the holes. He remarked that this was "really the first flipper."

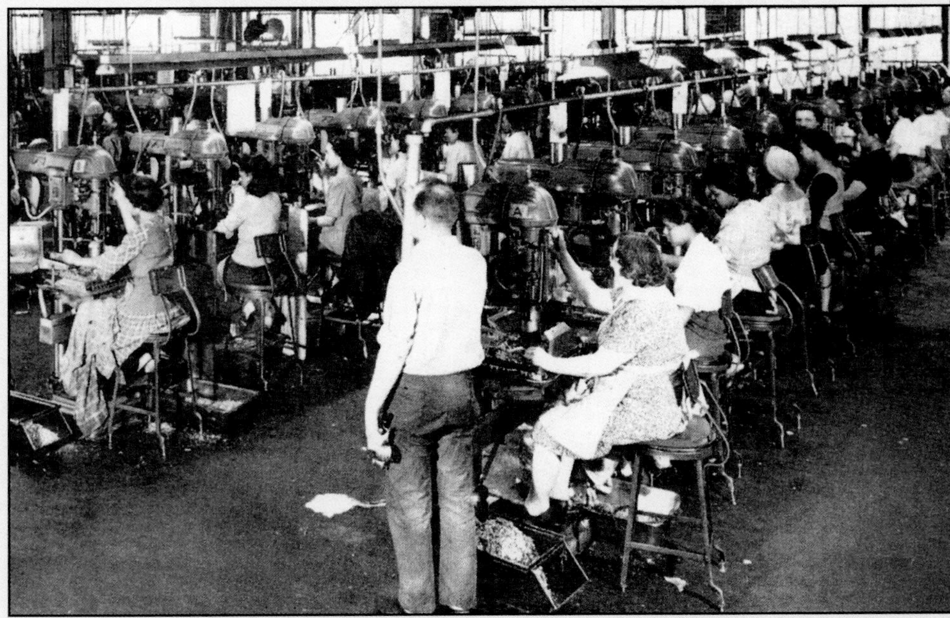

Genco factory goes to war. *Courtesy Steve Kordek.*

Harvey met Steve Kordek in 1937 and they are still friends today. Steve began working on the assembly line and when he was familiarized and competent in knowing all the parts of a game he joined Harvey in the designing room. While working at Genco, Harvey would go to the factory in the middle of the night and design games, as it was easier concentrating then. When the workers started arriving in the morning he would go back home, have breakfast, and then come back to work. Some of Harvey's classic games include the upright pinball machines that were released in the early 1950s: *JUMPING JACK*, *400*, and *GOLDEN NUGGET*.

Harvey had taken a vacation in Florida and decided to look up the Genco distributor on the East Coast. He met Bert Lane, who took him to see his plant. At the time, Bert had an order to produce 5-horse merry-go-rounds and offered Harvey a job; he accepted the offer and left Genco in 1955. There is a lot of recognition this man deserves; he even designed the original Pepe the Clown. Harvey also designed a digger (Crane novelty game), which was sold to Williams, and he went back to Chicago to help put it into production. The Bert Lane Company was eventually taken over by Continental Vending in New York. Harvey was on the design team that brought out the first machine to dispense ice into a cup.

This great man lives in Florida today with his wife Ethel and daughter Janice. On one occasion that I rang, his daughter answered the phone. I asked her if she would like to write a few words about her father.

My father shared most of his engineering background and inventive mind with my son, Stephen. This has been a determining factor in the direction in Stephens's life – "Gramps" was the father he never had. The two of them spent countless hours together. One time in particular I can remember was when dad would go around the neighborhood looking for castaway electronics, bringing home TVs, radios, old phonographs, etc. and would set Steve under the outside overhang. It was there that my dad taught "my five year old" how to solder! Hammering and sawing were already old hat by the time Steve was four. It was only recently that I learned about this and all the times he got injured. Dad felt it was important that he should learn such with his oversight – being a typical mother, they knew I would have flipped if I had known. Many a time "accidents" were retold as something much more benign. Little did I know what factors were at work forming my son.

"Gramps," as Steve calls him, gave him a sense of adventure and an insatiable curiosity for life and how things worked – or worked better. What a wonderful way in which to immortalize and honor the work and love Dad has than to include him in your book. God bless your work with success.

—Janice Forguson

Harvey Heiss, enjoying a break from the pinball industry. *Courtesy Jan Forguson.*

Harvey with his grandson Steve. *Courtesy Jan Forguson.*

What can I say after reading what Janice has written? There are many behind the success of pinballs whose work hasn't been recognized in books in the past. I feel I should have done more, but being so far away my resources are limited. I remember Harvey asking me to sign a book for him. I replied "it is you who should be signing it for me."

I asked Steve Kordek if he could name one of the games he had designed that he was most proud of:

The one that I feel most proud of was Triple Action, which Genco released in 1948. Gottlieb had released Humpty Dumpty, the first pinball with flippers, designed by Harry Mabs. I believe the flipper was the making of the pinball game. Suddenly the pressure was on all of Gottlieb's competitors to come up with their own flipper design. I was told to get a game ready for the Coin Machine Industry show at the Sherman Hotel and only had seven weeks to do it. On that game, I elected to use only two flippers, placing them in the center at the bottom of the playfield. At the show, everybody but me had copied the Humpty Dumpty feature and had six flippers on the playfield. Triple Action was named the hit of the show.

The one person who had the most influence on me was Harvey Heiss. I worked with him for twenty years at Genco and it was from him that I learned to make successful game layouts. Layouts are so important in keeping players interested, which is the basic idea of a pin game design. I've got to give him all the credit. He is still alive and I have visited him every so often. He has previously come to the Pinball Expo in Chicago that I attend on a regular basis but his health doesn't allow him to attend now.

—Steve Kordek

Niagara. *Alan Tate collection.* $3000.

D. Gottlieb & Co. released *NIAGARA* in December. This was the first machine to use "trap holes" and there were four of them on the playfield. Similar to a bingo machine, once the ball is trapped, it remains in the hole until the next game. Trapping the four balls would give you a replay. The backglass was animated, and featured a person falling down the falls as targets are hit. Notice the couple having a peck on the bottom left of the backglass: this was Roy Parker at his best. Wayne Neyens designed the machine and it is one of his favorite games.

Harry Mabs was responsible for some of Gottlieb's greatest games, highly desired by collectors today. Another fine example is seen on *MINSTREL MAN*, released in January. The center of the playfield featured three dropdown "Sambo" targets, which would be unacceptable today. Harry Mabs left the company and went to Williams Manufacturing in the middle of 1951, feeling he didn't get the recognition he deserved for inventing the flipper at D. Gottlieb & Co. The last machine he designed at Gottlieb was *WILD WEST*, which was released in August.

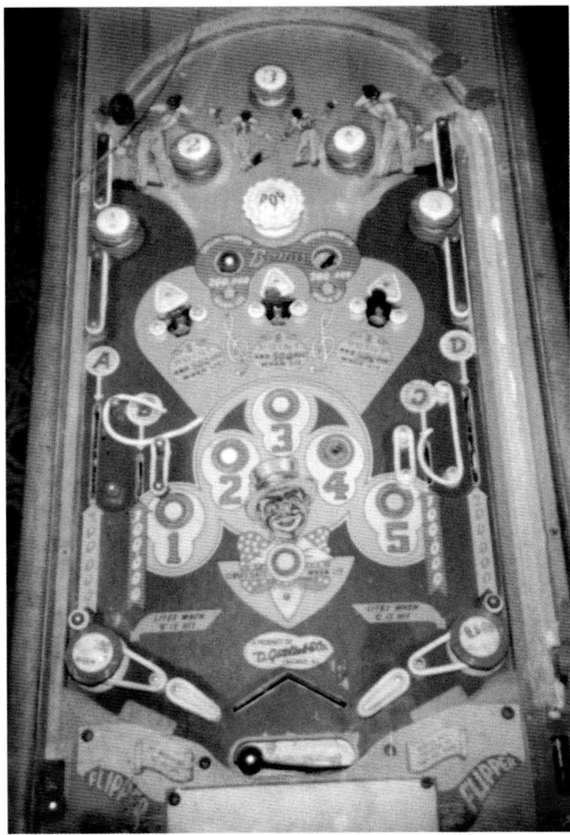

Minstrel Man. *Photo courtesy Russ Jensen.* $3500.

As soon as you mention the word flipper to me, I think of Harry Mabs. When Wayne Neyens sent me the photo of Harry, I truly couldn't believe it as I have never seen a picture of him before. I asked Wayne to write a few words about his friend, and his reply was as follows:

Harry Mabs was born the same year that Dave Gottlieb was born, 1901. They often talked about the fact that they were the same age. Harry was a great storyteller, very good at telling jokes and had a very outgoing personality. Harry was not only a great designer but he was an excellent artist. He liked to draw and spent many hours, perhaps days, painting on playboards and vellum; drawing was his hobby. So he would get ideas for a game and usually a theme to go with the idea and then he would draw and color the picture to go with the idea. Harry was a good enough artist that he took courses at the Art Institute in Chicago, a very prestigious Art School. He loved to draw clowns – one large beautiful one he gave to Dave Gottlieb. Harry left Gottlieb shortly after designing the flipper, which was Gottlieb's loss and William's gain. Although Harry never designed any great games at Williams he was a major contributor to their design department with many, many ideas.

—Wayne Neyens

Harry Mabs is on the right in this photo taken at the Gottlieb factory. Jim Mangum, a Gottlieb salesman, is holding a spanner to Harry's head. *Courtesy Wayne Neyens.*

1952

Williams Manufacturing released *SLUGFEST* in March, designed by Harry Williams. The backglass was animated, with men actually running from base to base. When the ball is trapped in the hole on the playfield, the men in the backglass are activated. Williams released *MAJORETTES* the next month; on the backglass for this game we see five beautiful women in a parade. Artist George Molentin even included a Williams cameraman on the right of the glass. The flippers are set on either side at the bottom of the playfield with a huge gap between them for the ball to be lost. A power bumper was placed in the middle to help save the ball. *HONG KONG* was released in September, combining pinball and bingo in one. On the upper right hand corner of the backglass there was a five row by three row card indicator and there were fifteen holes on the playfield. This machine proved to be a hit with players.

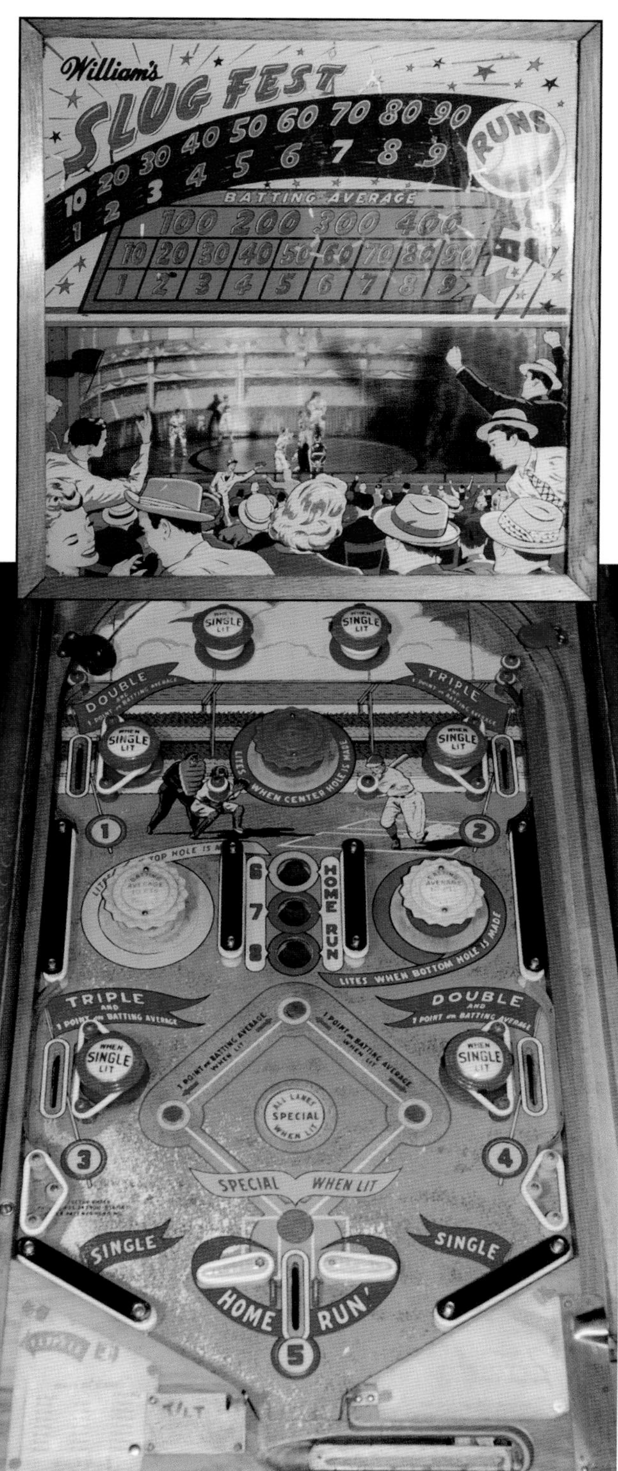

Slugfest. *Alan Tate collection.* $3000.

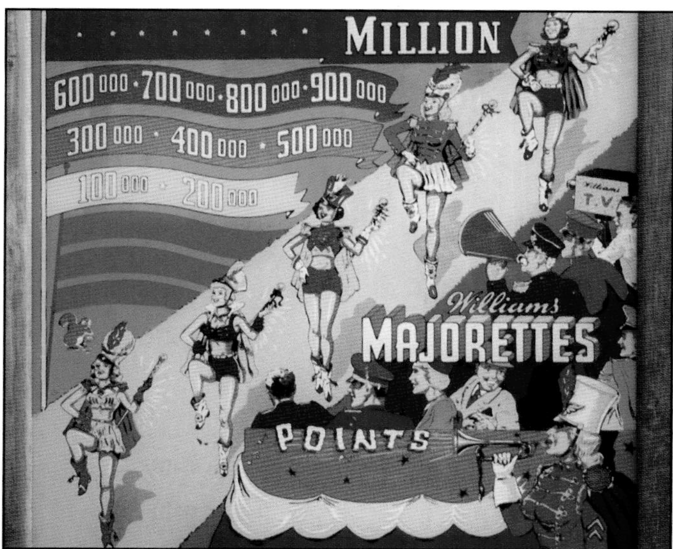

Majorette. *Jason Douglas collection.* $1300.

Hong Kong. *Alan Tate collection.* $1300.

In November, Williams released *DISK JOCKEY*, which also combined bingo with pinball. The holes are set a little differently than on *HONG KONG*. On this machine there are a group of nine holes in the upper center of the playfield and six below the flippers. *DISK JOCKEY* featured a "Double Score" feature: when bumpers 1 to 5 were hit in consecutive order they would light the double on the backglass and this would double the In-Line replays. When bumpers 1 to 7 were hit in consecutive order, this would give the player a free game and would light the side rollovers for special. Williams released *TWENTY GRAND* in December, which was also a hit with players. It featured "high scores and spell awards," meaning a player could win games by reaching certain scores or by spelling words on the playfield. There were nine trap holes on the center panel of the machine. If a player spelled "TWO" they would get two free games, if they spelled "FIVE" they would get five free games. The ultimate challenge was to spell "TWENTY," which would give twenty free games. This machine had four flippers on it. Only two could be controlled with the flipper button on the side of the cabinet. The two closest to the sides of the cabinet were activated as soon as the ball went in the eject hole; the flipper would send the ball back up the playfield. Harry Williams, who designed all the above machines, cleverly designed this machine and George Molentin did the artwork on all the games.

Disk Jockey. *Alan Tate collection.* $1500.

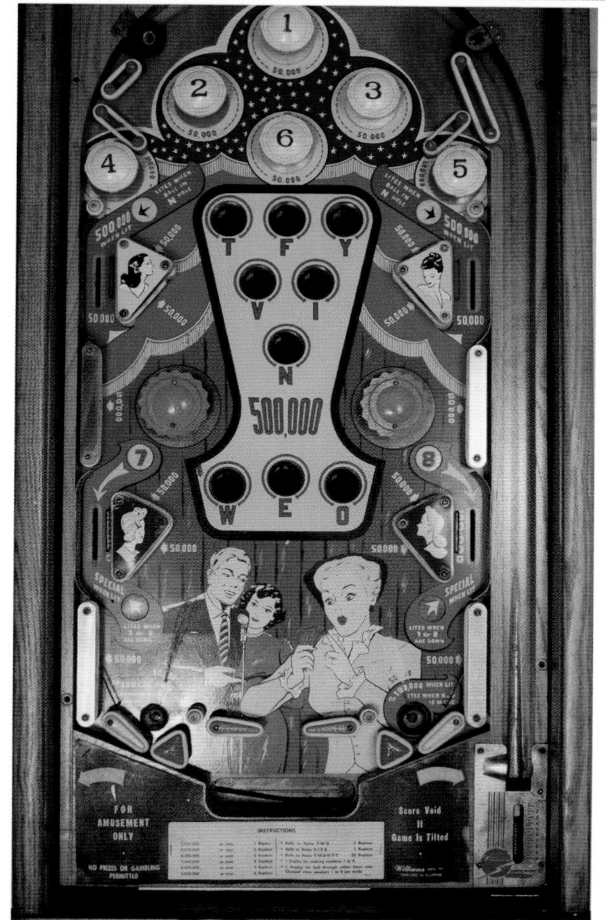

Twenty Grand. *Jason Douglas collection.* $1400.

Genco released three pinballs in 1952. The first was *SPRINGTIME*, released in March. Like *DOUBLE ACTION*, which had been released earlier, this machine had balls in the backglass that would be released when the player trapped the ball in the eject holes on the playfield. There is a beautiful woman lifting up her dress on the playfield, which would have caught the attention of all male players. In October, Genco released *400* and in December they released *JUMPING JACK*. These two were both upright games with a vertical playfield. They didn't take up as much room as a pinball, and could be operated in locations where space was limited.

400. *Alan Tate collection.* $1200.

D. Gottlieb & Co. released *CROSSROADS* in May. This machine had five trap holes on the playfield. When a ball was trapped it would light a corresponding rollover button for more points. If a player was able to complete the 1-7 sequence it would light up the special on the bottom rollover that was between the flippers. *CORONATION* was released in November, seven months before the crowning of Queen Elizabeth II on June 2, 1953. The machine had seven trap holes set in a (V) pattern. If a player got four balls in a line they would be given a replay.

We are now in the classical period of Gottlieb woodrails.

Crossroads. *Alan Tate collection.* $2000.

Coronation. *Barry Gooding collection.* $3000.

QUEEN OF HEARTS, released in December, was the first machine to use the "gobble hole." It had five of them in an arc across the center playfield. Again, we see the brilliance of Roy Parker on the backglass.

Queen of Hearts. *Author's collection.* $3000.

1953

Genco Manufacturing had success with their upright vertical pinballs, releasing *GOLDEN NUGGET* in February and *SILVER CHEST* in April. The backglass on *GOLDEN NUGGET* was appealing and captivating.

Williams released *SILVER SKATES* in February. This machine had an animated backglass and also five trap holes on the playfield. If a player trapped the ball in the penalty box (trap hole closest to the flipper), it would be released when balls were trapped in the other four holes. When this sequence was accomplished, the "extra special" would light up. As on *TWENTY GRAND*, released earlier, the player could only control the two closest to the outhole by hitting the flipper switch on the side of the cabinet. The two outer ones were automatically energized as soon as the ball landed in the hole adjacent to the flipper.

It was in this year that Williams Manufacturing began using score reels. They were first seen on *ARMY NAVY*, released in October. The scoring was done using score reels instead of lights behind the backglass. The players resisted them, however, and only a few more were made. *STRUGGLE BUGGIES* was released in November. Although the machine scored in millions, only the first three score reels would score – the last four were dummy ones that stayed on (0). By lighting the bumpers 1-7, the player would light up special. Scoring points on the playfield would advance the buggy around the track and making A-B-C would light up specials between the flippers. Williams Manufacturing released *DEALER* in December, which also featured card score. A player could win free games on reaching high score, getting special on the playfield, or by matching 21.

Golden Nugget. *Alan Tate collection.* $1200.

Silver Skates. *Alan Tate collection.* $1800.

D. Gottlieb & Co. released *GUYS DOLLS* in May; it was designed by Wayne Neyens and is usually known as "Guys and Dolls." The one thing lacking was flippers. By hitting the flipper button, the player would activate the six arrowed rebound posts at the bottom of the playfield. This is a unique and unusual game; completing the A-B-C-D-E sequence lights the bonus hole for replays. The artwork, again by Roy Parker, is very colorful.

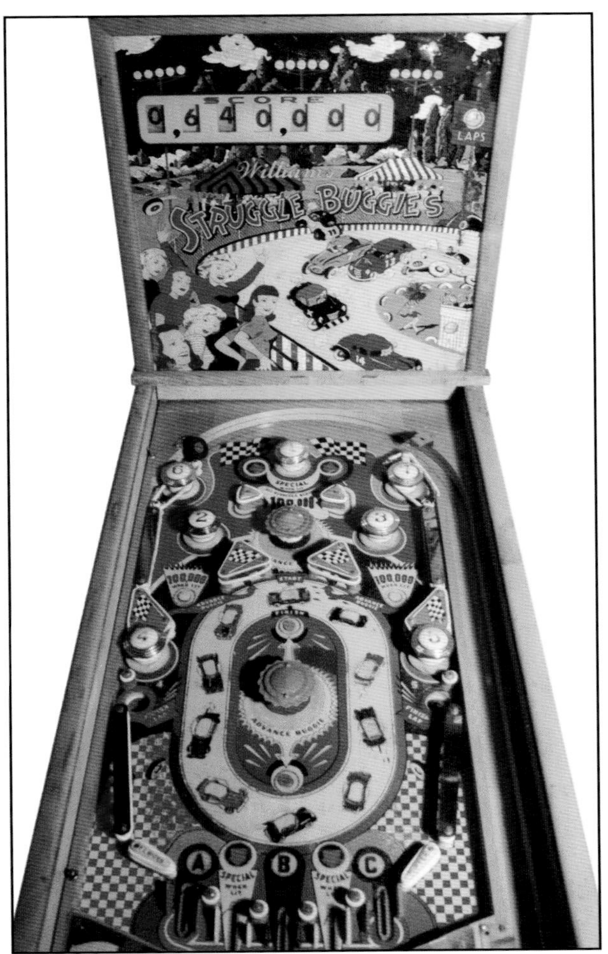

Struggle Buggies. *Alan Tate collection.* $2000.

Dealer. *Author's collection.* $2000.

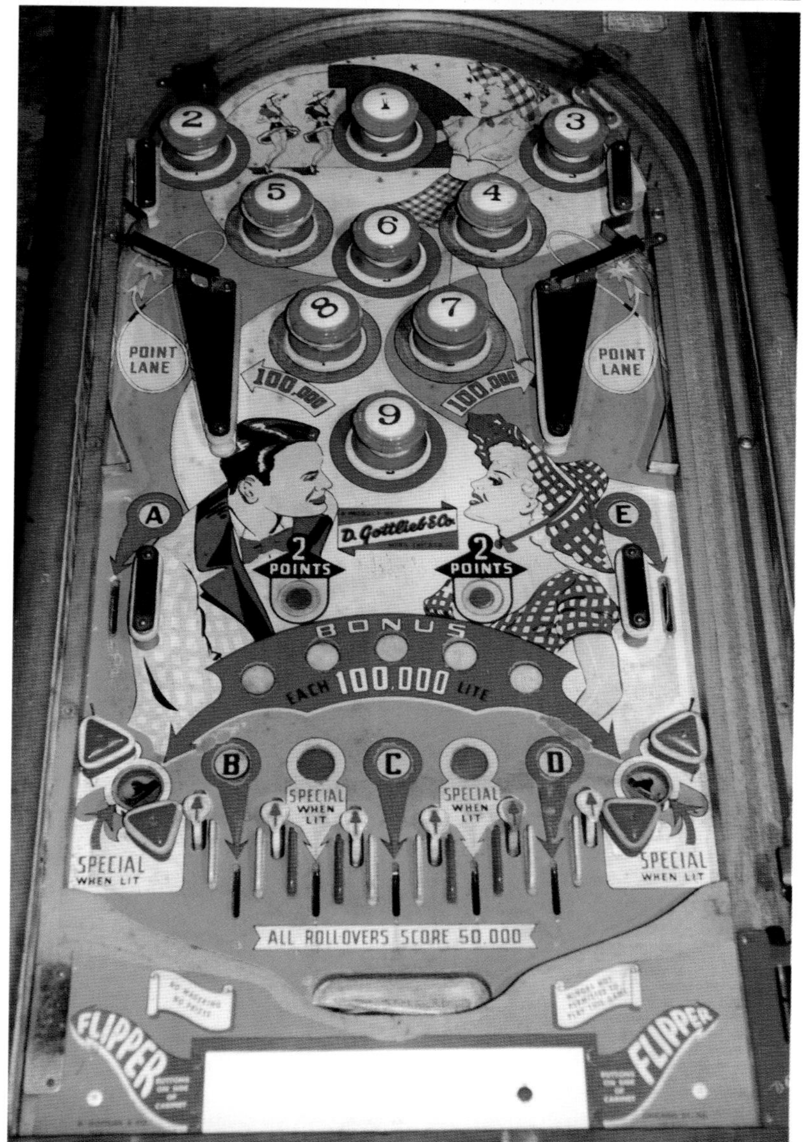

Guys Dolls. *Alan Tate collection.* $1500.

1954

Williams Manufacturing released *SPITFIRE* in December, designed by Harry Williams. It had a mini yellow playfield on the left side and a green one on the right side. By building up bonuses, a player could score replays. The flippers were still reversed and the machine could score up to two hundred replays. The artwork was by George Molentin,who fascinated players with this backglass.

Spitfire. *Jason Douglas collection*. $1400.

The commanding position held by Bally Manufacturing in producing bingo machines did not go unchallenged. United Manufacturing was also producing these games. In March, they released *MEXICO*. This game was the first to use the select button on the front of the machine. On the playfield were an extra three holes where the player could light up Mexico on the backglass.

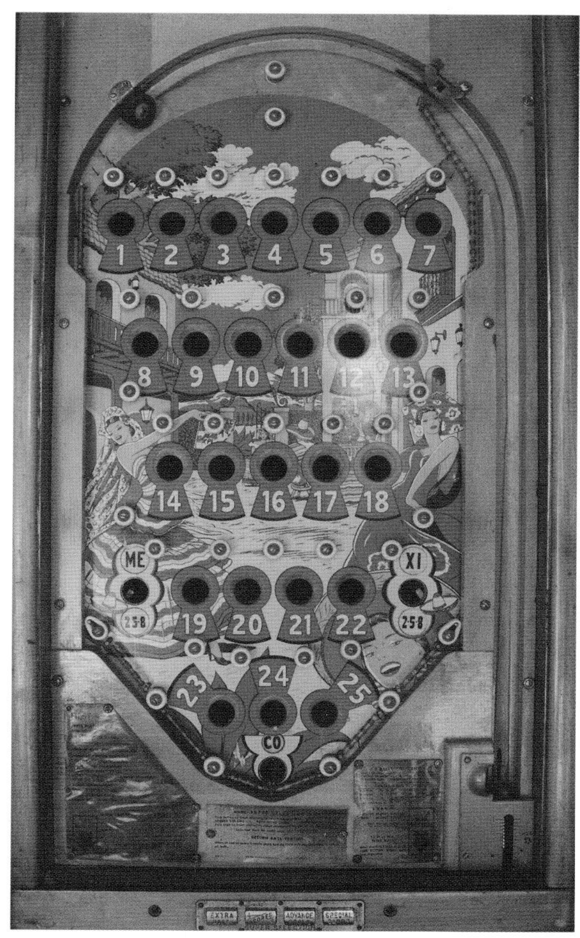

Mexico. *Jason Douglas collection*. $1000.

Hawaiian Beauty. *Alan Tate collection*. $2000.

Gottlieb released *HAWAIIAN BEAUTY* in May, designed by Wayne Neyens. He cleverly put the three pop bumpers at the bottom of the playfield, providing more action. The game was originally called Monkey Shine but was later changed. Wayne Neyens was the chief designer at D. Gottlieb & Co. and designed all their games. He was responsible for the one of the most significant changes to pinball, the introduction of the first multi-player game allowing four people to compete. *SUPER JUMBO* was released in October, using rotating scoring drums instead of the lighted scoring. The idea of reel scoring came from shuffleboards that were being used by United Manufacturing. Only five hundred were produced, making it a rarity today. Unfortunately the usual colorful backglasses that players were used to seeing by Roy Parker were not on this machine. Still, this game was a major breakthrough in the industry. It paved the way for the future, as today all games have multiple player option.

I asked Wayne Neyens how he designed the multi-player unit:

The first four player game circuit was a real challenge. I ended up, on my game, using our 86 point unit and did all the switching on the disc. Bob Smith, our Chief Engineer, thought that the unit was overworked and that it would be necessary to build a different, stronger unit. So it was decided it would be better to use relays instead, thus the player unit and player relays were the end result. I also built a six player and called it HIGH BOY. As I recall we only built one game – what a monstrosity that was and what a circuit.

—Wayne Neyens

Super Jumbo. *Alan Tate collection.* $3000.

I had the opportunity to contact Alvin Gottlieb on numerous occasions while writing this book. I asked him to write a few words about his father David, who founded the company D. Gottlieb & Co. Alvin considered the factory as his "second home." A funny thing Alvin shared with me was that he could always tell what mood his father was in by the angle of his cigar – the higher up it pointed the angrier he was. When I asked Alvin what section in the book would he like the story to appear, he replied next to *SUPER JUMBO* as it was a machine dad was proud of. Here is what Alvin had to say:

To write about David Gottlieb and the company he founded would take an extensive volume. First about the man and his legacy. Dave, as he was always called, was a man of high integrity who boasted that "His word was his bond," which was universally attested to by his family, his employees and his customers. A tough exterior belied the true kindness and consideration he extended to all.

As his son, I was privy to many intimate details of his generosity to those in need. He ran his company with an iron hand though, and he preached to us that there is only one way to run a business, that is, "the right way." He adopted the phrase "There is no substitute for quality" as the company's motto and it appeared on the games and in all the advertising. Dave's youngest brother, Nathan, "Nate" as he was called, became sales manager and was universally liked and respected by all in the business. Dave was intimately involved in game design and artwork. His chief engineer, Bob Smith, never said anything was "good" or "bad"; it was acceptable or not acceptable. Harry Mabs, a designer, worked many of Dave's ideas into very successful games. Wayne Neyens, the most prolific creative game de-

signer in the field, developed the art of design into a system that ran from "raw wood" to a finished product that was easily adapted to production by the engineering department. Roman "Doc" Garbark was the mechanical design engineer who created many intricate units that gave Gottlieb games "That touch of Originality and Dependability." Tony Jerard, plant superintendent, was originally a tool and die maker and ran production as a precise operation. These aforementioned people were the nucleus of Dave's company.

The factory was staffed with people, some of whom had started working for Dave in 1927. Over the years many families and individuals stayed with the company and belonged to the "25 Year Club" and some remained considerably longer.

Judd Weinberg, Dave's son-in-law, began with the company in developing the export market, which in later years became the cornerstone of the company's most successful period. He became president of the company when Dave eased off his management time to do more fishing. Judd's devotion to the business saw the firm grow to its position as the world's largest manufacturer of amusement pinball machines.

Judd and I wore many "hats" as was the case in the operation of a closely held business. My tenure started in 1947 when my father took me into the engineering department and told them to teach me everything there is to know about building pinball machines in two years. Of course I never learned it "all" but enough to understand what our goals were. I loved the business and plunged into whatever area I could to do what needed doing.

In 1956, Dave and Dorothy Gottlieb announced they were going to endow the construction of a hospital in memory of his parents, Samuel and Bertha Gottlieb. I was given the task to "Get our architects together with some doctor friends and get the planning going." When Dave Gottlieb gave orders, things happened. One of his favorite expressions was "Things just don't happen…you have got to make them happen." The Gottlieb Memorial Hospital opened in July of 1961 with 120 beds and a handful of doctors. Today the Hospital campus includes a 200-bed hospital; a multi-story physician office building; a health and fitness center; a Cancer Care Center dedicated to Marjorie Gottlieb Weinberg, Judds' wife who lost a valiant fight to cancer; a child care center; and various other entities that constitute the "Gottlieb Health Resources" organization. From a very modest start, the combined budget now reaches over $300 million and serves an ever-widening community. When asked why he started this project, he simply said he "Wanted to put something back into the land that has been so good to him."

In as brief a manner as possible, I have tried to encapsulate what D. Gottlieb & Company was about. As you know, the company was sold to Columbia Pictures in 1976, but both the Gottlieb and Weinberg families are active in the operation of Gottlieb Hospital just as Dave Gottlieb wished. In a different way the "Legend Goes On."

—Alvin J. Gottlieb

Pioneer Dave Gottlieb. *Photo courtesy Wayne Neyens.*

Another favorite of mine is *DIAMOND LILL*, released in December. The center of this machine had a horseshoe with ten different colored diamonds around it, and the machine had reverse flippers. The balls played would collect in the tray when they were lost. Another machine released by D. Gottlieb that month was *STAGE COACH*, one of the early single player games that indicated the balls played. The small white buttons on the bottom left would light up as each ball was lost. The machine had five gobble holes in the center of the playfield. The artwork was brilliant, capturing the American West on both the backglass and the playfield.

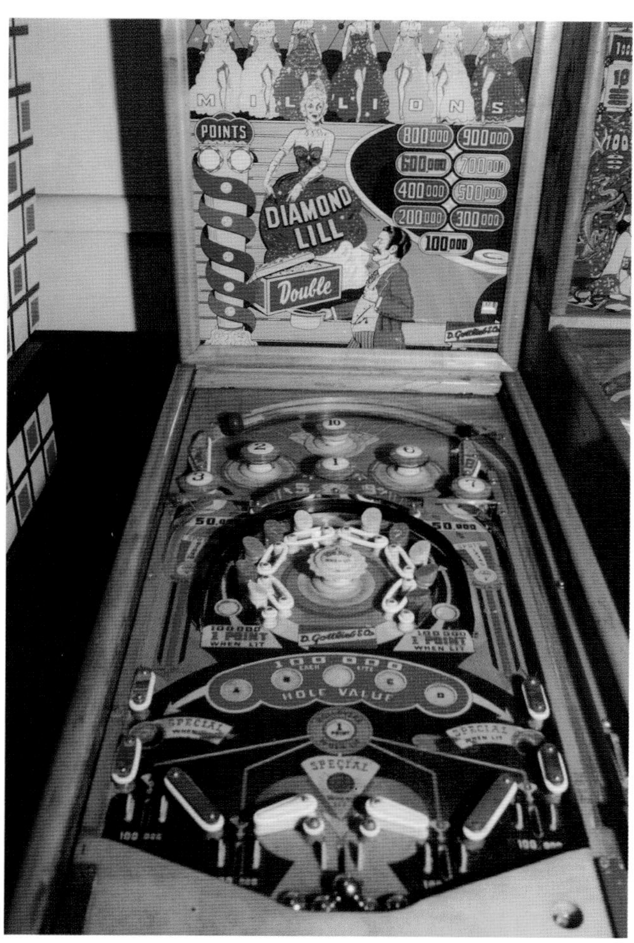

Diamond Lill. *Paul Brisbane collection.* $2000.

Stage Coach. *Jason Douglas collection.* $2000.

I asked designer Wayne Neyens where he got his ideas from and whether he was ever under pressure to design games:

You asked me about design pressure and where ideas come from – I'll try to answer those two questions. First the easy one about pressure. When I was the only designer I often thought about the number of families and family members that were directly dependent on my work, not only the employees of Gottlieb but all the employees of the companies that supplied us with cabinets, coils, plastics etc. It was a responsibility I never took lightly. When I moved up to Chief Engineer I was still responsible for the designs, the artwork etc.

Where did ideas come from? They came from every where. One of my favorite places to go on a Sunday afternoon was the Museum of Science and Industry in Chicago, a place full of ideas. Just driving along and seeing a billboard as an example might suggest something. Even dreaming if you can believe it. Songs, movies etc. – the world was full of ideas. I just had to look for them and recognize them. You ask a song writer where he gets an idea for a tune and he wouldn't really know – it just comes from out there, you just have to recognize it. In response to my priest who once asked the same question I told him I always got my best ideas during his sermons. That brought quite a laugh but you know there is some truth there.

—Wayne Neyens

1955

Williams Manufacturing released their first four player machine, called *RACE THE CLOCK*, in March – five months after Gottlieb released *SUPER JUMBO*. This was the company's first multiple player game with score reels. The multi-player games offered players a chance to challenge each other, thus making them more competitive. *WONDERLAND* was released the following month. Although multi-player games were popular, they added to the production costs. To keep expenses down, the company continued with the light up backglass scoring. Harry Williams designed the machine and artwork was by George Molentin. The backglass was exceptionally attractive and the game challenged players. On the top of the machine are four rollovers numbered 1 to 4. If a player lit these up it would light the middle rollover for special. The machine had one gobble hole (also known as the skill hole), which was in the center of the playfield. In August, Williams released their first two-player pinball, called *CIRCUS WAGON*. The gobble hole was placed just below the center on the playfield. Although it awarded 10-100 points, it also meant the end of the ball.

Above & right: Wonderland. *Author's collection.* $4000.

D. Gottlieb & Co. released *DUETTE* in March, designed by Wayne Neyens. This was their first two-player pinball machine. The artwork on the backglass is not necessary catchy as compared to previous games. The focus appeared to be on the score reels, which made *DUETTE'S* backglass uninteresting. Gottlieb made two versions, a standard and a deluxe model. The backglass was larger on the deluxe model, with the word "deluxe" appearing on the left and the right sides. The body also was larger and used shuffle style legs.

Circus Wagon. *Jason Douglas collection*. $1800.

Duette. *Author's collection*. $2500.

Sluggin' Champ. *Alan Tate collection.* $3000.

SLUGGIN' CHAMP, released in April, also came out in both standard and deluxe models. This game is based on the great American sport of baseball. The game shows eight teams in the National League (New York, Brooklyn, Milwaukee, Cincinnati, Philadelphia, Chicago and Pittsburgh) and eight teams in the American league (Cleveland, New York, Chicago, Detroit, Boston, Washington, Baltimore, and Kansas City). The object is hitting rollovers and contacts to complete either league, which lights the special hole on the center of the playfield. As soon as a rollover is activated the corresponding city on the backglass lights up. This is one of my favorite games. The next four-player game was *JUBILEE*, released in May. This was a low production game, with only five hundred made, as score reels added to the production costs of pinball machines. This was the second four-player machine the company produced.

SOUTHERN BELLE, another classic pinball from the golden era, was released in June. The backglass is both beautiful and colorful and the game had plenty of player appeal. Completing A-B-C rollovers would light up special; a player could also light up special by completing the 1-2-3-4 rollovers. *WISHING WELL* was released in September. Gottlieb's flyer for this game states: "Earn a shower of coins from this fountain." The machine had an open playfield and players had to be aware of the gobble hole in the center that scored 500,000 points and awarded special when lit.

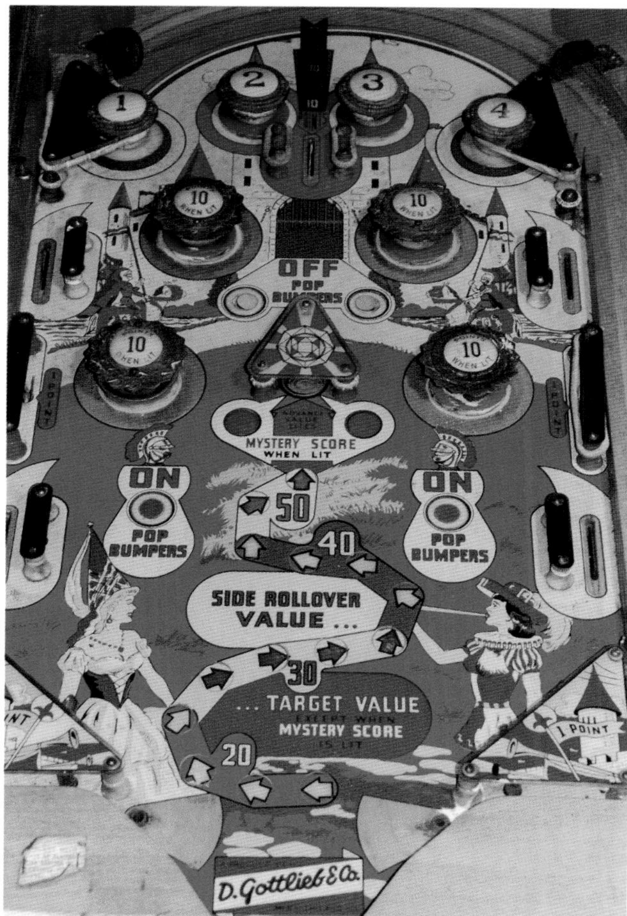

Jubilee. *Alan Tate collection.* $1800.

Southern Belle. *Alan Tate collection.* $2000.

1956

Wishing Well. *Jason Douglas collection.* $1700.

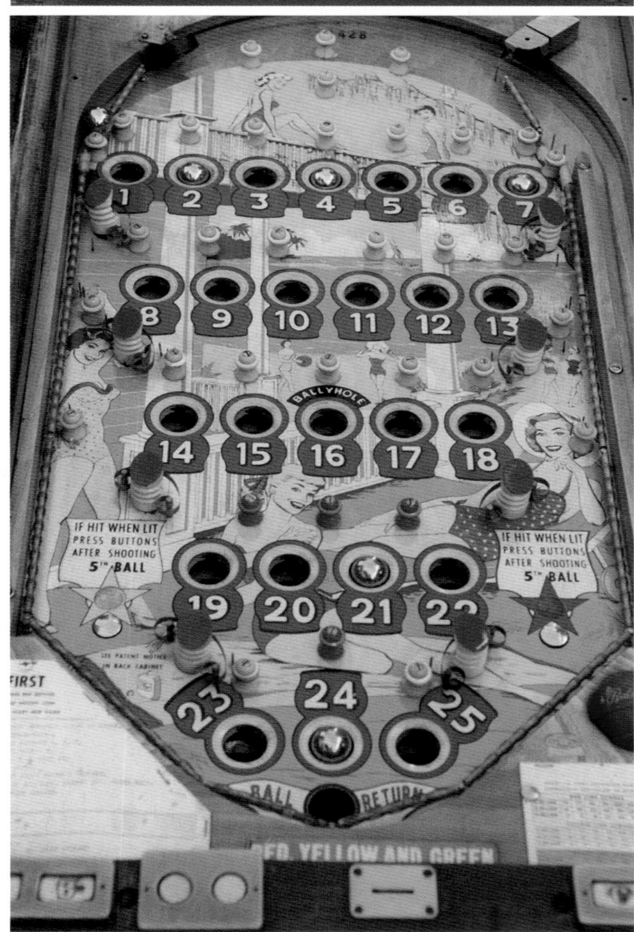

Key West. *Jason Douglas collection.* $1200.

In June 1955, D. Gottlieb & Co. started their own campaign to rescue pinball machines and give them the respect they deserved, as they were not gambling machines but amusement machines. Pinballs were by no means the same as bingo type gambling machines. In 1956, the federal court ruled that bingo machines were gambling machines and the number being produced dropped dramatically. The ruling also declared that there was a difference between pinball and bingo. D. Gottlieb had won the battle that had marred pinballs from the beginning. They started advertising that amusement pinball machines were a product of Yankee engineering and quoted on the backglass "Amusement Machines, as American as Baseball and Hotdogs."

With the court ruling going against them, companies like Bally and United now had to look for a new market and different type games that were legal. Unfortunately, this didn't happen for United and they were soon out of the bingo and pinball business. The company now focused on Shuffle Alleys.

During this period, American products were wanted all over the world, so Bally seized this opportunity and exported their bingo games on a larger scale all over Europe, especially to Great Britain, Germany, and even down here, Australia, where they stayed legal until the late 1980s. A popular game produced by the company was *KEY WEST*, released in October. It was also in this year that Bally re-entered the pinball market with one of the most brilliant games to date: *BALLS-A-POPPIN*, released in August. This was the very first machine to feature multiball. It was a two-player game and, unlike all other two-player games, had light up backglass scoring. Up to six balls could be played at a time, with the balls fired from the left side of the playfield. Bally was back in the pinball market and would challenge the dominance of the others in the years to come.

Williams released *TIM-BUC-TU* in January, featuring six eject holes on the top of the playfield. By lighting up the different suits of aces, kings, and queens, the player lights up the special on the side rollovers. The flippers were set to the sides of the cabinet, thus restricting the player's control.

REGISTER was released in October by Gottlieb. The flippers on this machine were reversed. Wayne Neyens cleverly designed the playfield, which featured two bullseye targets. The machine also had a smaller backbox compared to earlier four-player machines.

Red White Blue, an extremely rare game manufactured in 1956 by Williams. *Shay Assad collection.* $5000.

Balls-a-Poppin. *Photo courtesy Paul Brisbane.* $4000.

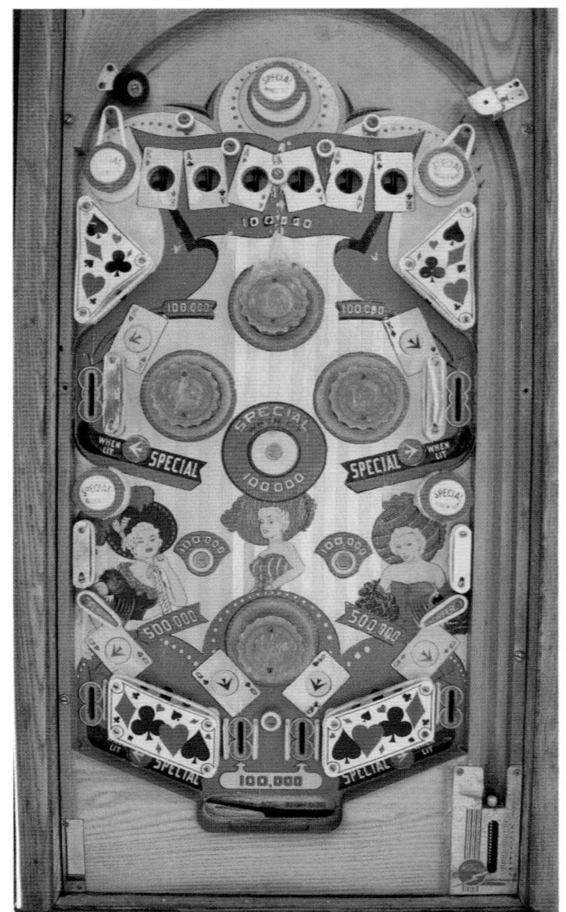

Tim-Buc-Tu. *Author's collection*. $1800.

Register. *Alan Tate collection*. $2000.

1957

The Genco Manufacturing Company had been in production since the 1930s, but fell victim to a series of disastrous fires in 1957 that eventually closed them down. They did release two machines, the first being *FUN FAIR*, released in May. This machine had a 3-D backglass which emulated a carnival atmosphere. By completing 1-7 (ducks) and 8-14 (rabbits), the player would light the corresponding one on the backglass and light up the specials. The last machine made by Genco was *SHOWBOAT*, released in December. These two machines were both challenging and appealing to players and are two of the most sought after Genco pinballs.

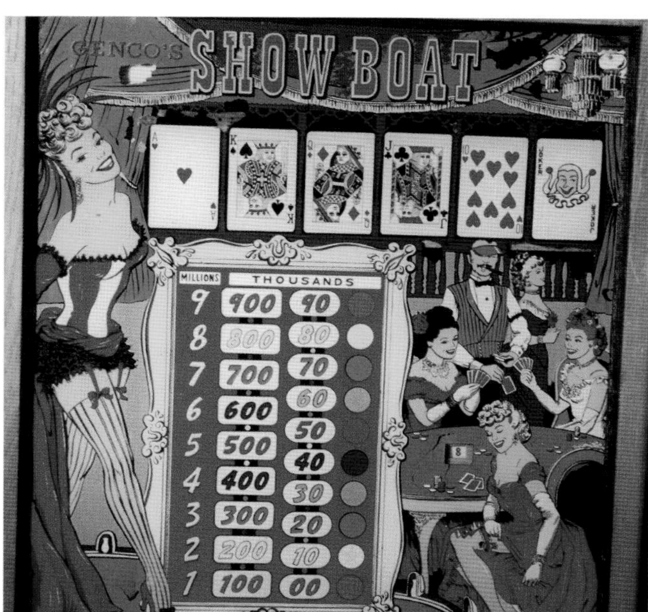

Fun Fair. *Author's collection.* $3000.

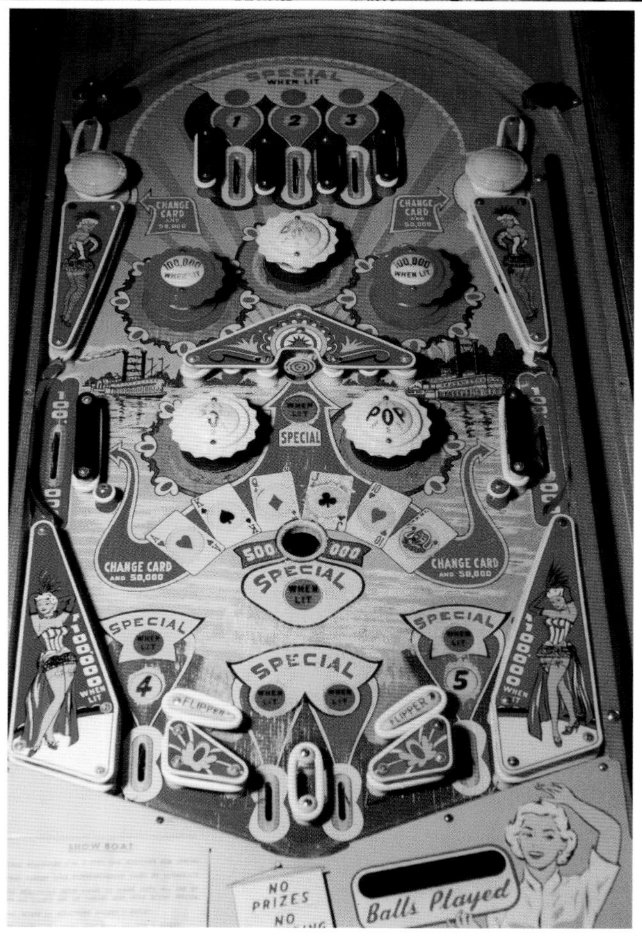

Showboat. *Alan Tate collection.* $3000.

Circus. *Alan Tate collection.* $4000.

Bally was back producing pinballs, releasing *CIRCUS* in July. Like *BALLS-A-POPPIN*, this was a two-player machine with light up scoring that also featured multiball action with balls being fired from the left of the playfield. Another feature of the machine was automatic ball lift – the ball was kicked out to the firing pin. No other pinball manufacturer in the 1950s used this feature. The next and final machine Bally released in the 1950s was *CARNIVAL*, released in August. This was Bally's first pinball using score reels. It had a wide-open playfield, four flippers, and twelve targets to shoot for. Bally released an unusual game called *TARGET ROLL* in November: it resembled a miniature pinball machine with a roulette wheel on the playfield. The machines released by Bally in the 1950s are extremely rare and treasured in anyone's collection.

Bally Manufacturing had been started by Raymond T. Maloney, one of the great pioneers. A great businessman and salesman, he was president of the company until his death in 1957, when his heirs took over the company. The Bally name would continue into the future, the hard work establishing this company having been done by the legend, Ray Maloney.

Circus. *Alan Tate collection.* $4000.

Williams Manufacturing released *GAY PAREE* in January. This four-player machine was very colorful and offered players a bonus score. The player could advance the bonus from 10 points to 100 points by hitting various targets on the playfield. In June, Williams released *HI HAND*, a combination of a pinball and a bingo machine. *KINGS* was released in September; in this game, a player needed "4 of a kind" to light the special for one replay. There were two gobble holes on either side of the playfield. These were common on machines of this era; although they awarded the player points or replays, this ended the player's ball. *STEEPLE CHASE* was another popular horse game, released in October. In November, Williams released *JIGSAW*. This was a fascinating game, featuring fourteen rollovers that would light up picture sections in the backglass and add score. The backglass was masterfully completed with mirrors, an additional attraction to players.

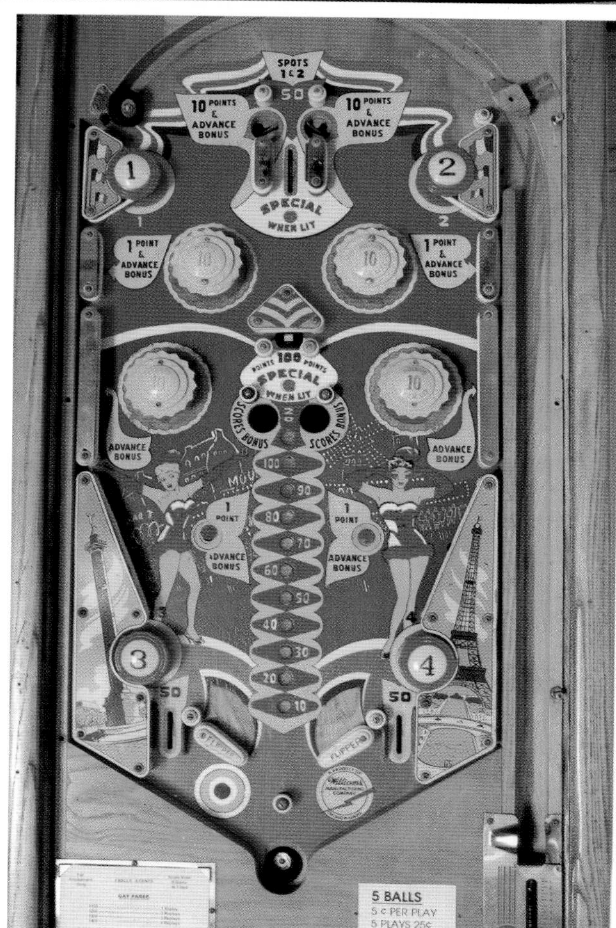

Gay Paree. *Jason Douglas collection.* $2500.

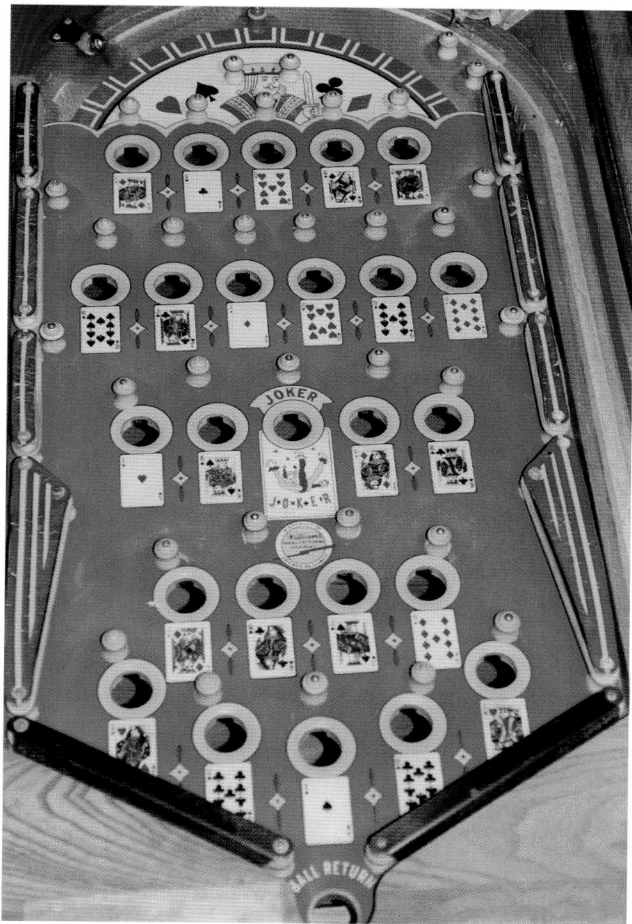

Hi Hand. *Alan Tate collection.* $1400.

Steeple Chase. *Alan Tate collection.* $1500.

D. Gottlieb & Co. released *FLAGSHIP* in January. This colorful game shows two beautiful girls standing on either side of a ship's steering wheel. *MAJESTIC* was released in February. It was designed by Wayne Neyens and was the first machine to introduce the roto-target. The roto-target had fifteen colorful rotating targets with scoring values from 30 to 300, which greatly challenged the skill of all players. This novel skill feature proved to be a huge success as it increased player's scores.

Flagship. *Author's collection.* $1300.

CONTINENTAL CAFÉ, a two player game with three gobble holes in the center of the playfield, came out in July. This machine featured a unique design for its bulls-eye target. These targets were dual scoring; if players hit the target directly in the center they would score 50 points. If they hit left or right of center they were awarded 5 points. This challenged the players' flipping accuracy. Gottlieb released *SILVER* in August, also with a roto-target. The roto-target feature was very popular with players and Gottlieb was the only company using it. The player, by completing 1-4, adds a letter to S-I-L-V-E-R on the backglass. This holds over from game to game until S-I-L-V-E-R is lit; completing the name lights targets for special.

Continental Café. *Author's collection.* $1400.

Silver. *Alan Tate collection.* $2000.

WORLD CHAMP was released in August. Here we see why Gottlieb was dominating pinballs in the 1950s, as the artwork and design was outstanding. On the backglass, the boxer is shown knocked down, the referee is doing the count, and his corner has thrown in the towel. This is one of my favorite games.

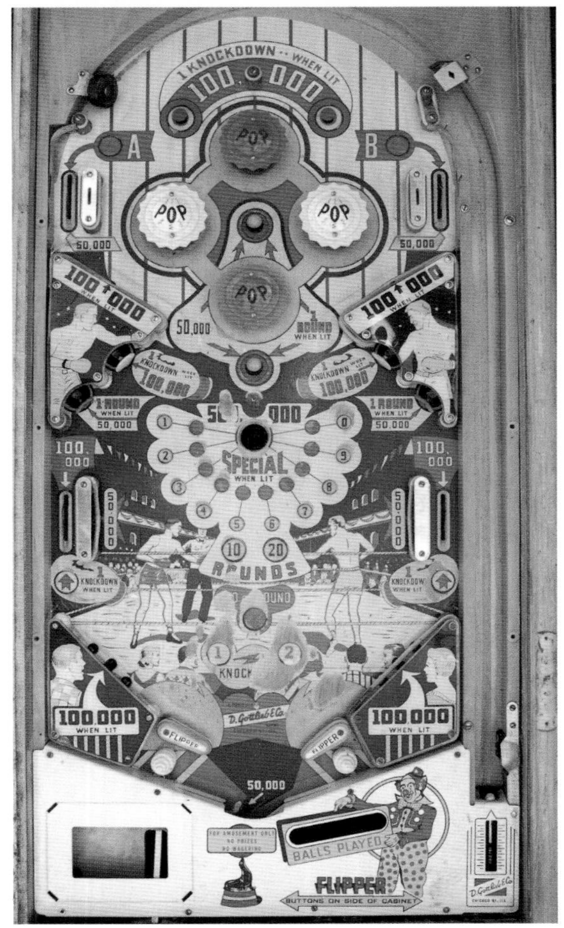

World Champ. *Author's collection*. $2500.

My son Cameron holding the promotional advertising for "The '57 Shake" pinball competition.

As a side note, I was asked to provide two pinballs for a competition in 1997. The competition was promoting milkshakes and was called "THE '57 SHAKE." The company handling this asked me to restore two games for them to give away: one was *WORLD CHAMP* and the other was *CAPTAIN KIDD*.

Gottlieb released *FALSTAFF* (who was a Shakespearean character) in October. The machine is very colorful and featured the roto-target, which challenged players in their skill and timing. The roto-target was also used on Gottlieb's next two games: *STRAIGHT FLUSH*, released in November, and *WHIRLWIND*, released in December.

Falstaff. *Alan Tate collection.* $2000.

Straight Flush. *Alan Tate collection.* $2000.

Whirlwind. *Jason Douglas collection.* $2000.

I asked Wayne Neyens if he designed all the circuits on the machines he designed:

Yes, I always designed and drew my own circuits. I took great pride in innovating new circuitry. In designing games I usually knew in my mind approximately what the game was going to be, at least to start out with. After laying out the whiteboard I would always wire up the action part of the game and then for several hours or days I would play a mind game making modifications in the action. Then I would sit at my drafting table and draw the circuit. That was always a challenge to figure out simpler and better ways to accomplish something. I always tried to put the complete game together and have it work the way I wanted it to without any errors. I only accomplished this on one game – usually an error would creep in either in my circuit drawing or in my soldering.

—Wayne Neyens

1958

Williams Manufacturing released *KICK OFF* in March. In this game, a player could score points on the red and blue team. The red and blue teams would alternate throughout the game. Each advance made by the player was indicated on the machine's soccer playfield. Williams released *SATELLITE* in June, the theme capturing the imagination of the players as the space age was just around the corner. This machine had a monkey orbiting around the earth. In July, Williams released *4 STAR*, another colorful game. All credit for the captivating artwork on Williams's pinballs goes to George Molentin, who again adds charm to the machine.

The disappearing jet bumper was introduced by Williams on *GUSHER*, which was designed by Harry Williams. Players took to this new feature, as it required a skill shot to raise the jet bumper so the number sequence 1-12 could be completed for replays. The backglass shows a couple driving their convertible through an oil field.

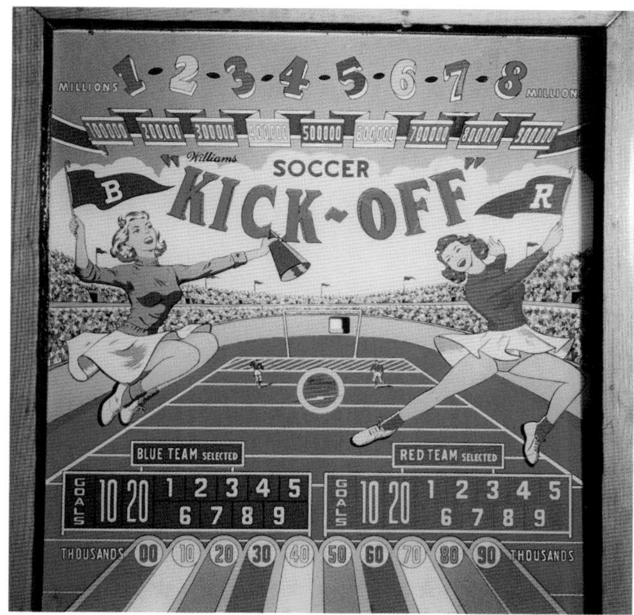

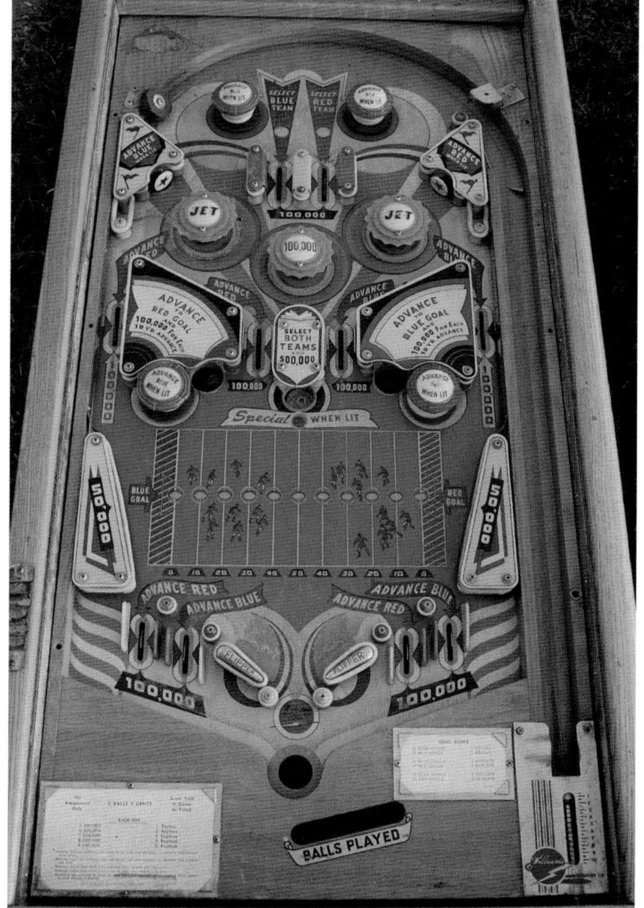

Kick Off. *Author's collection*. $1500.

Satellite. *Jason Douglas collection*. $1800.

4 Star. *Author's collection*. $1500.

Gusher. *Jason Douglas collection*. $3000. Steve Kordek and Norm Clark both confirmed that Gusher was designed by Harry Williams, not Gordon Horlock as usually stated. Gordon Horlock was Chief Engineer at the company and didn't design any games.

In February, D. Gottlieb & Co. released *BRITE STAR*, a very attractive two-player machine. Gottlieb continued using roto-targets as they were quite popular with players. On this machine, if a player hit the star on the roto-target it would increase all targets by ten times. *PICNIC* was released by Gottlieb in April. The company was releasing some of the most exciting and unique games in the world, thanks to the inventive mind of chief game designer Wayne Neyens. Roy Parker's artwork captures the crowd enjoying fun and games on a picnic.

Gottlieb released *ROCKET SHIP* in April; it was designed by Wayne Neyens with artwork by Roy Parker. This is one of the games most prized by Bob Borden, of Borden's Home Amusements (see Chapter Five).

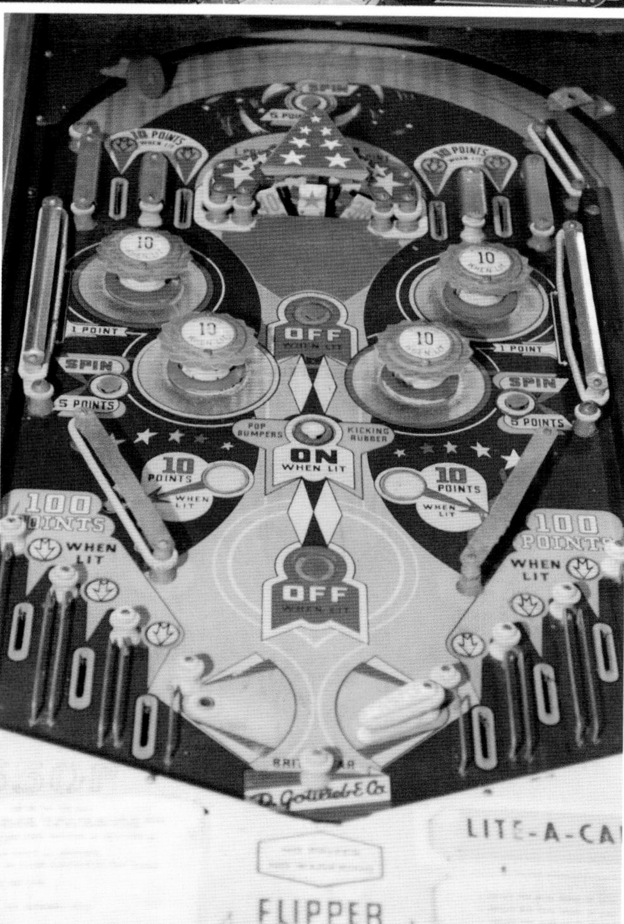

Brite Star. *Alan Tate collection*. $1400.

Picnic. *Jason Douglas collection*. $2000.

Rocket Ship, one of the many restored games Bob Borden (of Borden's Home Amusements) has for sale. $3000.

Robert Young next to his favorite game, Roto Pool. *Courtesy Marco Rossignoli*. $2000.

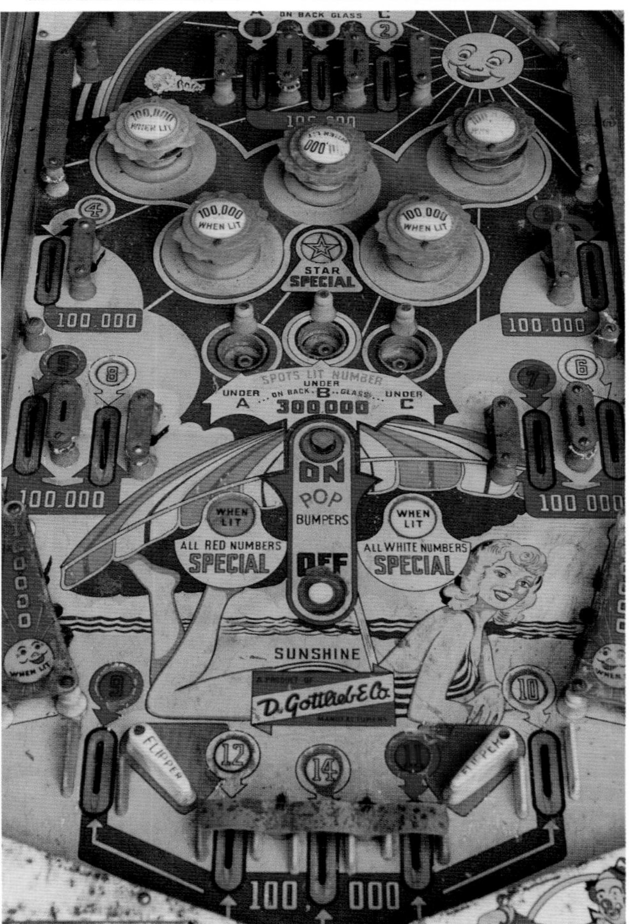

Sunshine. *Author's collection*. $2000.

ROTO POOL was released in July 1958, designed by Wayne Neyens with artwork by Roy Parker. The top center rollover and the roto-target spot pool balls on the backglass. A friend of mine, Robert Young, is pictured next to *ROTO POOL* in the photo.

SUNSHINE was released by Gottlieb in September; this was the first machine to rate players' scoring, which was done automatically as they accumulated points. At

the end of a game, the player would be ranked, Fair, Good, Excellent, Super, or Genius – of course it was every player's desire to be a Genius. *CONTEST* was released in October. This machine had four nicely placed flippers that gave the player greater ball control. The backglass, though colorful, lacked artwork.

Since the introduction of legs in the 1930s, they had always been wooden. In 1958, we see a structural change to the appearance of pinball machines, the legs being made from metal.

1959

Bally released *TARGETS* in September 1959; this was a bat and ball game with a shooting theme. Bally was continuing to make bingo machines, but releasing novelty games like this one kept them in the pinball scene.

Contest. *Jason Douglas collection.* $2000.

Targets. *Alan Tate collection.* $1400.

By this year, Williams Manufacturing was being run by Sam Stern, who had bought out Harry Williams's half share in the company. Harry Mabs was still working for the company in the design department. Sam Stern was leading the way for the future. Williams Manufacturing released *TIC-TAC-TOE* in January. It was another exciting game, featuring large Xs and Os lighting in a grid on the backglass. When a player completes the line, the center hole lights up for special. *CROSSWORD*, designed by the genius Harry Williams, was released in April. A player could spell words horizontally or vertically for replays; if all words were spelled the player would be rewarded with "extra special."

Williams was the king when it came to baseball machines and one of the most desired is *PINCH HITTER*, released in April. This was a two-player game with 3-D animation in the backbox. The company also released *TOUCHDOWN*, a game based on another favorite sport – gridiron. It had an animation unit in the backbox. On the playfield, players shot at targets for 25, 50, and 75 yards. If they timed the shot to perfection they would score a touchdown going up the center ramp. Williams released *SEA WOLF* in July; like *GUSHER*, this machine had a disappearing bumper. *SEA WOLF* had an animated backglass – the lit submarine would rise and dive as the bumper went up and down. The machine had two sets of flippers: one was set down the bottom of the playfield, the other was just below the disappearing bumper. The object of the game is to get the red 1-7 out and the blue 1-7 out; this lights up the special. The hardest number to make is 5, as the bumper needs to be down, and the ball is automatically lost when the number 7 is made. *ROCKET* was released in November. At the top of this game's playfield are five eject holes numbered 2-6; the numbers 1 and 7 can only be made when the ball is lost in the outside rollover lane. If a player could "orbit" any three successive rockets, this would earn them a free game.

Tic-Tac-Toe. *Alan Tate collection.* $1600.

Crossword. *Alan Tate collection*. $2000.

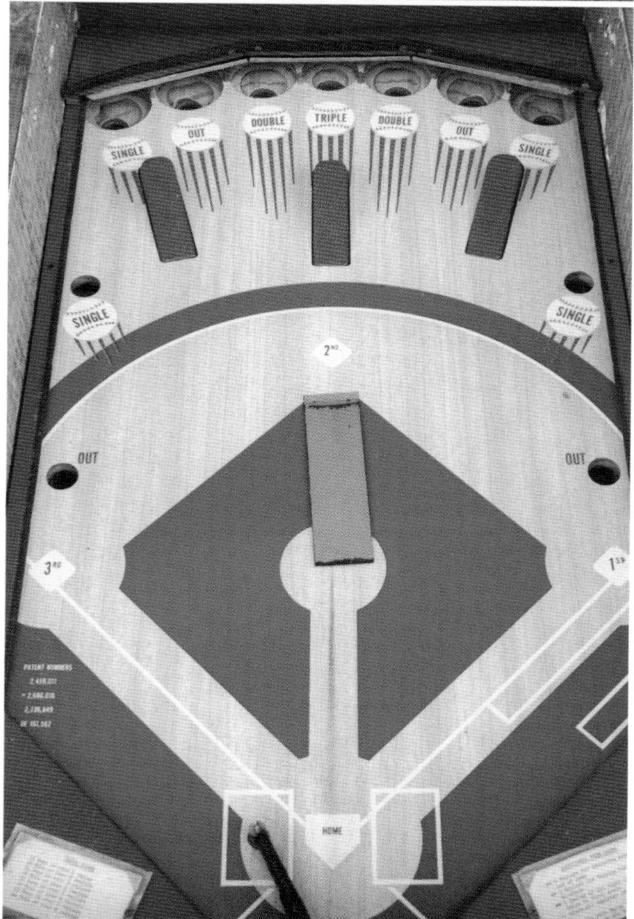

Pinch Hitter. *Author's collection*. $2000.

Touchdown. *Alan Tate collection.* $1500.

Rocket. *Jason Douglas collection.* $1600.

Sea Wolf. *Alan Tate collection.* $2500.

D. Gottlieb & Co. released *ATLAS* in April 1959. Gottlieb were on a winning streak with their roto-target pinballs. This machine had two sets of well positioned flippers and four places that enabled the player to shoot the ball to spin the roto-target.

Atlas. *Jason Douglas collection*. $1400.

Gottlieb released *QUEEN OF DIAMONDS* in April, featuring animation in the backglass. Lighting all the cards awards the player 400,000 points and a free game. This machine had three gobble holes and a large gap between the flippers. *AROUND THE WORLD* was released in July. It had an interesting playfield layout. There were three targets in the center, yellow, red, and purple, and the player could advance the value of each target from 10-50 points. Artist Roy Parker added humor to the backglass, showing people playing pinball machines even on Venus. Gottlieb released *MISS ANNABELLE* in August, their first single player game with reel drum scoring. Wayne Neyens designed the game and it featured an animated unit where a fan would slowly unveil and reveal a Gottlieb beauty behind it. The playfield had a gobble hole in the middle, four flippers, four bumpers, and a double bonus feature. The score to beat was also featured on the backglass; this now challenged players to beat this score. The western theme was used on various machines and always proved to be a hit. On *SWEET SIOUX*, which was released in August and again used the roto-target, this was no exception. The machine had five rollovers on the top of the playfield that would score double indicated value when lit. It also had four different contacts that would spin the target.

Backglass animation was used to attract players to the game. On *UNIVERSE*, released in September, two spaceships blast off into space and orbit the earth on the backglass. The machine had four flippers and an open style playfield. If a player completed the 1-8 sequence on the playfield they would receive a free game and the special lit up, enabling the player to win a free game by shooting the ball in the center gobble hole. The ship in the backglass advances every time the ball goes over a rollover and when the two targets on the upper side of the playfield are hit.

Gottlieb released *LIGHTNING BALL* in December. With this game, designed by Wayne Neyens, the company went back to light-up backglass scoring. The backglass also featured animation on a roto-disk: colorfully dressed soldiers pull the letters around the disk, spelling out "Lightning Ball." The player could shoot the ball around the playfield in a diamond pattern, adding a letter on the roto-disk. Artist Roy Parker drew lightning bolts that trace the shot around them. Game designer Wayne Neyens told me this was one of his favorite games, as it offered the players a true challenge. There are three contacts in a vertical line: green on the top, yellow in the middle, and blue on the bottom. Hitting either one advances the roto-disk in the backglass. Completing the name "Lightning Ball" scores special; a player could also score special by completing the 1-6 sequence. There are two gobble holes on the left and right side of the playfield just above the kickers.

Queen of Diamonds. *Alan Tate collection.* $2000.

Around the World. *Author's collection.* $1400.

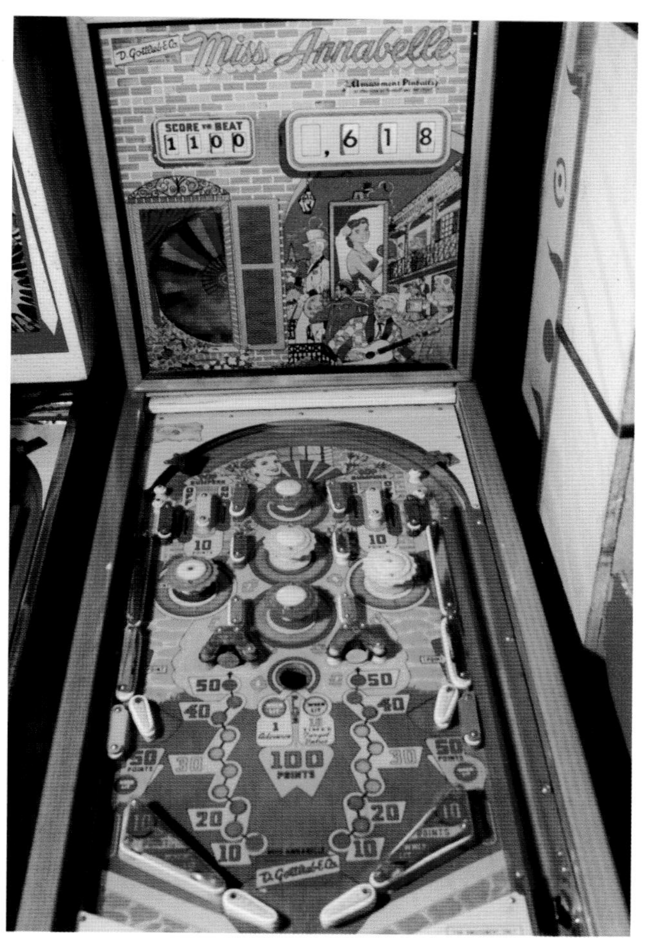

Miss Annabelle. *Alan Tate collection.* $2000.

Sweet Sioux. *Author's collection.* $1600.

Universe. *Jason Douglas collection*. $2000.

Lightning Ball. *Alan Tate collection*. $2000.

I spoke with Wayne Neyens regarding controlled distribution of the Gottlieb product and whiteboards:

Whiteboard is not a name that I ever used. I used a blank board, which is what it really was. I usually had an idea for doing something to make a game versus a machine. An example that comes to mind is LIGHTNING BALL. There I wanted to arrange rebound rubbers in such a way that a continuous action could occur. Sometimes games just evolved around something I had heard or seen.

Dave Gottlieb came up with the idea of gauged production and controlled distribution, which simply means calling up the distributors and asking them how many they wanted of a particular game. From their responses we would know how many to build; that is why some of the quantities built were odd numbers such as 970 or 1525. This was different than other companies, who told their distributors how many of a number they were going to get – then they either sold them or ate them.

—*Wayne Neyens*

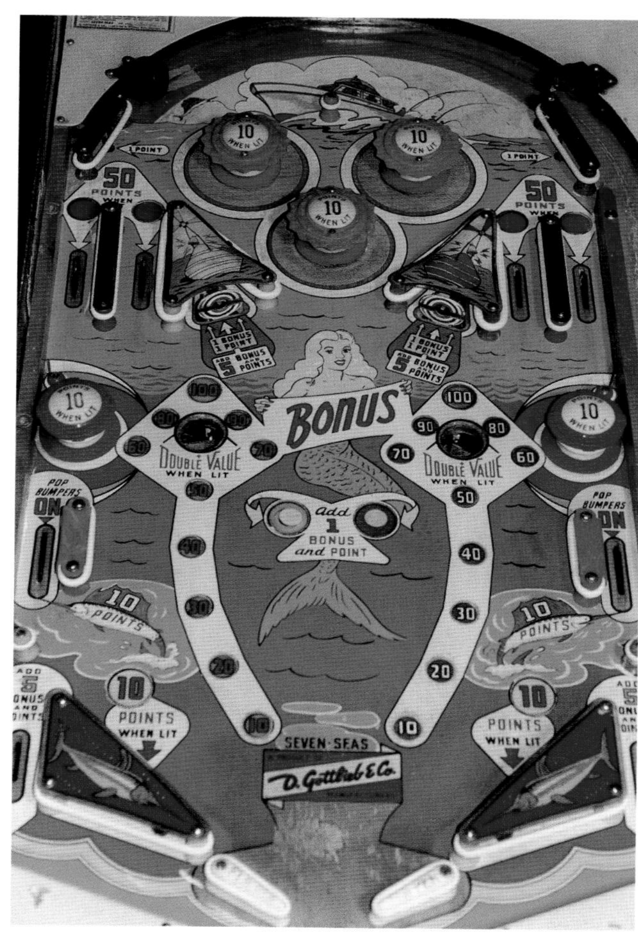

Above & right: Seven Seas. *Alan Tate collection.* $1600.

Gottlieb's next machine was *SEVEN SEAS*, released in December. Notice the two boats on the backglass, both called S.S. Gottlieb. Again we see the brilliance of Roy Parker filling the game with imagination and exciting the player with brilliant artwork. This machine had a low production run; only 750 were produced.

During the 1950s, we have seen Roy Parker at Gottlieb and George Molentin at Williams doing the artwork; combining this with the brilliant designs of Harry Williams, Harry Mabs, and Wayne Neyens resulted in the "Golden Age of Pinball." As the backglasses proclaimed, these games were indeed "Amusement Pinballs as American as Baseball and Hotdogs."

CHAPTER FOUR
THE 1960S

By this decade, pinball machines had come a long way; there was a demand now for more creativity and more challenging games. In 1960, there were only two manufactures producing pinball machines: Gottlieb and Williams. A few years down the track, Bally and Chicago Coin would start producing pinballs and together with Gottlieb and Williams these companies would be referred to as the big four. Machines in this era were influenced by leisure activities, fashion, and sport, and they captivated the imagination of the players. In this period, we also see more games being sent overseas and distributors being established all over the world. The machines went to Europe, Italy, Spain, Japan, and down here – Australia.

1960

At Williams Manufacturing, Sam Stern was in charge and the company had gone through some financial problems. Sam had bought out Harry Williams's share and was on the road to entering the company into its own Golden Age. He had designer Steve Kordek join the company and was working with legendary designer Harry Mabs. The name was also changed from Williams Manufacturing to Williams Electronic Manufacturing Corporation. The company released *GOLDEN GLOVES* in January, which was designed by Harry Mabs (who had designed another classic boxing machine for Gottlieb, *KNOCKOUT*, in 1952).The artwork was by George Molentin, who designed all the artwork in the 1950s for Williams. It enchanted the players and had great appeal. A player could win free games on the machine by reaching the score indicated or by lighting the word "GLOVES" on the playfield. When this is accomplished the player earns a free game and lights up the bottom two rollovers to score special. The machine had three jet bumpers and a well set out playfield.

The next machine released by Williams was *21*, designed by Harry Williams. Released in February, the machine combined the two types of scoring: drum and light up. Players build up their scores in the game of 21; if they score 21 or beat the dealer they win a free game. The dealer's score is indicated on the backglass.

Williams also released *OFFICIAL BASEBALL* in February. Baseball games proved to be very popular with players and are still in demand today. This machine had a 3-D animated running man unit in the backglass, which was another form of attracting player's attention to a game.

NAGS, released in April, was the last machine Harry Williams designed for the company in this period, as he went back to California. I feel this was the best horse race pinball ever produced. It had a rotating disk on the playfield that would rotate throughout the game. On the disk were six bumpers numbered 1-6; as a ball hits the bumper the corresponding horse would move towards the finish line. Combine this with 3-D animation and the player is totally enthralled. *NAGS* was the machine mentioned earlier in the introduction – it's the one that I purchased and my wife wasn't happy that I had spent $1000 on it. I subsequently restored it and sold it five years ago to a very good friend of mine, Gary Coleman, who has a love for racehorses. The machine is in his gamesroom and is his pride and joy. Gary is pictured here with the machine.

Golden Gloves. *Jason Douglas collection*. $1600.

21. *Jason Douglas collection*. $1800.

Official Baseball. *Jason Douglas collection*. $2500.

Nags. *Gary Coleman collection.* $3000.

Gary Coleman with his prized machine.

Darts. *Paul Brisbane collection.* $1800.

Williams released *DARTS* in June; this was the first machine Steve Kordek designed for the company. *DARTS* was the first of a series of machines that had a new look cabinet, referred to by the company as "Styling of the 60's style Cabinet Design." The game had attractive artwork and was the first to feature the popular game of darts. Lighting up all the numbers on A B C lights up special. *VIKING*, a two player game with reel scoring, was released in July. *JUNGLE* was released in June. Designed by Harry Mabs, it featured backbox animation. In the center of the playfield is a target. Whichever animal is displayed in the window above, if the target was hit it would knock the animal down in the backglass. The animals in this window rotate when advance is hit. The object of the game is to knock all the animals down. At the start of a game, the animal targets reset.

Viking. *Jason Douglas collection.* $1600.

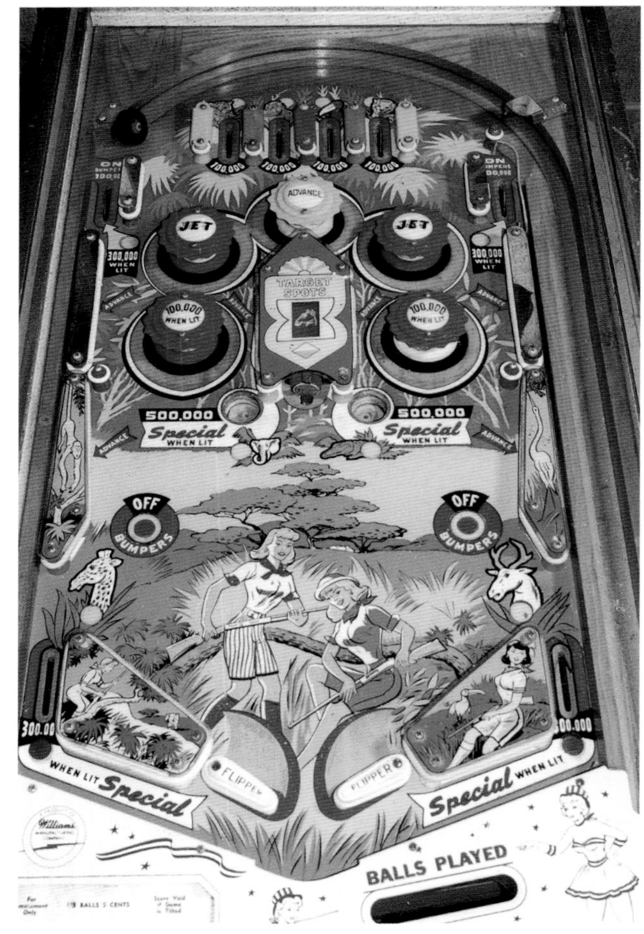

Jungle. *Alan Tate collection.* $2000.

BLACK JACK was released in November with a theme the same as a machine released earlier in the year: *21*. This game was such a success that the company came out with a more updated version. A great card game, the machine also combined reel scoring with the light up backglass. The next month, Williams released *MAGIC CLOCK*, the very first pinball with a moving target. Steve Kordek and Harry Mabs designed this machine. The moving target was a hit with players as it challenged their skill. If a player hit the target they would score between 50-100 points, if they missed they would only score one point.

This was the last machine Harry Mabs designed before he retired and moved to Florida. Since coming to Williams he had designed many of their games with Harry Williams. I asked Wayne Neyens, a good friend of Harry's, why Harry Mabs wasn't recognized as having designed games when he worked at the company, as the majority of the credit went to Harry Williams. Wayne told me the games produced at the company were more or less a team effort. Harry Mabs was an idea man and really didn't care about the details. Sadly, Harry Mabs and Harry Williams are not with us today. Harry Williams will always be remembered in the pinball world. He was a pioneer in the industry, becoming part of it in 1929. He started Williams Manufacturing in 1947 and was responsible for many contributions to pinball machines, such as the pedestal tilt and the kicker. He was a great designer of pinball machines and was referred to as the "master pin game psychologist." Harry Mabs was also a great designer. He was the man who invented the flipper: for the first time a player could control the course of the ball, making it a game of skill.

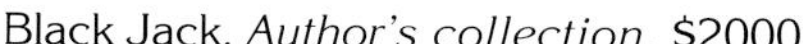
Black Jack. *Author's collection*. $2000.

Magic Clock. *Alan Tate collection*. $2000.

D. Gottlieb & Co. were the kings of pinball machines; their games were highly successful and the players loved them. Their machines were designed by Wayne Neyens with artwork by Roy Parker in this period. The company released *LITE-A-CARD* in February, promoting the game as the first two-player card game. The playfield had a target in the upper center that would either score 50 points or 100 points. If a player hit it in the center it would score 100 points, if it was hit off center it would only score 50 points. This was cleverly done, using two sets of switches behind the target: one on the center, and the other on the outside of the center. The machine had four flippers and three gobble holes in the center of the playfield.

Lite-A-Card. *Alan Tate collection.* $1600.

TEXAN was released in April. On the playfield, Gottlieb again used the popular roto-target – this time adding three eject holes on the playfield, two on either side of the roto-target and one above it. The machine could be set by the operator to either three or five ball play. *TEXAN* was the last four-player woodrail pinball made by Gottlieb.

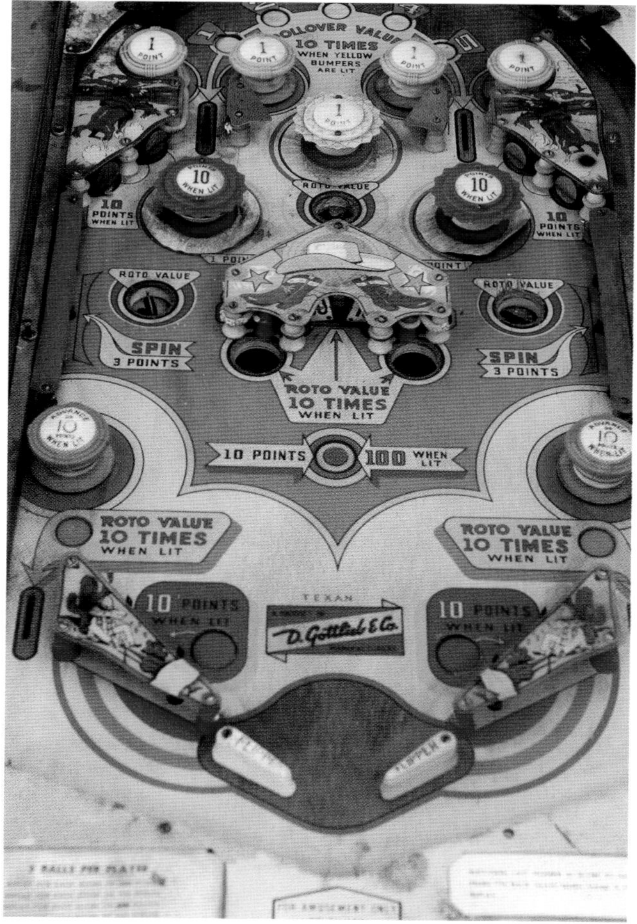

Texan. *Alan Tate collection.* $2000.

Wagon Train. *Jason Douglas collection*. $2000.

In the same month, Gottlieb released *WAGON TRAIN*, which was a great challenge for players. Notice that on the playfield there are no gobble holes. A player had to light up the numbers 1-5 in both the red and white feathers on the backglass to win a free game. This would also light up the top rollover for special. On the roto-target, two numbers appear at the same time. This machine also had the score to beat panel, which attracted players to the game.

Gottlieb released *DANCING DOLLS* in May. A machine highly desired by collectors today, it was also the last machine produced by the company that had light up backglass scoring. A feature that attracted players was the animation on the backglass: behind the stage are two silhouetted dancers that would dance behind the screen as targets were hit on the playfield.

CAPTAIN KIDD was released in July and featured a female pirate on the backglass. On top of the playfield in the center, Gottlieb first used the "Circle Five" pop bumper. With the right shot, a player could bounce the ball around this pop bumper and complete the sequence 1-5 that advances towards the special.

In October, Gottlieb released *KEWPIE DOLL*, which was their last woodrail pinball machine. The rails that held the glass on were to be replaced with metal ones. The backglass on this game featured an illuminated shooting gallery with five rabbits on the top and five ducks on the bottom. As soon as a player hit a target the corresponding rabbit or duck would light up in the backbox.

A major breakthrough occurred in the pinball industry with the introduction of *FLIPPER* in October. In some states, pinballs were still illegal to operate as the free game was still classified as a gambling device and was prohibited. *FLIPPER* was the answer to these states and was inspired by Alvin Gottlieb. The game was designed by Wayne Neyens and featured "Add-A-Ball." Instead of winning free games for high score, the player would receive an extra ball. The length of the game was extended as players could keep playing as long as they kept getting free balls; up to ten could be registered and were indicated on the backglass. This machine also came out with the "Hard-Cote" playboard finish. In addition, scoring was different on this machine. Prior to *FLIPPER*, when the score reached 999 a (1) would light up to indicate that a thousand had been reached. As a player could continue playing as long as they got free balls, we see the introduction of four wheel scoring. Another first on this machine was the introduction of the wedge head shape for the backbox.

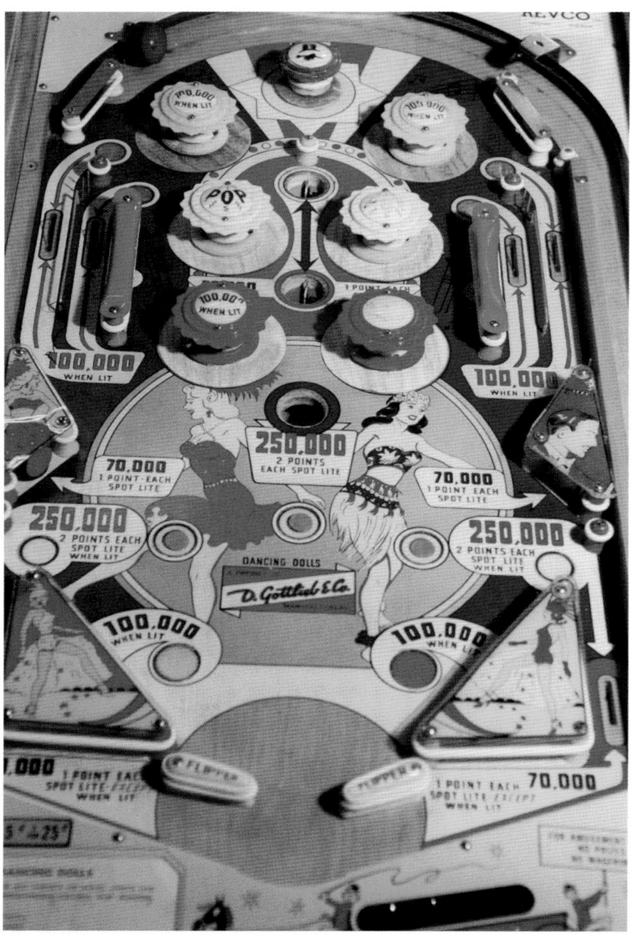

Right & above: Dancing Dolls. *Alan Tate collection.* $3000.

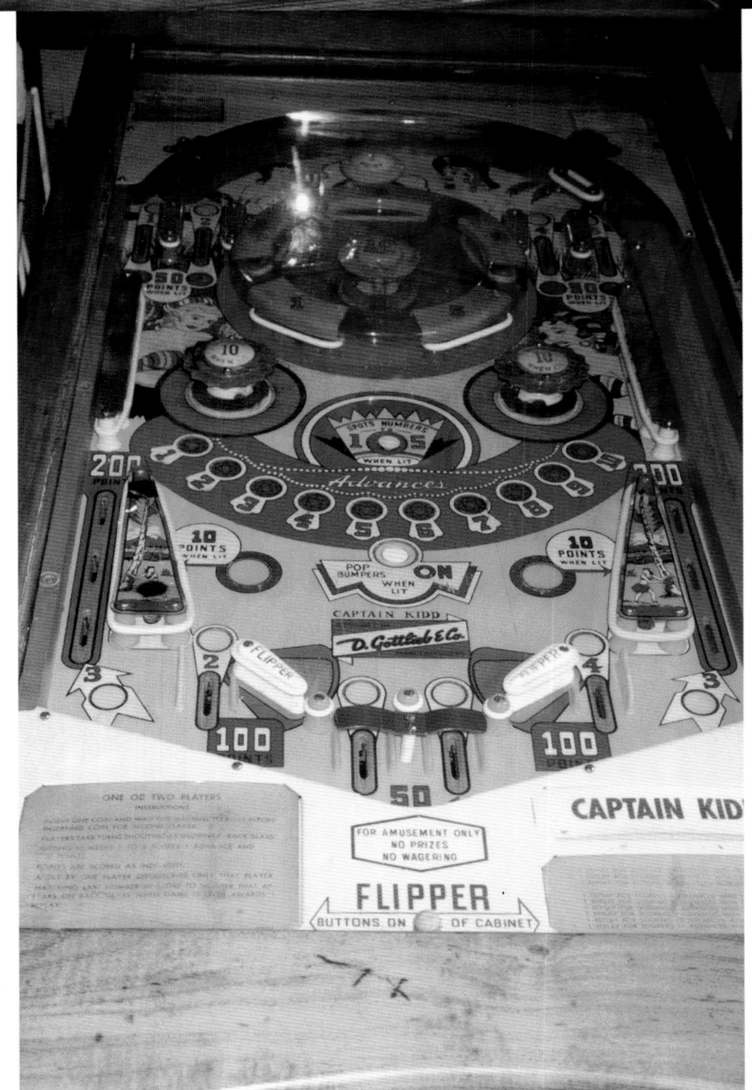

Captain Kidd. *Troy Meredith collection.* $2000.

Kewpie Doll. *Jason Douglas collection*. $2000.

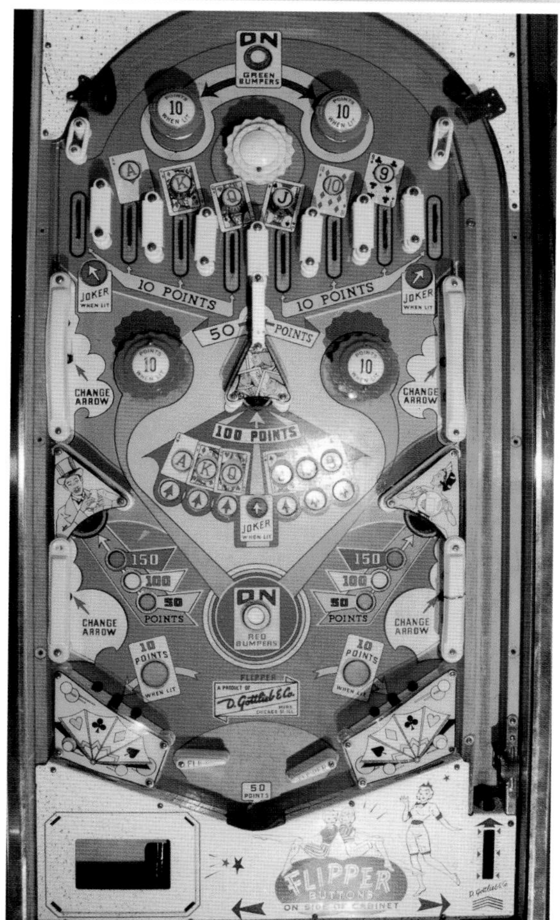

Flipper. *Jason Douglas collection*. $3000.

Alvin Gottlieb was the inspiration behind *FLIPPER*. I asked him what else he did while working at the plant, and how his dad accepted the Add-A-Ball:

Some of the things I became involved in after leaving the engineering department might be of interest. At that time, the only information on spare parts was a single sheet of paper that had a few part numbers and some vague descriptions. I took it upon myself to put together a parts catalog, which was a first in the pinball business. The company bought a small lithograph printing press and some layout accessories. After photographing most of the parts that the parts department said were most in demand, I laid out a multiple page catalog and printed several hundred of them. Our commercial printer printed the cover and we sent the finished book to all of the Gottlieb distributors.

The company never made much money on the parts business but the ability to order spares and receive them quickly enhanced the value of our games. One of the problems I ran into in preparing the catalog was that many assemblies and sub-assemblies did not have part numbers because there were no numbered assembly drawings. I started a numbering system using "SA" as a prefix (meaning Special Assembly) and just gave numbers to the units we sold already assembled. The catalog grew substantially over the years and was turned over to the engineering department and a commercial printer for production. All of our competitors had to come out with catalogs not long after ours was sent out. Dave Gottlieb once quoted someone who said, "Imitation is the most sincere form of flattery" every time we did something that others copied.

A problem that became more serious as the games became more complicated was "contact bounce," which occurred when a switch was rapidly closed. It would occasionally cause the game to miscount the score or not activate a game feature. After seeing the actual bounce using a strobe light and oscilloscope, various modifications were tried to stop the bounce but I decided that a whole new relay was needed to cure the problem. The old relay was just too slow. Doc Garbark, our engineer draftsman, came up with a brilliant design using small tapered switchblades and a lightweight armature. The tapered blades would not have any strong harmonic vibration characteristics and the light armature with its attached switch actuator was very rapid in operation. Doc named the relay the "AG relay" after yours truly and so marked my place in history. At least to me.

Alvin Gottlieb with his granddaughter Lisa. *Courtesy of Alvin Gottlieb.*

The engineering department was always on a quest to develop a front door for our games that could not be easily broken into. I took great delight in coming into the department after engineering had come up with a new design carrying a huge long screwdriver. In seconds I would have the door popped open. Doc then came up with a double cam lock door that looked great. I couldn't open it without ripping out the whole front of the cabinet. Samples were built and sent out for test. One of the test reports that came in said the door on his game was not broken into but a thief had broken out the whole bottom of the cabinet and stolen the cash. He asked that we go back to our old door system because it was cheaper to repair a door than the whole bottom of the cabinet.

Harry Mabs, the Gottlieb designer, came up with the Flipper, which radically changed the pinball business. He was working on an electrically operated bumper to kick the ball. He had a bumper activated by a solenoid coil and was testing it by just hitting two wires together. I always spent a lot of time chatting with Harry, who was a source of many fascinating stories, and I think I was the only one to see what Harry was doing. I didn't attach much significance to it until a short time later when he asked everyone into his room to look at something. There was a raw wood playboard with six flippers on it that later became "Humpty Dumpty." Dave Gottlieb was totally taken by the game and said he would come up with a name for it himself. He told me to bring in a book of "Fairy Tales" from our house the next morning. That was the genesis of the line of games with Fairy Tale names.

Dave came up with many ideas, including the first multiple player pinball, "Super Jumbo." Again, all the other pinball companies jumped on the idea and just about all games were multiple player thereafter. One playboard "gimmick" I came up with was the "turret shooter," which was first seen on "Just Twenty One." What I put together was a very crude attempt, but the designer and engineers refined it into a novel device that was used on several games and used by other companies in later years.

Another idea of mine was the "Add-A-Ball" game, which was born out of a legal problem. In one area, a free game was considered "A thing of value" because at the end of a game a "Free Play" was indicated on the score glass. The ruling meant that free-play pinballs could not be operated there. I was there for the ruling and I saw that the operators were devastated. I told our distributor that I had an idea for a game that might help. Upon return to the factory, I discussed the idea with Wayne Neyens, our chief designer, who thought there was some merit to it but couldn't take time from his work to develop it without Dave's OK. After a long discussion with my father, he grudgingly gave the approval to let Wayne work on it. He maintained that "nothing will replace the Free Game." He was right, but in areas where free-play was not allowed, Add-A-Balls were profitable. Dave was so taken by "Flipper," the first Add-A-Ball, that he enjoyed playing it at length. Over the years, several versions were widely sold into the export market, which eventually led to the acceptance of free-play games.

This is the first time I have put down some of my involvement in the game business. You can imagine what memories my 34 years at it gives rise to. This may be much more than you asked of me, but once I started, the thoughts kept coming.

—Alvin Gottlieb

MERRY-GO-ROUND was released in December. This new style pinball had steel rails and a fancy locking bar. Circus themes were popular with players and this machine was no exception. It had a disc just above the center of the playfield that would rotate, and the player could score 100, 200, or 300 points, Gottlieb called this scoring feature "Round Robin" scoring.

Merry Go Round. *Alan Tate collection.* $2000.

The Bally company was committed to bingos, however they released a one ball machine called *BEAUTY CONTEST* in January. This machine looked like a pinball but didn't have any flippers. Instead it had two powerful kickers that would push the ball back up the playfield. The player would have to light the girls on the backglass by either hitting the bumpers or by spotting the lit number in the eject hole in the middle of the playfield. A minimum of six lit girls awarded the player two replays, seven lit awarded four replays, eight lit awarded eight replays, nine lit awarded twenty replays, and all eleven girls lit awarded 100-180 replays. This would be hard to accomplish due to the fact there was only one ball per game. This was a gambling machine that was different from bingo machines; even turning off the machine resets all the credits. The machine also featured automatic ball lift and an "Auto Mission" coin divider: the operator's percentage of coins was diverted into another coin box on the left side of the cabinet. This is an unusual machine and is a good talking piece in any collection.

Beauty Contest. *Paul Brisbane collection*. $1200.

1961

Dave Gottlieb was born in Milwaukee shortly after his parents emigrated there from their native Lithuania, and their enthusiasm for the freedom and opportunities they found in the United States was passed along to Dave and his five brothers and two sisters. He founded D. Gottlieb & Co. in 1927, a company that dominated the industry for decades. He was a marketing genius, inspirational leader, and a man of vision. In 1956, Dave and his wife Dorothy announced they were going to construct a hospital in memory of his parents, Samuel and Bertha. In July 1961, this dream became reality with the opening of the Gottlieb Memorial Hospital in Melrose Park, Illinois. Many told him he would never get the project off the ground, but Dave Gottlieb rarely set out to do something that he didn't accomplish. When Dave's son Alvin was asked why his dad wanted to build a hospital, he replied, "He wanted to put something back in the community." I have mentioned the hospital in this book as I hope it reflects on the type of man David Gottlieb was. He will live on in the hearts of all those who knew him, just as he lives on in the institution he built.

David Gottlieb and his wife Dorothy broke ground in 1959 for a non-profit community hospital in Melrose Park, Illinois that would be a memorial to David's parents. The hospital opened in July 1961. *Courtesy of Alvin Gottlieb.*

Bobo. *Author's collection.* $2000.

In 1961, Williams was playing catch up to Gottlieb. *BOBO*, released in January, was designed by Steve Kordek and the artwork was by George Molentin. The playfield was plastic coated, a feature Gottlieb had advertised on *FLIPPER* three months previously. The company still used the stylish fancy cabinet. This machine had light up backglass scoring and a low production run of 400.

HIGHWAYS, released in September, was the first machine used by Williams that could be set to either 3-ball play or 5-ball play. On the flyer for this machine, the company states that setting the game to 3-ball creates *SUSPENSE* and *EXCITEMENT and REPEAT PLAY.*

On *HOLLYWOOD*, released in May, we see the last machine to use the stylish 60s style cabinet – this design didn't go over well with players. This machine featured the "moving target:" by hitting this, the player would advance both the score and the bonus value. On either side of the moving target are gobble holes that award players 50-350 points.

Williams released *METRO* in December. This was the last machine to use the disappearing bumper. To activate the bumper, the player must get the ball in either eject hole called "Action" on the playfield.

The last machine to use light up backglass scoring was *SPACE SHIP*, released in December. It was designed by Steve Kordek, who was known for earlier space theme pinballs that he had designed at Genco Manufacturing (these were *MERCURY*, *FLYING SAUCER* and *ROCKET*). The playfield is well set out, with four rockets at the lower end. By advancing a rocket to the top, the player lights up the skill hole for special; by lighting up the entire rocket, the player lights up the center target for special.

Highways. *Alan Tate collection.* $2000.

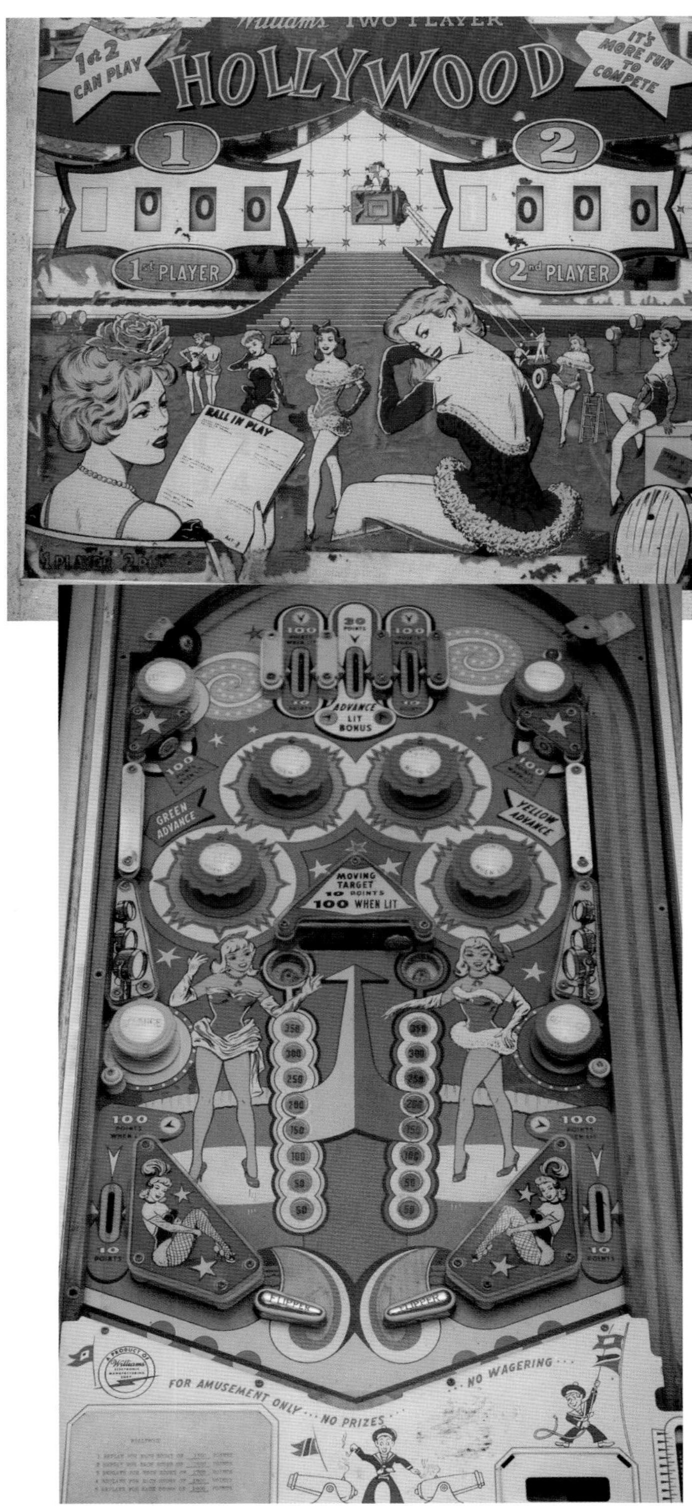

Hollywood. *Jason Douglas collection.* $2000.

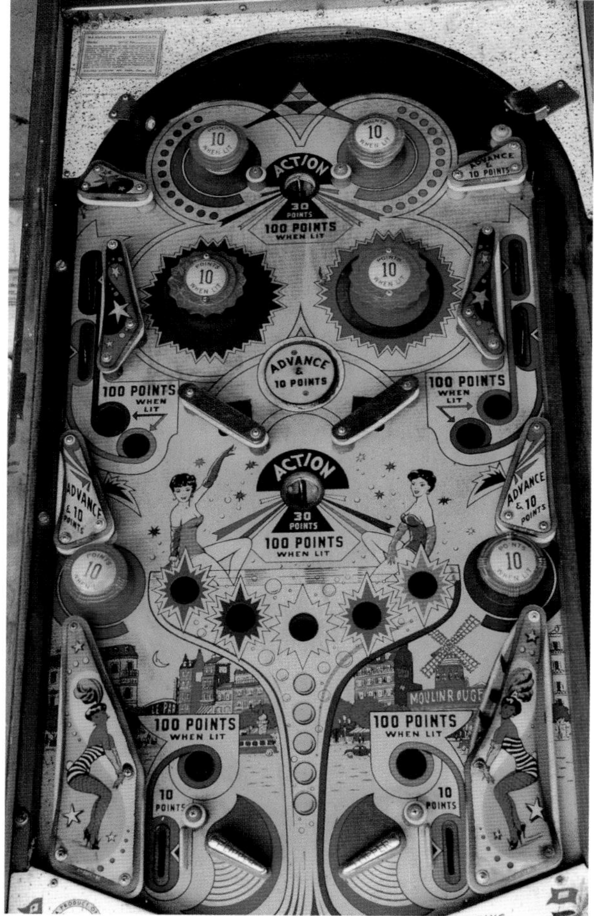

Metro. *Author's collection.* $2000.

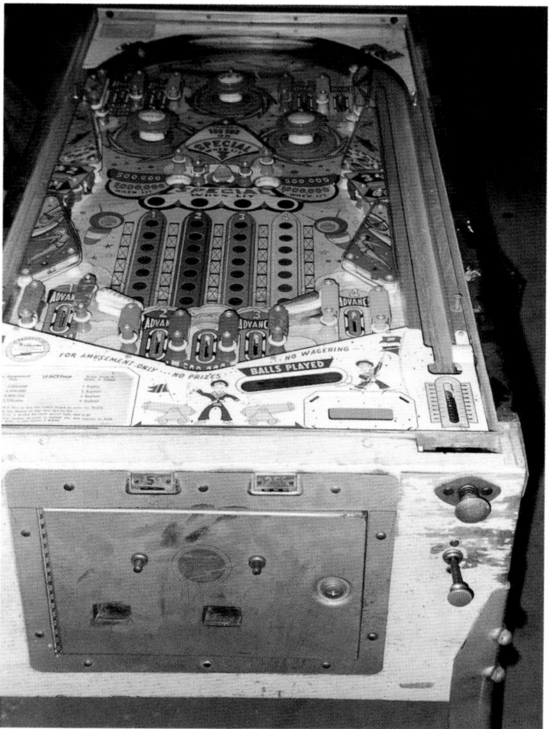

Space Ship. *Author's collection.* $2000.

Gottlieb released *FOTO FINISH* in January; this machine had a carry on feature that continued till all four horses reached the finish line, which is the objective of the game. There are four rollovers at the top of the playfield. Two of the red horse score bumpers on either side of these rollovers light at the same time. Throughout the game, as points and targets are hit, the lights rotate. If a player goes down the rollover which has the lit bumpers on either side, the horse moves one step towards the finish line. At the end of the game, the horses that have not reached the finish line remain in that position and don't reset at the start of a new game. When all the horses have made it to the finish, line they reset back into the start position. This is how the carry on feature works, and the players loved it. Bringing all four horses to the finish line scores a free game. By completing A-B rollover and C-D targets, a player lights the center gobble hole for special. The backglass featured the score to beat panel. The four horses featured on this machine are Citation, Whirl Away, Man O War, and Sea Biscuit.

Gottlieb produced *SHOWBOAT* in April. On the backglass is a boat named "Flipper Queen" sailing down the Mississippi and a bathing beauty sitting on a pier waving at it. The picture portrays a variety of people joining in the showboat atmosphere. The playfield had an unusual layout: in the center were four colored roll-unders in a vertical line; rolling under these and completing the sequence lights the bottom rollover for special. The machine had four flippers at the bottom of the playfield. Hitting the left flipper button activates the two on the left hand side together, while the right flipper button activates the two on the right hand side. Players found it difficult to control the ball with the flippers and were inclined to press both flippers at the same time. Completing the A-B-C sequence lights up a "Duo-Match" feature at the end of the game, giving players double the chance at winning a free game on lucky number. The lucky number is displayed on the backglass at the end of a game. If it matches the last number on the player's score, a free game is awarded. During the game a stepping unit is activated, usually when 1 or 10 points are scored. It is impossible for a player to keep track of what the lucky number might be.

Foto Finish. *Jason Douglas collection*. $1500.

Gottlieb released *LANCERS* in September 1961. The top of the playfield featured six rollover lanes; each one except the center would light up an extra scoring feature. Another feature on the machine were the four eject holes: one on the top center, the others in the middle of the playfield. On this playfield there are no specials. To achieve a free game, a player must either reach the score set or match the lucky number.

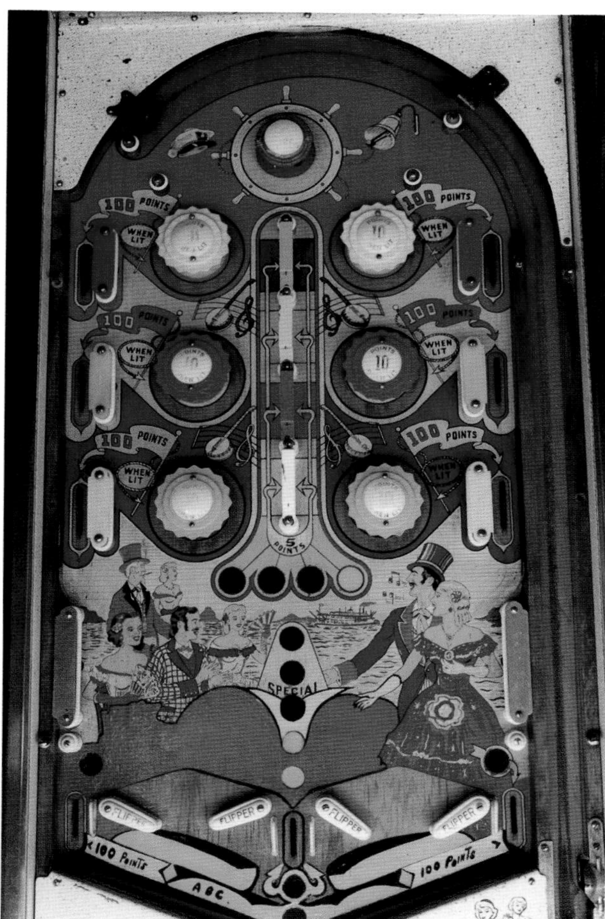

Showboat. *Jason Douglas collection*. $1500.

Lancers. *Alan Tate collection*. $1600.

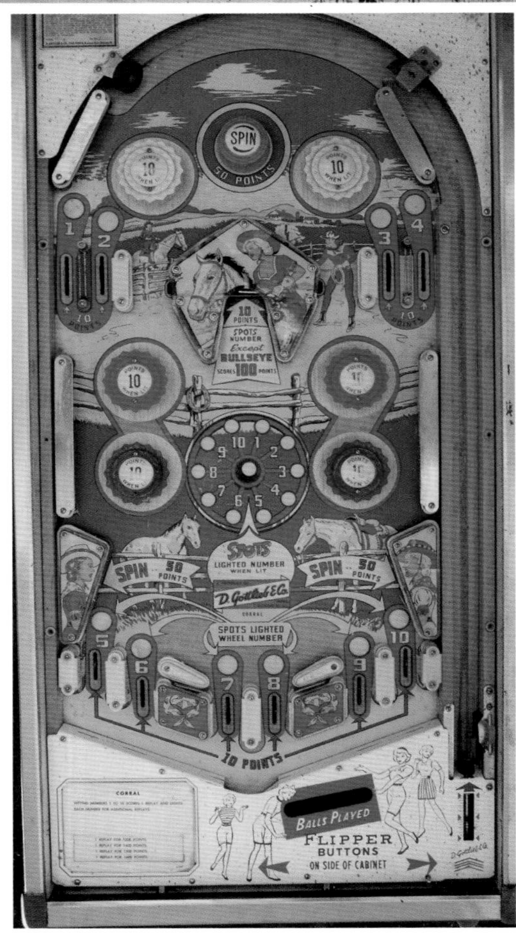

Corral. *Author's collection*. $1600.

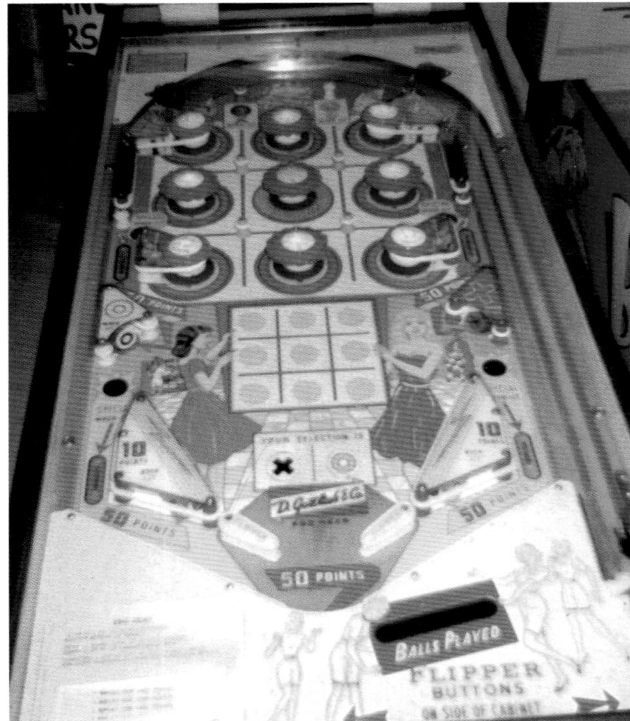

Egg Head. *Photo courtesy Russ Jensen*. $2200.

CORRAL, released in September, was the last machine with the score to beat feature on the backglass. Completion of the rollover sequence 1-10 would score an extra game or an extra ball (the operator could adjust the game to award free balls or free games). The roto-target is well positioned in the upper center of the playfield; by hitting this target, a player spots the indicated number. The bull's eye target scores 100 points.

Gottlieb released *EGG HEAD* in December, based on the game tic-tac-toe. The artwork on this game makes it stand out. It shows a mad professor trying to control his robot as a beautiful young woman is playing his tic-tac-toe game. By completing horizontal, vertical, or diagonal lines of X's or O's, a player scores special and lights rollovers at the bottom of the playfield for additional special.

I asked Wayne Neyens to explain what artists contributed to game design.

Most collectors think that the artist had a lot to do with designing games – nothing can be further from the truth. The artist never saw the game during the design stage; they never even got into the design area. Our artists always worked in studios at the companies that did our silk screening, such as Advertising Posters or Reproduction. Generally, the designer designed the game, drew the back glass complete with his name selection, drew a design, and colored the play board (very roughly). When the game was chosen to go into production, drawings were made and a number assigned to it in place of the name. This was done because the name was usually changed several times and we could not go back and rework all the drawings. (A good example of this would be that the name of Humpty Dumpty was Flipper up until the last minute. That is another story however.)

Once the drawings were done and a theme and name decided on, the artist was called in and told what we wanted and he was given a set of drawings from which he worked.

Yes, we always made prototypes before every run, which had several advantages. It gave us, the distributors, and the operators an idea of what the game would do, how much money it would make etc. It helped the engineering room to check out all the test fixtures, the circuits, the cables etc. When you were building maybe three hundred games a day and you changed games from one model to the next, things had to go together smoothly or else you had a lot of people standing around and things piling up. Again, this is only touching on a little bit and really needs a lot of explaining. All prototype games, or samples as we called them, had an S before or after the serial number.

—Wayne Neyens

Old Plantation. *Jason Douglas collection*. $2000.

J. H Keeney Company, owned by Jack Keeney, started making machines in 1932. The company only made a few pinballs in the 1950s, concentrating more on amusement machines. In February 1961, they released *OLD PLANTATION*, a gambling machine cleverly disguised in a pinball style cabinet.

1962

Chicago Coin released *SUN VALLEY* in October 1962, after not producing a pinball since *CAPRI* in 1956. The company was producing baseball machines, shooting galleries, and other amusement machines. *SUN VALLEY* was designed by Jerry Koci and John Gore and the artwork was by Roy Parker. The game featured "NINE-A-LITE" rollover targets: the number being hit when the ball rolls over the targets on the playfield lights the corresponding number up on the backbox.

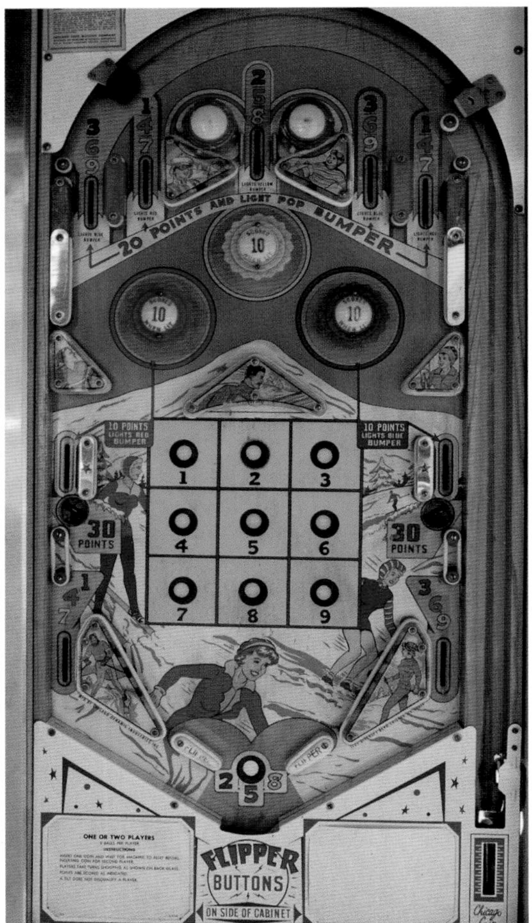

Sun Valley. *Author's collection*. $1600.

In May, Williams released *COQUETTE*. It was a two player game that had a playfield packed with features, including the popular moving target that would score 100 points when hit. On the top of the playfield between the four advance bumpers there is a rollover button that would light the two bumpers, increasing their value from 1 point to 10 points. There are two rollover buttons on the lower section that turn them off. If a player was able to hit both the A and B target, it would double the score of the eject hole value. A player could get 30, 50, and even 100 points in the eject hole.

Williams released *FRIENDSHIP 7*, designed by Steve Kordek, in July. The backglass art included a picture of John Glenn, who had navigated the Mercury space capsule in February 1962. This was the first American orbital flight and Glenn's capsule was called "Friendship 7". As the capsule flew over Australia, John Glenn reported seeing lights – residents from the city of Perth had turned on all their lights in his honor. This machine was an Add-A-Ball game that was great to play; a player could win an extra ball by making 1-4. The player's greatest challenge in playing the machine was to match the letter on the reel (in the center of the playfield between the bumpers) with the lit playfield letter. This would light the center target up for extra ball. On either side of the playfield are side rebounds: the top rebound advances the reel and the lower rebound advances the letter. Lining up the two proved to be a challenge to players and they loved it. This machine is in the classic class category and had a low production run of only 800.

Norm Clark's first attempt at designing a pinball machine for Williams was *KING PIN*, which was released in September and became a huge hit, quickly establishing Clark as a promising new designer at the company. There were ten pins on the playfield; as the ball rolled over them it would light the corresponding pin on the backglass. Hitting all the rollover buttons 1-10 would score a strike. The machine had two sets of flippers and a kick-out between the lower set of flippers that fired the ball back up the playfield.

Coquette. *Author's collection.* $1600.

Friendship 7. *Alan Tate collection.* $2000.

King Pin. *Jason Douglas collection*. $2000.

Another great pinball designer that I contacted was Norm Clark; further on in the book you will read more about his achievements. I asked Norm to write a few words about his career in the industry. When I asked him under which section he would like his story to appear, he replied "Next to King Pin, as it was the first machine I designed."

Here is a review of my career from the time I left Montreal to come to Chicago. I was working in Montreal at Canadian Aviation Electronics; we did overhaul and repair work mainly for the RCAF. My friend Abe Richmond also worked there; he left Montreal to come to Chicago and started working for Hallicrafters Radio in the engineering department. He persuaded me to come to Chicago, which I did because I could see no advancement in Montreal. I had a wife and two very young children, which made the move a little difficult for both the family and me. My friend Abe got me into Hallicrafters's engineering department where I was working on the development of a single sideband transmitter. Abe's wife at the time was working at Williams. One day while picking her up after work he got to talking with Harry Williams (the owner). Harry asked Abe to come to Williams to put electronics into pinball games. Abe got me into Williams and in 1954 I started working there.

Norm Clark in his office. *Courtesy Norm Clark.*

The idea of putting electronics into pinball proved to be too expensive. Abe left the company and went to Bell and Howell, another electronics plant, where he asked me to join him. By this time, I was getting interested in pinballs although I had never played one in my life. I worked as a technician putting the whitewoods (engineering models) together and wiring them. A little later I was also doing the circuitry on the games. Harry Mabs was the only in house designer. Harry Williams was liv-

ing in California, where he did some pinball design as well as novelty games such as Peppy the Clown.

Sam Stern bought Harry Williams out and shortly after that Harry Mabs retired, leaving Sam Stern without a designer. Sam then hired Steve Kordek to do the pinball design, leaving Williams with only one designer. A little later, Sam approached me and asked me to try my hand at design; this was approximately in mid 1960. I made a couple of whitewoods, which were a little too far out for the games being built at the time. In 1961, I designed a game called King Pin. This was the first game that I did and it was produced in 1962. The game turned out to be a success and paved the way for me as a designer.

I remained at Williams till the end of 1974. The last game I designed there was Satin Doll. Bill O'Donnell had approached me and asked me to go to Bally and run the Design Department; I started work there in January 1975. I was made Vice President and remained at Bally for ten years. leaving to join a flipper design business with a friend. The name of that business was Flipper Ltd. Business wasn't too good, as the other manufactures had their own design groups. We terminated the business a year later and I went into retirement. I was offered several jobs with other small and up and coming companies but turned them down, as I wanted to take it easy.

—Norm Clark

Portrait photo of the legendary Norm Clark. *Courtesy Norm Clark.*

VAGABOND was released by Williams in October. Steve Kordek designed this machine, which had a relatively low production run of only 600. This machine was the first to use the drop target: hitting the target when it was lit gave the player an extra ball. Players loved this feature, as they could now see the result of a perfect shot. In years to come, the drop target would be on a majority of pinball machines. To light the center target on *VAGABOND*, a player needed to hit all ten rollover buttons. A player could also earn an extra ball by completing the A-B-C-D sequence. The game had five jet bumpers and two eject holes on either side of the playfield. By landing the ball in the eject hole, the player scores and raises the drop target.

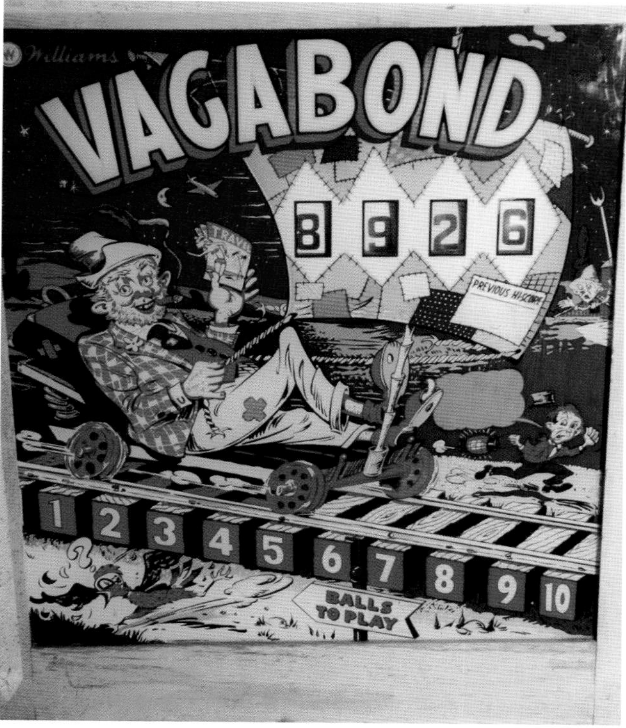

Vagabond. *Alan Tate collection.* $2000 *(playfield shown on folowing page).*

Vagabond. *Alan Tate collection.* $2000.

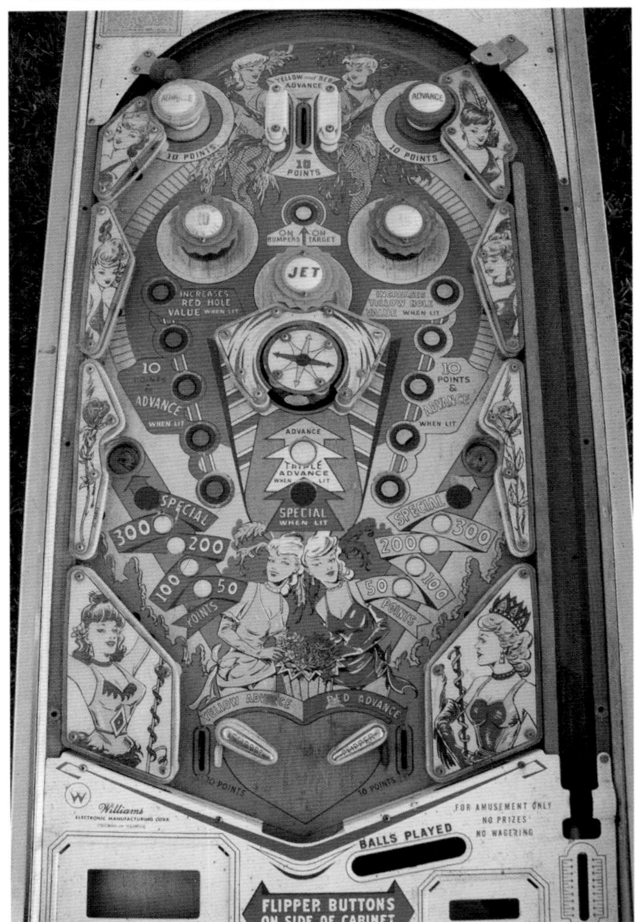

4 Roses. *Author's collection.* $1800.

Williams was in its own "Golden Age" now, giving the players games that were diverse and had challenging features. On *4 ROSES*, released in December, we see rotating targets being used in the center of the playfield. The rotating targets turn and change from red to yellow alternately when hit. The player could advance either color and increase the value of the side hole from 50 to 100 to 200 to 300, then to special. The machine also had two advance bonus systems on opposite sides of the playfield; getting the ball in the top rollover lights the jet bumpers for 10 points. The artwork was by George Molentin; his brilliance and creativity is demonstrated yet again.

Gottlieb was still dominating the market in this period. In January they released *LIBERTY BELLE*, featuring "Double Twin" roto-targets. This machine also paid tribute to Astronaut John Glenn, the first American to blast into space and orbit around earth. The machine had four flippers: two in the middle and two at the bottom of the playfield. Wayne Neyens designed the machine and added an extra target on the popular roto-target, adding to the challenge. When hit in the middle, the center target lit the bumpers for extra scoring.

One of my favorite machines is *TROPIC ISLE*, which was released in April and had backglass animation where three monkeys climb up the tree. A player, by completing the sequence 1-5, lights the side rollovers for special and the outhole for 200 points. Considering there were only five balls to play, this challenged the players. The A-B-C-D targets advance the monkeys up the backglass, and there is also a circular roll-under in the middle of the playfield that scores either 5 points or, if lit, 50 points. Once all three monkeys have climbed the tree, the player receives a free game and the monkeys are reset. The monkey feature carries over from game to game: if at the end of the game the monkeys are only halfway up the tree, they stay there at the start of the next game.

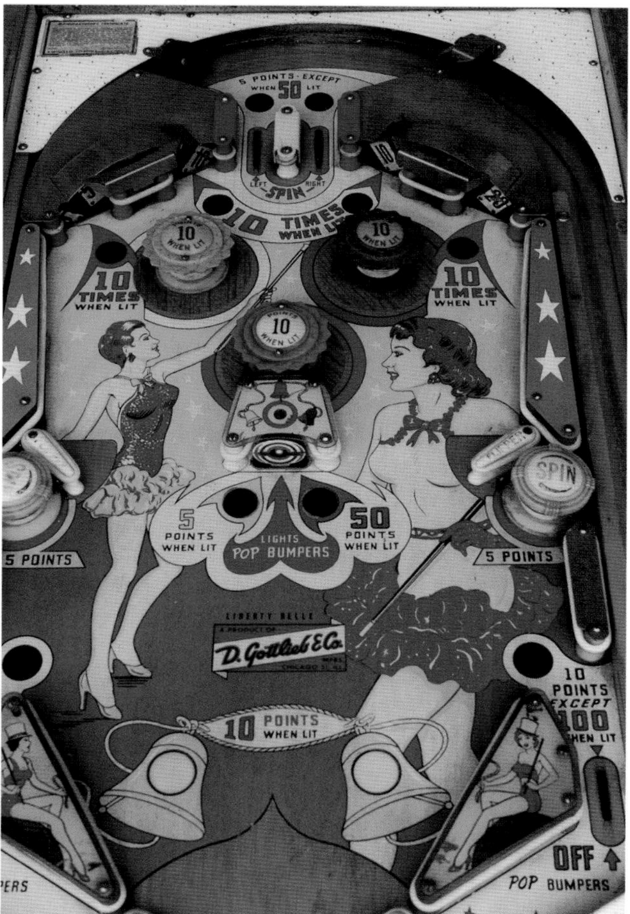

Liberty Belle. *Author's collection.* $1800.

FASHION SHOW was released by Gottlieb in June. It featured a roto wheel in the upper center of the playfield. A player advances the value of the wheel by hitting the bull's eye target in the center of the playfield. The value starts at 20 points then advances to 30, 40, 50, and even 100 points. The four side rollovers also score the target's value.

Gottlieb released *PREVIEW* in August. There is a Parker girl right in the front center that automatically attracts you to the game. On all multiple play games, Gottlieb would add on the backglass "It's more fun to compete! A game of skill." The machine had six rollovers at the top of the playfield that scored 10 points – or 100 when lit. There were five targets numbered 1-5 on the playfield. Each time one is hit, the corresponding button lights up, giving the player 10 points instead of 1 point. Hitting all these targets lights up the outhole to score 100 points. The only way a player could earn a free game on this machine was by reaching the score set or by matching the lucky number at the end of the game. There were no specials on the playfield, a feature that players missed.

Gottlieb released *OLYMPICS* in September, with a theme used back in 1952 by Williams Manufacturing. Each rollover on the playfield designates an "Olympic City" and is lit up on the backglass. Lighting up eight cities earns a free game. If all targets are completed, this lights up the two specials. On the backglass, a diver is getting ready for her jump. There are five cities on either side of the backglass, each with a picture of an Olympic sporting event (boxing, soccer, basketball, hockey and swimming). Roy Parker even blends the track and field and the swimming into the backglass, a truly unique, spectacular piece of artwork with the crowd in the background cheering the athletes on.

RACK-A-BALL, released in December, is based on the popular game of pool. This machine was such a hit with players that it was later re-released in different themes; this occurred in 1964 (*BOWLING QUEEN*) and 1969 (*MIBS*). At the beginning of a game, the 12 rollovers are lit. By scoring any lit rollover, a player racks a ball in the backglass. An operator sets the number of balls required to receive a free game, usually set at 9 and 12. Another way to win free games is to hit the red, green, and blue targets: this lights the bumpers and the side kickers to score 10 points and also lights the bottom rollovers for special. The special light would alternate as points are hit. A player could also win free games on reaching the score set for a replay and by matching the lucky number. This machine appealed to players, offering them a challenge. Add the backglass animation and you come up with another classic Gottlieb game.

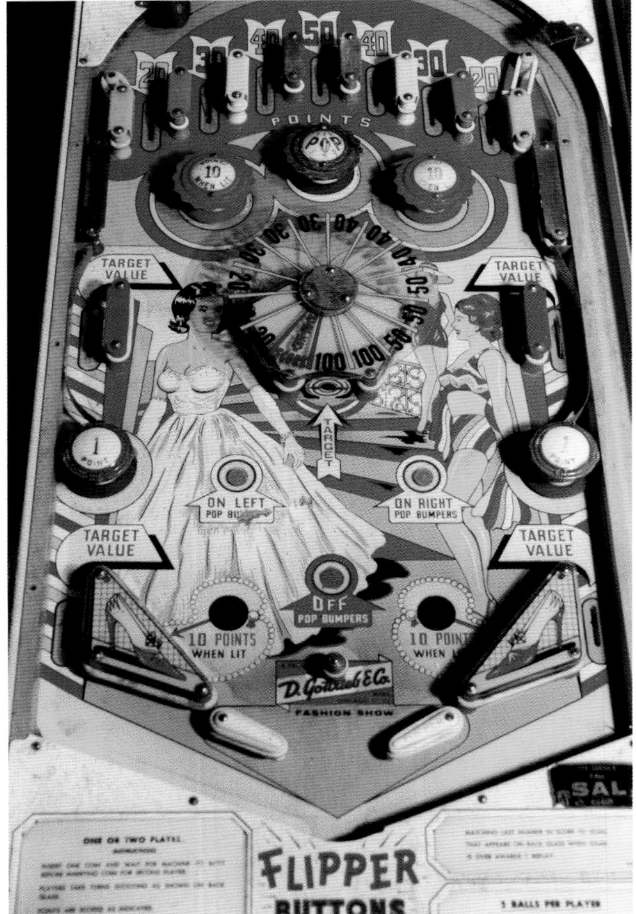

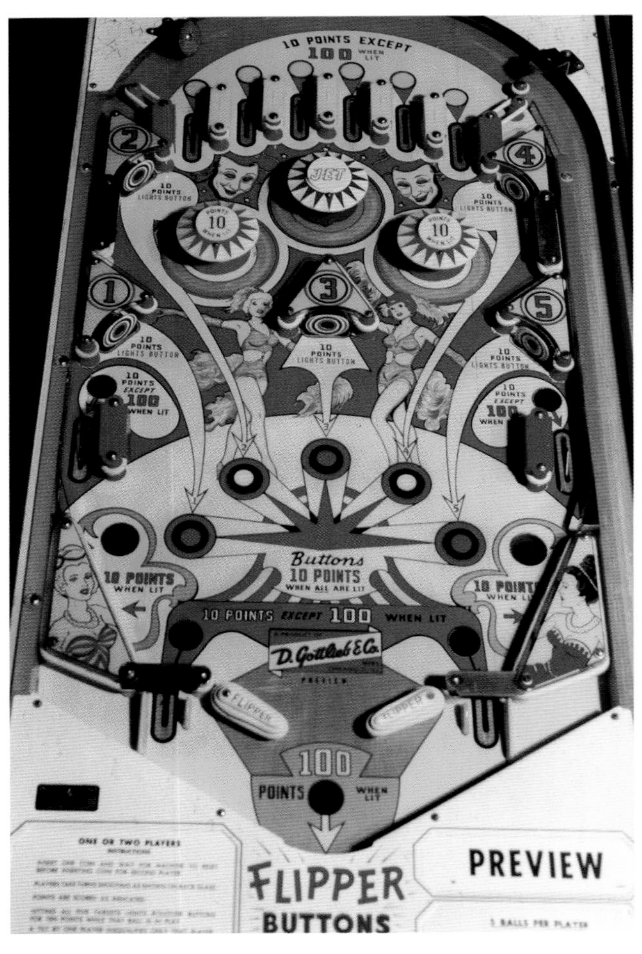

Fashion Show. *Jason Douglas collection*. $1500.

Preview. *Alan Tate collection*. $1800.

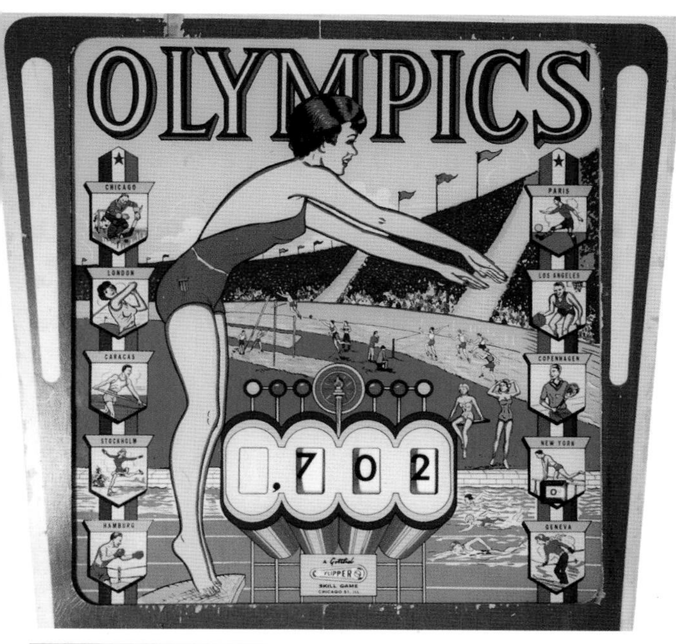

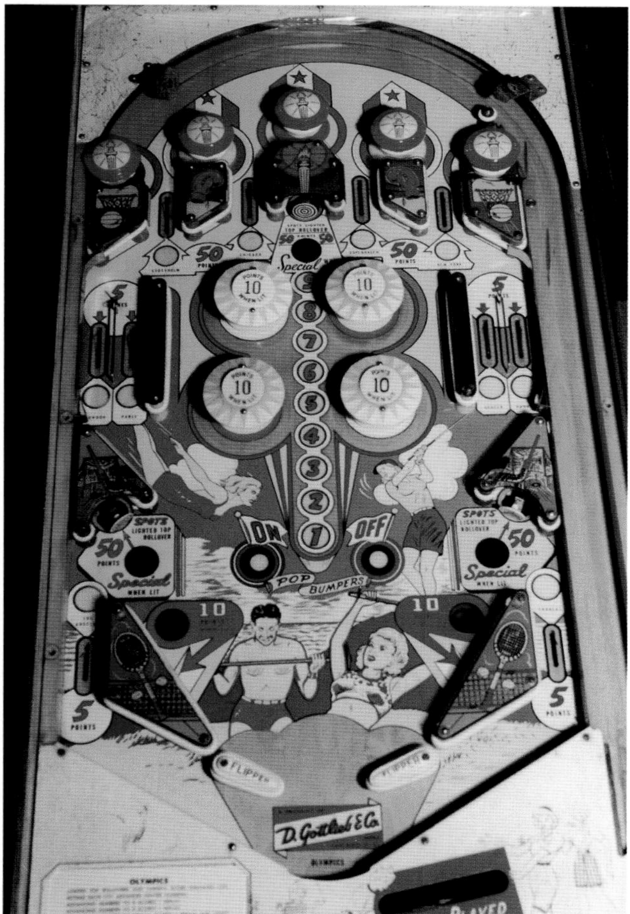

Olympics. *Alan Tate collection.* $2000.

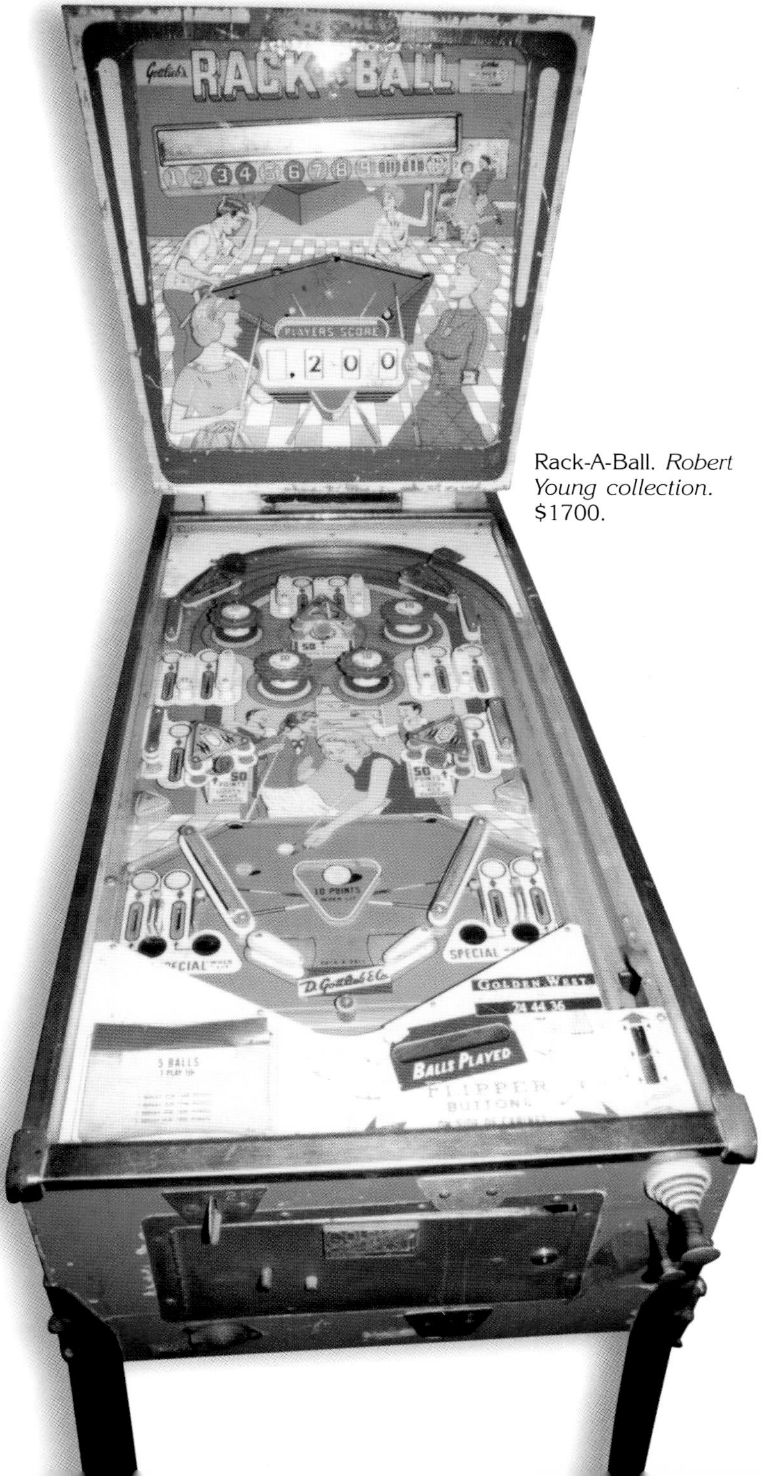

Rack-A-Ball. *Robert Young collection.* $1700.

I asked Wayne Neyens what his wife thought of pinball machines and what were some of his favorite games:

My wife never played pinball; not that she didn't like them but she kept busy running the household. My three kids loved pinball and I kept several games at home at all times. I had a Niagara for several months and then traded it off for a set of encyclopedias; they were not too happy over that. I had an aunt who told me, in front of all my relatives, that I should quit playing games all day and go out and get a real job.

Favorite games that I designed? Well, that is most difficult because I have several and they were favorites for different reasons. I think from a design standpoint "Queen of Hearts" has to be my favorite game, but for the fun of playing it would have to be "Slick Chick" or "Lightning Ball."

—Wayne Neyens

Wayne Neyens with his wife Muriel and daughter Patricia on the left. This picture was taken at the Pinball Expo 1999. *Courtesy Wayne Neyens.*

1963

This was the year that Bally Manufacturing seriously entered the pinball market and challenged the dominance of the "Big Two:" D. Gottlieb & Co. and Williams Electronic Manufacturing. It was in this period that the market for "in line" bingo machines was drastically limited by United States' legislation. Since the death of Ray Maloney in 1957, his heirs had run the Bally company. In 1963, the sales manager at Bally, Bill O'Donnell, got a team together and bought the company. With the government putting the squeeze on bingo games, the company started focusing on the pinball market. The difference in Bally pinballs was that they used a 50 volt circuit instead of the 24 volt used on games made by Gottlieb and Williams, thus giving the flippers, bumpers, and kickers that extra bit of power.

The first machine released by Bally was *MOONSHOT*, released in January. Ted Zale designed it, and the game was identical to Gottlieb's *TROPIC ISLE*, released in April 1962. The same month, Bally released *CROSS COUNTRY*; it had a production run of only 500. Bally machines were known for the "Free Gate," a feature that would be on a majority of their games in the 1960s. A player, by hitting A-B-C-D, opens the gate. Ted Zale reintroduced the use of asymmetrical playfields, where the left side of the playfield is not identical to the right side. *CROSS COUNTRY* was an interesting game. At the start of the game, shooting over the red, green, or blue rollover selects the player's route. The objective is to get to the end to win a free game. This machine had the carry-over feature: at the start of a new game, all the advances on the routes would not reset. This feature promoted repeated play.

On *HOOTENANNY*, released in November, we see the introduction of the mushroom bumper. It can be seen in the center of the playfield, just below the three pop bumpers. The mushroom bumper is a 1" mushroom shaped plastic post that scores when the movable top is raised by contact with the ball; this was another Ted Zale design. Bally machines looked different than the others produced; the score reels are yellow and the head took on a different shape, distinguishing it from the others. They have many different variations of gates and the playfields are asymmetrical. The aim of this game was to spell the name H-O-O-T-E-N-A-N-N-Y on the backglass. The machine has two gates on the right hand side of the playfield; a player only scores 10 points going down the free ball gate on the top right of the playfield. If one of the gates is open the player scores 30 points; if both are open the player scores 100 points and advances a letter on a backglass. To open a gate a player must complete the A-B-C-D rollovers at the top of the playfield. Hitting the number 1-2-3 targets opens the gate as well. This machine also has the carry on feature, where lit letters remain lit from game to game until the name has been completed. If a player manages to complete the name, a free game is awarded and the letters reset.

On *MONTE CARLO*, released in December, Ted Zale put five mushroom bumpers on the playfield; these bumpers were different and players enjoyed the change. By hitting the top five rollovers, a player lights the special on the lower end of the playfield. Lighting the letters B-I-G W-I-N lights the next number on the casino table. The aim is to light all ten numbers on the casino table to earn a free game. At the end of the game, whatever number is lit on the casino table will remain lit until the next game. This feature encouraged players to keep inserting coins to accomplish the Big Win and receive a free game.

Cross Country. *Troy Meredith collection.* $2000.

Hootenanny. *Alan Tate collection.* $1500.

Monte Carlo. *Jason Douglas collection*. $1300.

Chicago Coin released two machines in this year: *FIRECRACKER* in October and *BRONCO* in November. The company only produced a few pinball machines, concentrating on other amusement games. *BRONCO* had an attractive backglass. On the center of the playfield is a jet bumper surrounded by four plastic shields. The player could keep bouncing the ball around the bumper scoring points. Also on the playfield are two eject holes, which fire the ball into the corral area for fast ball action. A player, by hitting the A and B target, lights the center bumper for additional scoring. Al Schlappa and Jerri Koci designed this machine.

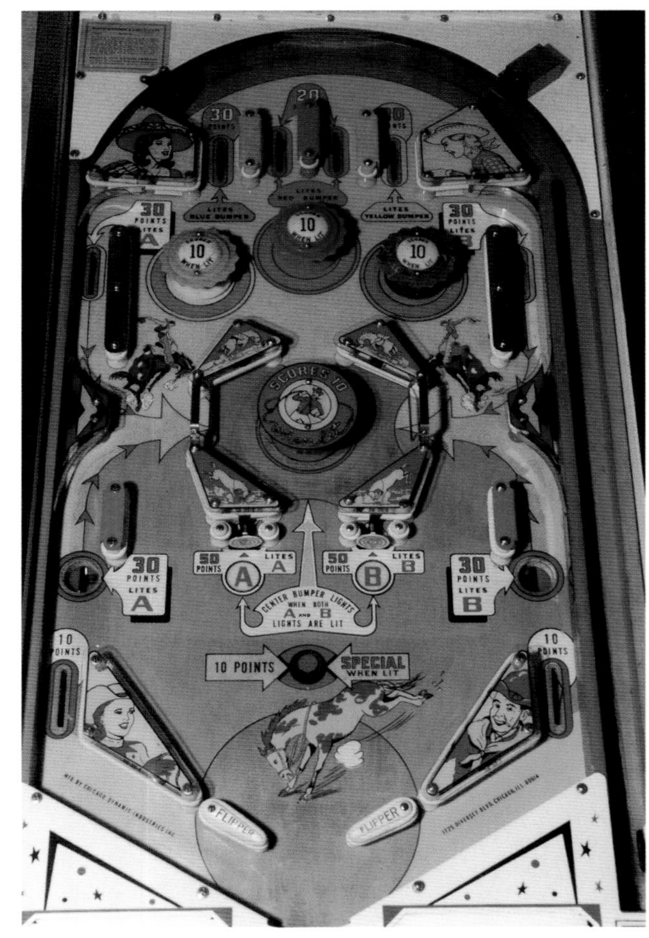

Bronco. *Gary Coleman collection*. $1800.

Williams released *TOM TOM*, a two player game, in January. This machine had two moving targets on either side of the playfield and two ball shooters on either side of the flippers. Once the ball enters the ball shooters, it advances the target value and propels the ball back up the playfield. The American West is well portrayed in the backbox. Artist George Molentin cleverly added Tom Tom drums around the score reels while Indian girls dance around the fire.

The next machine from Williams was *BIG DEAL*, released in February. The drop targets feature was an instant hit for Williams, after first appearing on *VAGABOND* four months earlier. On *BIG DEAL* there were four drop targets on the playfield; by hitting all four a player lights a joker and the next card in the royal flush on the backglass. By completing the royal flush, a player earns a free game. The machine has an open playfield. The two flippers are set apart with a rebound plastic in the center of the playfield between them. The cards in the royal flush remain lit from game to game until completed. Steve Kordek designed this game. Notice the small banner reading "Steve's Diner" in the top left hand corner of the backglass.

The next machine released by the company was *SWING TIME*, an Add-A-Ball game with a low production run of only 500. The Add-A-Ball games were very popular with players as they could win extra balls. If a player lit up T-I-M-E on the playfield by rolling over the rollovers they got an extra ball. There is a jet bumper in the center and two pop bumpers a little further down on the playfield. The jet scores 10 points and 100 when lit. The pop bumpers score 1 point and 10 when lit. The two lower bumpers are referred to as dead bumpers; unlike pop bumpers have no electromechanical action.

SKILL POOL was released by Williams in June. in the middle of the playfield there are fifteen rollover buttons set out in a rack. By hitting all the rollover buttons, a player lights up special. The machine had a target in the upper center of the playfield, which scores 100 points or special when lit. The target resets when the ball lands in the kickup shooters on either side of the flippers. The machine had two gobble holes on either side of the playfield, which score 50 points or special when lit. Williams referred to these as "skill holes."

BIG DADDY was released in September, again featuring the drop target. The company was taking full advantage of this device that appealed to players. The drop target in the center of the playfield scores 100 points. Completing the 1-10 sequence lights up the target for special. There are two eject holes on either side of the drop target. When the ball lands in either hole, this resets the target and scores 50 points. This machine was packed with features and is desired by players even today.

The last machine to be produced in this year by Williams was *BEAT THE CLOCK*, released in December. This was the first multi ball game giving the player two balls in play at the same time. It was designed by Steve Kordek and also featured an animated backglass. The positioning of the four flippers at the bottom of the playfield made it hard for the player to keep the ball in play.

Tom Tom. *Author's collection.* $1400.

Left & above: Big Deal. *Jason Douglas collection.* $1400.

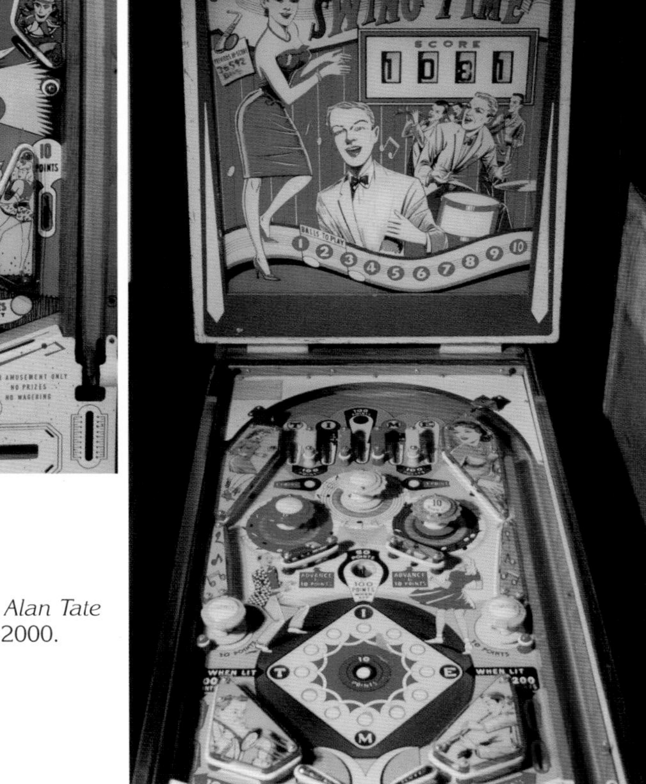

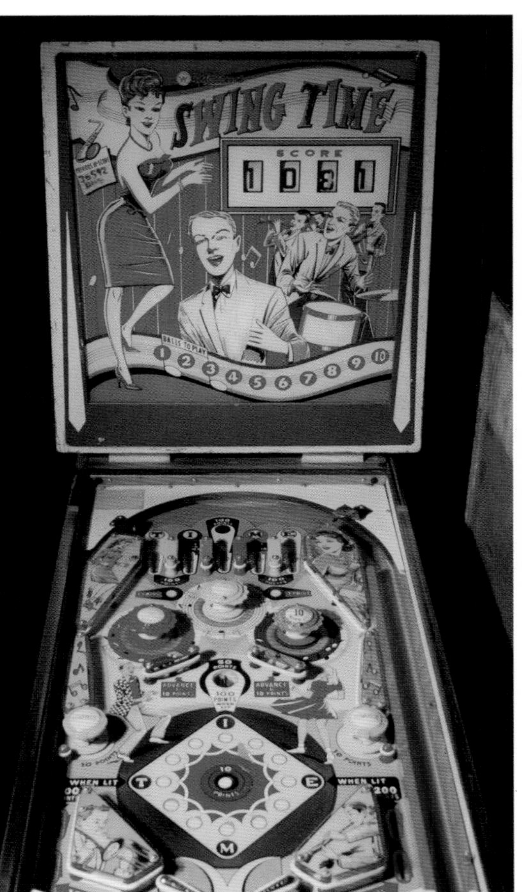

Swing Time. *Alan Tate collection.* $2000.

Skill Pool. *Jason Douglas collection.* $1500.

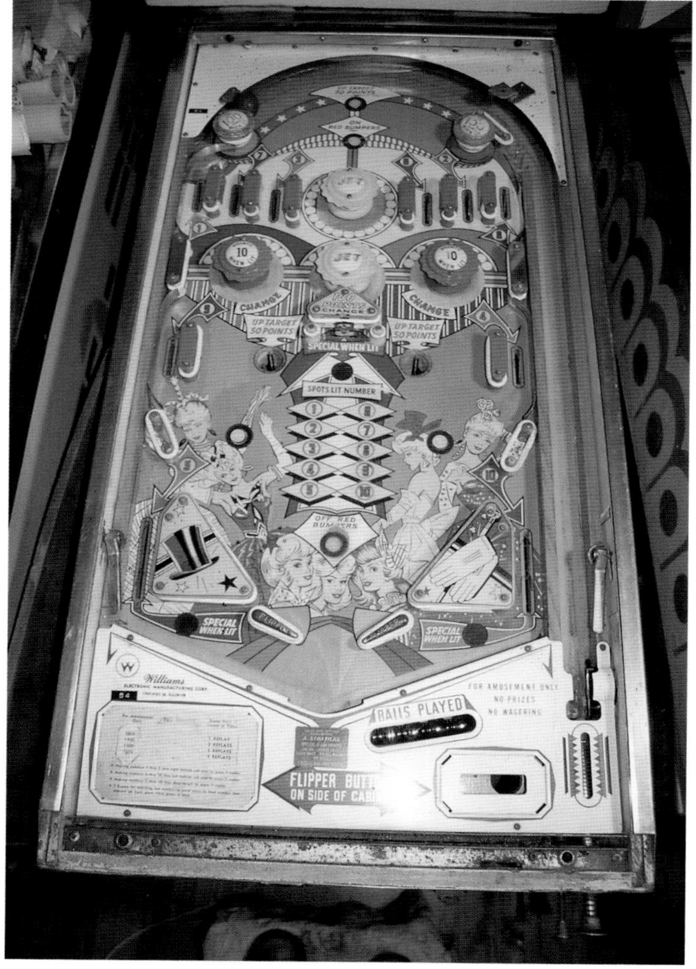

Big Daddy. *Alan Tate collection.* $1500.

Beat the Clock. *Author's collection.* $2000.

The combination of designers Wayne Neyens, Steve Kordek, Norm Clark, and Ted Zale, along with artists Roy Parker and George Molentin, were creating some of the most memorable machines ever produced. As I'm working on these machines, I often think of the endless creativity shown by these great designers/artists and their inspirational works of art. America's economy was booming. People around the world loved the American culture and fashion and they got a glimpse of this in the pinball machines being exported worldwide.

Pinball themes showed the American "Wild West," American cities, American recreation, American cars, American sports, and American fashion. Collectors today treasure these games. Private homes are where the majority of pinball machines are found today and every day more and more people are collecting them.

Gottlieb released *GAUCHO*, a four player game, in January. In the early four player machines, Gottlieb had a detachable marquee that explained the instructions for play. After a successful run of four player machines, we see these instructions being added to the backglass. In both the left and right lower corners of the backglass these instructions are lit up. On the left is printed "It's more fun to compete! Choose partners for team play." For team play, four players need to be playing. At the end of a game, the scores of player one and player three are added up and so are the scores of player two and player four; the team with the higher score wins. In the middle of the playfield is the popular roto-target, where the player could score on either the left or right side. There were five power bumpers on the playfield and four dead bumpers that would spin the roto-target when hit.

Gaucho. *Author's collection*. $1600.

Gottlieb released *SLICK CHICK* in April. This machine is another Gottlieb classic, and the girls in the backglass look like Playboy bunnies. The head of Playboy, Hugh Hefner, started his business in 1953 with a magazine called *Playboy* being sold every month. In 1960, the company called Playboy Enterprises opened up playboy clubs in Chicago – you could go there for a drink, lunch or dinner, and have a bit of fun. The ladies in these clubs were dressed in the traditional playboy costumes with rabbit ears and tails. Roy Parker brilliantly captures the imagination of the pinball player with artwork that lures you to play the game. The game was designed by Wayne Neyens and is another of his favorites. Completing S-L-I-C-K C-H-I-C-K in rotation lights one of the five rollover buttons and resets the sequence. Lighting all five rollover buttons lights the center hole for special. There are two rollovers on either side of the playfield numbered 1-4. By hitting the four numbered rollovers consecutively, a player wins a free game. Players have to be wary of the gobble hole in the middle of the playfield that awards 100 points and special when lit.

Slick Chick. *Jason Douglas collection*. $2500.

Slick Chick was another Wayne Neyens masterpiece; it is a machine that challenges the player's skill and ball control. I asked Wayne about the game and how he came up with the name.

Slick Chick is not only a very good game but a lot of stories have been told about the name. Why, I don't know. But the true story, and I should know, is that I was searching for a two word name, five letters long, with a common letter in the middle. The game was well along when on a Sunday night I happened to be going to a friend's house for dinner. As I rounded the corner leading to his house there, staring me in the face, was a big neon light reading "SLICK CHICK" and advertising a new restaurant. The next morning I drew up the backglass with the name and it has been there ever since.

—Wayne Neyens

SWING ALONG was released by Gottlieb in July and was the first machine to use spinning targets. These targets were suspended by a fine wire. Making the target spin by hitting it would award points; the harder it was hit the more points the player would receive. On the playfield there were three in a row. There were also four bumpers; to light the bumper, which would give a higher score, the player must first hit the corresponding colored target. Rock 'n' Roll had begun in America in the 1950s – this form of entertainment took the world by storm and everybody loved it. Artist Roy Parker portrays rock 'n' roll dancers in full swing on the backglass of *SWING ALONG*.

Sweethearts. *Paul Brisbane collection*. $2000.

Swing Along. *Author's collection*. $1800.

SWEETHEARTS, released in September, was the last Gottlieb machine to use the gobble hole, which was common in most 1950s games. Players didn't like the fact that once the ball landed in the gobble hole it was lost. Gottlieb was the "king of card games" and this machine was one of their best. On the backglass there are three rows of cards. Every time a player makes a rollover on the playfield, the corresponding card lights up. Completing a set of cards lights up a special on the gobble hole. This was a skillful game to play; completing all three rows would light up three specials in the gobble hole, and every rollover on the playfield earned the player a free game.

FLYING CHARIOTS was released in October and featured a target alley in the center of the playfield. When the mystery feature is lit, the target scores between 50 and 300 points. Gottlieb called this the "Mystery Score." Looking at the backglass makes me feel as though I were in the great chariot race from the 1959 movie *Ben Hur*, which starred Charlton Heston as Juda and Stephen Boyd as Marcella.

The last machine by Gottlieb this year was *GIGI*; it was released in December and is another classic game. There are seven yellow bumpers and seven red bumpers. The objective of the game is to light up all seven of one color to score special and score an advance. At the start of a game, the yellow two, four, and six are lit, and the red one, three, and five are also lit. The problem is that if a yellow bumper is lit, the corresponding red bumper light goes out, and once the red bumper is lit the corresponding yellow bumper goes out. At the end of the game all the advances accumulated add bonus scores. *GIGI* was the first machine to use this "Bonus Score" feature.

Flying Chariots. *Michael Bowden collection.* $1800.

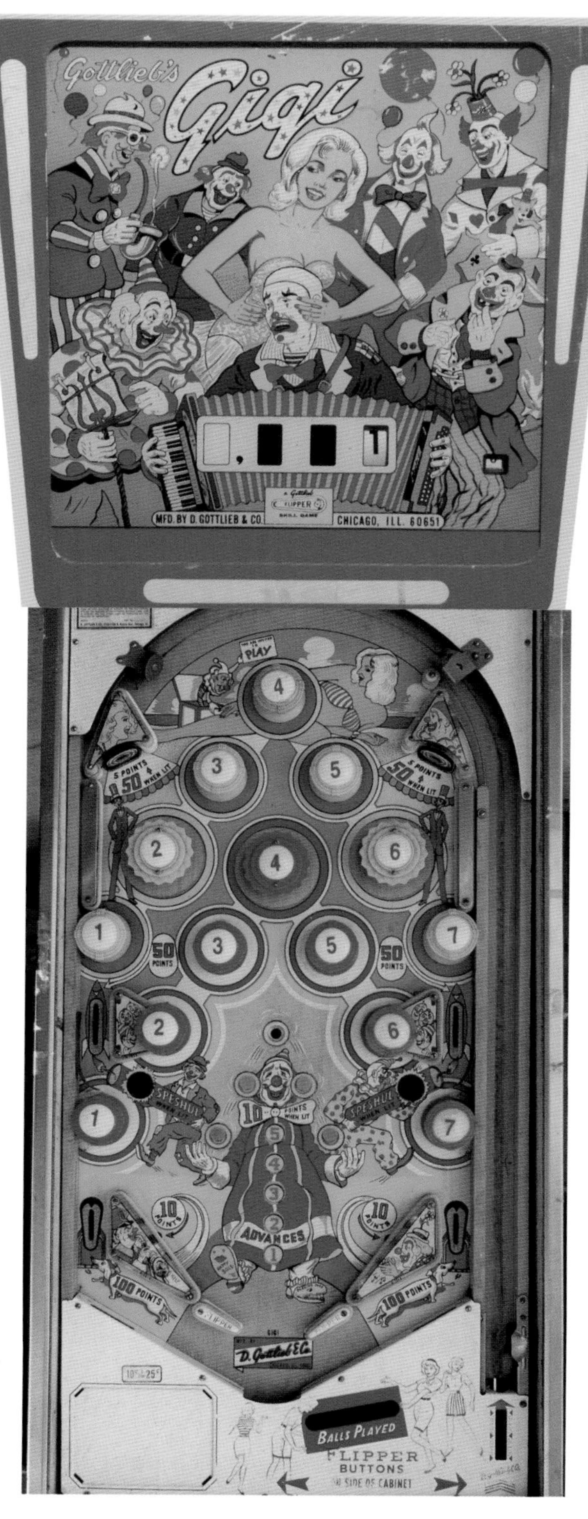

Gigi. *Author's collection.* $2500.

Poker Face. *Jason Douglas collection*. $1600.

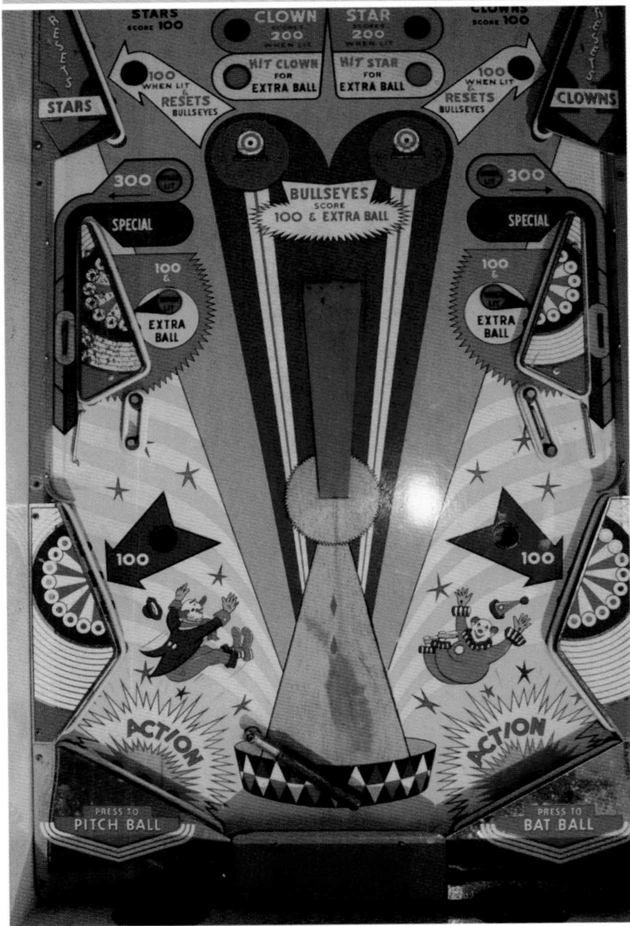

Carnival. *Jason Douglas collection*. $1500.

Race-Way. *Alan Tate collection.* $2500.

Keeney released *POKER FACE* in August. Lighting up royal flush or full house awarded the player a free game. This game featured an automatic ball lift. All pinballs to date, with the exception of the three machines released by Bally in the 1950s, had manual ball lifts. The player would have to manually push the ball up into the runway, where it was then propelled by the plunger. Keeney only produced a few more pinball machines, the last being *COLORAMA* released in November. This was the end of an era for Jack Keeny's company, which had started making pin games in 1932.

The Midway Manufacturing company was formed in the late 1950s by Iggy Wolverton and Hank Ross, who were formally at United Manufacturing. Their first arcade game was *RED BALL*, released in 1959. They released a few pitch and bat games in 1962: *DELUXE BASEBALL* and *SIXTY-TWO BASEBALL*. In June 1963, the company released *CARNIVAL*, another bat and ball game.

The most famous Midway games were the ones featuring a 3-D animated backglass. There were two formula one racing cars that would race around a racetrack in the backbox. This can be seen on *RACE-WAY*, released in September. This game was so popular, it was re-released as *CHAMP* in December. Magnets under the racetrack in the head move the cars in the backglass. At the start of a game both cars would move to the starting position. A player, by hitting certain targets on the playfield, advances the car one length, two lengths, or three lengths in the backglass. The playfield also featured a bonus system: the bonus could be collected in the middle two eject holes, referred to as "Pit Stops," and the two inner rollovers at the bottom of the playfield. For players to win a free game they would have to accumulate the number of laps set by the operator. Unlike other pinballs that score 1 point, 10 points and 100 points, this machine only scores laps. Once the car has crossed the finish line, one lap is added to the player's score.

Midway did not have the rights to use the "spring shooter assembly" (known as the plunger), so the player had to push a button to launch the ball onto the playfield.

Champ. The playfield on this game is identical to Race-way. *Author's collection.* $2500.

1964

While writing this book, I would often ring people regarding my research with a question or two. I rung Wayne Neyens one evening and left a message on his answering machine. He e-mailed me the following day to relay this story: "One evening my ten-year-old was climbing on top of one of the pinball games in my basement when the playfield glass broke and I had to rush her to the hospital for emergency repair. It was quite a serious series of lacerations. Well, the next day I switched all playfield glass over to tempered glass and from then on all glass was tempered. Other companies followed our example. Who knows how many law suits we could have had."

I asked Wayne what year this was and he replied' 1964. As a result of this incident, he was responsible for what is common on all pinballs today, tempered glass. (His daughter Phyllis was okay, but it gave the family a bit of a scare.)

In January 1964, Bally released *MAD WORLD*. Ted Zale designed the machine and the artwork was by Art Stenholm. Ted Zale incorporated his own ideas into the game. He used an asymmetrical playfield, two mushroom bumpers, and the free ball gate, which is seen on most Bally machines of this period. A player, by completing the A-B-C-D, lights the rollover on the top left of the playfield to open the free ball gate.

On the next machine released by Bally, *SKY DIVERS*, Ted Zale added the thrill and excitement of that sport to the pinball machine. This machine features a Double-Skill selectable carry-over feature where the player can select the skydiver closest to landing at the start of the game. The machine has an animated backglass – the skydivers dive from the plane and make their way down. The aim is to get them to the landing pad for specials. There are three mushroom bumpers on the playfield. If a player hits all three, the bonus gate on the top left of the playfield opens. By shooting the ball in, a player is awarded 100 points and advances the skydiver closer to the landing. There is another gate on the playfield called the Free Ball gate. By rolling over the rollover on the right of the playfield when lit, a player opens that gate. When the shot is made into the gate the player gets his ball back, scores 100 points, and advances the skydiver towards the special. This machine was the last Bally pinball to use the manual ball lift.

Mad World. *Jason Douglas collection*. $2000.

In May, Bally released *2 in 1*, which featured the automatic ball lift. Gottlieb, "king" of card machines, was now being challenged by newcomer Bally. The playfield on this game had five mushroom bumpers, which alternated between scoring in the game of 21 and giving points for high score. The four top rollovers also alternated between scoring in the game of 21 and giving points for high score. This is a brilliant game, in which the player plays the game 21 against the machine; when satisfied with their score they "stand" by pressing the hold button (on the front of the cabinet) before shooting each remaining ball. By doing this, the five mushroom bumpers are made inactive for "21" score and only give points. However, the top rollovers are still active; the only way to change them to give points for high score is to hit the skill rebound when the ball is fired up into the playfield. The player's score in the game of 21 is shown on the backglass and on the playfield when the score reaches 16. By reaching 21 at the end of a game, the player earns a free game.

Sky Divers. *Jason Douglas collection*. $1800.

2 in 1. My son Anthony is holding the backglass. *Author's collection*. $2000.

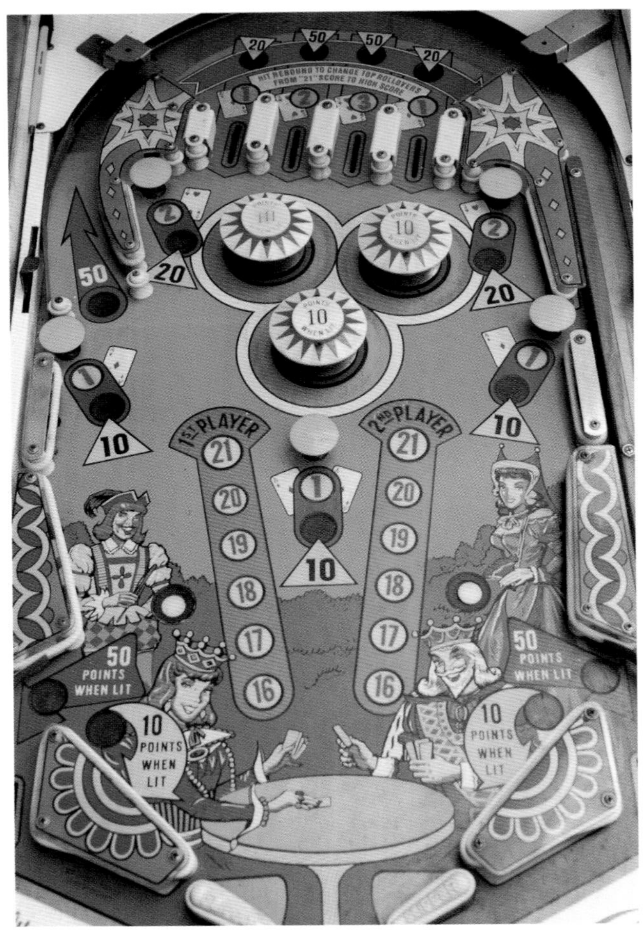

2 in 1 playfield.

HARVEST was released in August. Designer Ted Zale used a traditional symmetrical playfield, adding four slingshot kickers just above the flippers to give the game plenty of action. There are five mushroom bumpers on the playfield, each one with a letter next to it. Hitting the mushroom bumper lights the corresponding letter in the word "BALLY" on the center of the playfield. Lighting A-L-L, opens the free ball gate, which is on the lower side of the playfield; lighting B-A-L-L or A-L-L-Y opens the free ball gate and lights the star, which is in the center of the playfield. By completing the sequence and lighting B-A-L-L-Y, the player opens the gate, lights the star, and also lights the special at.the bottom left rollover.

Harvest. *Jason Douglas collection*. $1700.

As a side note, voltage in the United States is 110 volts, however there are countries around the world where voltage is 240 volts; such is the case in Australia. To get a machine to work from this period, you would have to install what is called a "step down transformer," which steps the voltage from 240 volts to 110 volts. For their machines made in this period, Bally Manufacturing used a universal transformer that operated on either 110 volts or 220-240 volts; to switch the voltage, the primary lead of the transformer just needs to be rewired.

At this time, Sam Stern had full control of Williams Electronic Manufacturing. In 1964, he sold the company to Seeburg Industries Incorporated, a jukebox manufacturer, but remained there as president until 1976.

Williams released *SOCCER*, designed by Norm Clark, in March. This machine featured an animated backglass – every time a goal is scored, the player in the backglass kicks a ball. Players select either the blue team or red team when the ball is fired onto the playfield, and this in turn lights up the correspondingly colored bumpers. The left rollover selects the red team and the right rollover selects the blue team. Players moves the ball towards the goal by hitting the two rollover buttons, the lit bumpers, the red or blue target, and the top advance. There is a center shooter that scores a goal between the bumpers.

Soccer. *Alan Tate collection.* $1600.

The next machine released by Williams was *PALOOKA*, an Add-A-Ball game with a low production run of 700. Steve Kordek designed the machine and the artwork was by Art Stenholm. It has five drop targets that are worth 100 points when hit. If a player knocks them all down, the targets reset and the center target's value increases from 100 to 300 to 500 to 1000 and then special. There are two shooters at the bottom next to the flippers that shoot the ball back up the playfield.

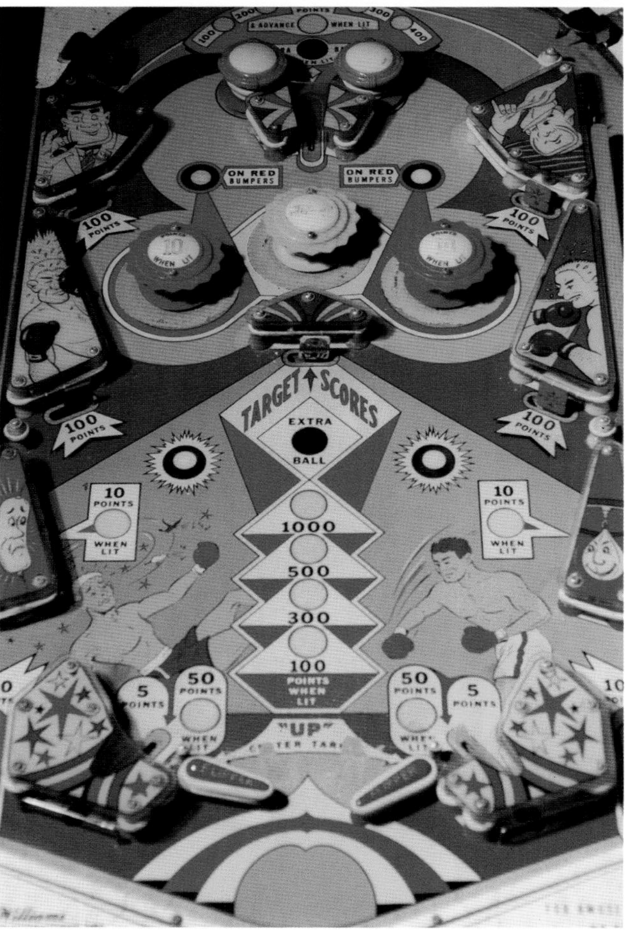

Palooka. *Alan Tate collection.* $2000.

SAN FRANCISCO was released in May; this was the last machine produced by any manufacturer to use the gobble hole. The gobble hole was popular with operators but disliked by players. This machine featured an animated backglass – the moving arrow in the backglass lights up corresponding buttons on the playfield that increase their value. Every lit button increases the value of the gobble hole in the center of the playfield by 100 points. The two eject holes on the playfield move the arrow five steps to either the left or the right. The six dead bumpers and the two targets also move the arrow.

San Francisco, the last machine to use the gobble hole. *Alan Tate collection*. $1700.

Heatwave. *Author's collection*. $2000.

HEATWAVE was another classic game, released in July. Steve Kordek designed it and the artwork is by Art Stenholm. The machine had backglass animation emulating a hot summer's day. A feature on the playfield was to hit the advance temperature swinging targets or rollovers. This results in an increase in the temperature on the thermometer in the backglass, thus increasing the drop target value in the center of the playfield from 100 to 500 points. When the thermometer reaches its highest level, the center target and the two side rollovers light up for special.

The company released an unusual game in September called *MINI GOLF*, designed by Steve Kordek. Under the playfield glass is a realistic 9 hole putting green. The player putts hole by hole till all 9 are made or 27 shots are used.

RIVER BOAT was released in September and was designed by Norm Clark. It has a great playfield layout: a player spots the cards by hitting the moving target in the center of the playfield or in the top center rollover. The cards are spotted, then light up on the backglass. Lighting the 5-9 cards lights up the special in the bottom left rollover; lighting the 10-Ace cards lights up the special in the bottom right rollover. By lighting all the cards, a player scores a replay at the end of the game. Another challenge of playing this game is to light up the three jokers, which can be done by hitting the two red targets on either side of the playfield. When all three have been spotted the top rollover lights up for special; if the player looses the ball the three jokers reset.

Williams Electronics had two great designers working together in this period – Steve Kordek and Norm Clark – and were turning out classic games. These games are still enjoyed today by players and are considered highly collectible.

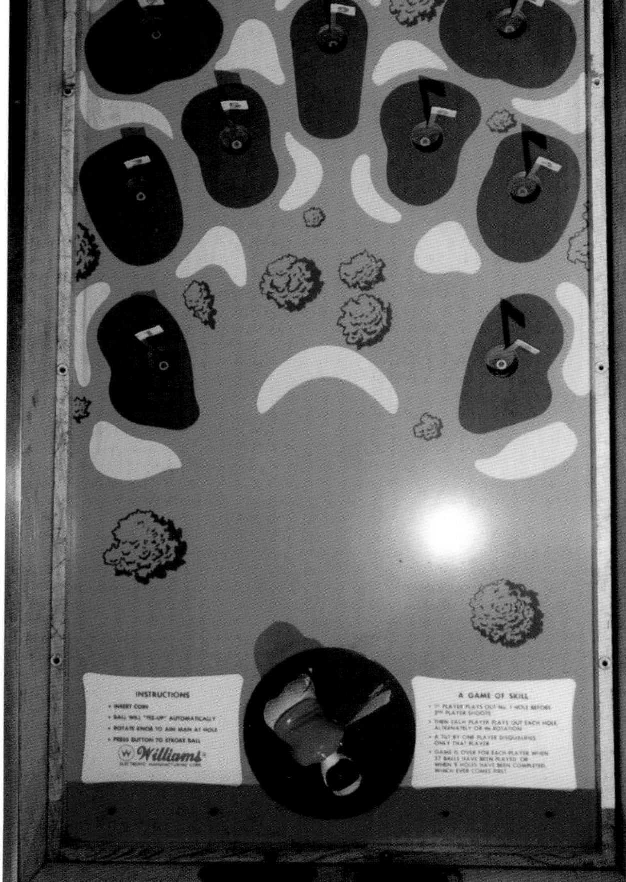

Mini Golf. *Jason Douglas collection*. $2500.

River Boat. *Jason Douglas collection*. $2000.

Williams next released *WHOOPEE* in October. This machine had "two lane center trap ball action." There are five balls trapped here; when balls go from lane to lane the target value increases from 100 to 500 points. If a player can shoot all five balls in the lane that has special lit, they win a replay. On either side of the flippers are ball shooters that shoot the ball back up the playfield, creating tantalizing play action.

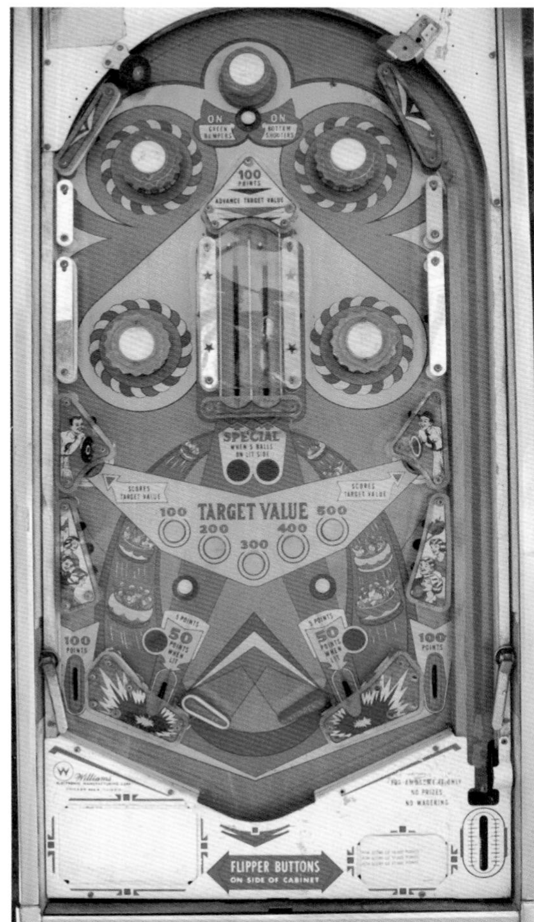

Whoopee. *Author's collection*. $1600.

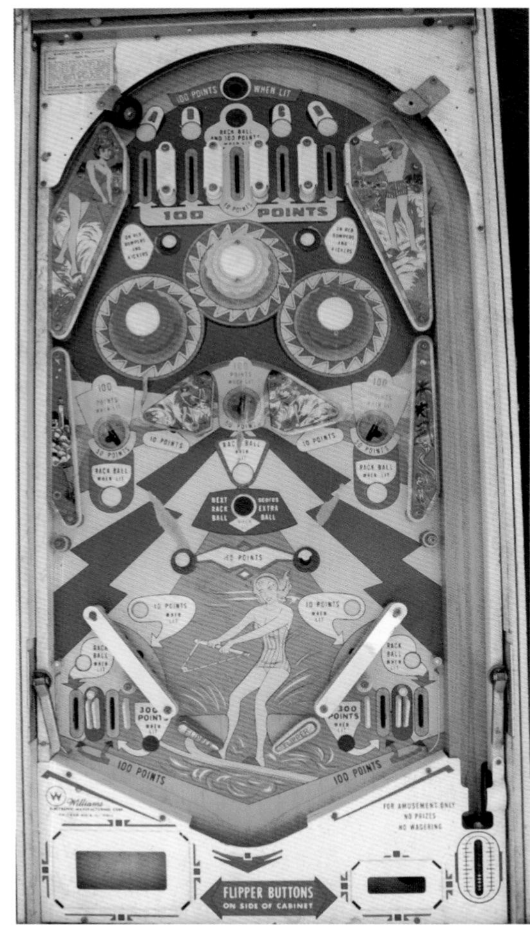

Zig Zag. *Author's collection*. $1500.

ZIG ZAG was released in December and the company released *WING DING*, the Add-A-Ball version, in the same month. The only difference in the two machines is that *ZIG ZAG* awards the player a free game and *WING DING* awards a extra ball. *ZIG ZAG* had a production run of 1674 and *WING DING* had a production run of 626. The game had backbox animation where multi colored balls rack up when the ball lands in the lit eject holes and lit rollover lanes. When all nine balls are racked up in the backbox, the center eject hole lights up for special; by completing the A-B-C-D, a player lights the bottom rollovers for special. The artwork on both of these machines is very captivating and was done by George Molentin. These were the last machines to use the reverse-head shape in the backbox.

In February, Gottlieb released *SHIP-MATES*, the first multi-player machine to have a re-settable tilt. On machines prior to this, when a player tilted the machine the game would be over; on *SHIP-MATES*, the tilt only penalized the ball in play and not the whole game. On the playfield there were six rollovers and six targets that determined the roto-target value. The value could be increased from 1x to 10x to 100x. By completing the 1-2-3 sequence on the playfield, the player lit up the "shoot again feature." There are two eject holes on either side of the roto-target; landing the ball in here spins the target. The sailor on the backglass automatically catches people's attention and lures them into having a game.

The next machine released was *WORLD FAIR* in April, released in time for the World's Fair held in New York. This machine features a "spin disc," activated by the lit red bumpers on the playfield and the outhole. There are eleven rollovers on the playfield, numbered 1-11; making the rollover lights the corresponding Ferris wheel in he backbox. The spin disc also spots the numbers. If a player lit all eleven numbers, they would get a replay.

Western themes were very popular with players and were frequently used in the 1950s and 1960s. On *BONANZA*, released in June, the artwork by Roy Parker includes the Cartwright family (from the television series *Bonanza*, popular in the late 1950s and still popular today) in the lower right hand corner of the backglass.

Wing Ding, the Add-A-Ball version of Zig Zag. The playfield is identical to Zig Zag. *Author's collection.* $1700.

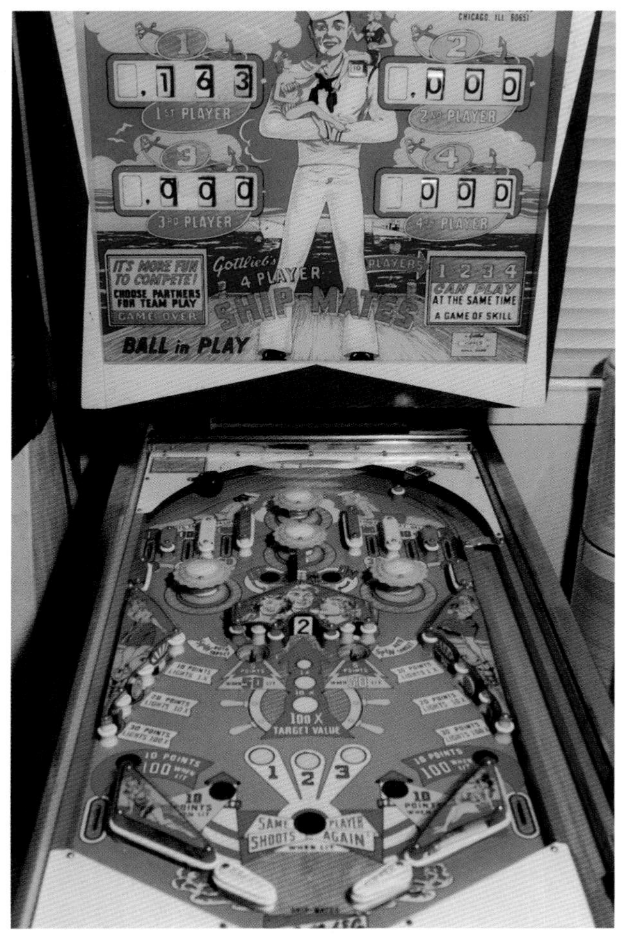

Ship-Mates. *Paul Brisbane collection.* $1800.

World Fair. *Alan Tate collection.* $2000.

Bonanza. *Author's collection*. $1800.

BOWLING QUEEN was released in July and was based on the popular American game of bowling. This machine is identical in play to a machine released in 1962 by Gottlieb called *RACK-A-BALL*. This machine had been very successful for the company so they re-released it under a different theme. The backglass artwork includes three pinball machines being played just under the score reels; these are Gaucho, Slick Chick, and Bowling Queen. Roy Parker even included himself in the picture – he is the gentleman under the scoreboard with cigar in mouth, wearing a cap, and carrying the bowling bag. At the start of a game, the twelve rollovers are lit up; by scoring any lit rollover, a player racks a ball in the backglass. Each rollover only racks one ball. An operator would set the number of balls required to receive a free game, usually set at 9 and 12. Hitting the left target lights up the blue bumpers; the right target lights up the red bumpers. This increased the value from 1 point to 10 points. Hitting the target in the upper center of the playfield lights up the kickers to score 10 points. Hitting all three targets lights the special on the bottom rollovers. The special light alternates as points are hit.

NORTH STAR was released in September. The artwork was by Art Stenholm, who added color and humor into the glass with a beautiful Eskimo and her pet polar bear, a walrus, and a sailor singing. Players mistake this backglass for that of Roy Parker, as Roy Parker had painted every Gottlieb pinball machine from before World War II till now. The machine was designed by Wayne Neyens and is another classic. The game had five rollovers at the top of the playfield; each one would light up a bumper for extra scoring. Completing all yellow and green rollovers lights the special on the two eject holes. Completing all the top rollovers as well lights the rollover button between the bumpers for special.

SEA SHORE was released by Gottlieb in September. The theme is people having fun in the sun and the backglass features another gorgeous Parker girl in the center. The playfield had a roto-target in the middle and two red targets on either side; two consecutive hits on the red targets multiplies the roto-target value by 100. The top rollover and eject holes spin the roto-target and light the corresponding colored pop bumpers.

Bowling Queen. *Jason Douglas collection*. $1600.

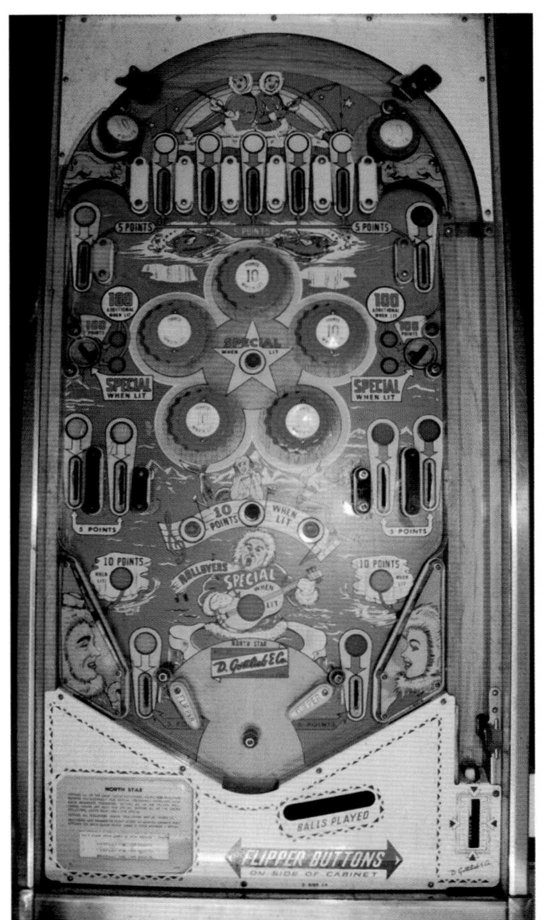

North Star. *Jason Douglas collection*. $2000.

Sea Shore. *Author's collection*. $1800.

1965

Bally Manufacturing, with Ted Zale as chief designer, was now moving into Gottlieb and Williams territory; this company was the only manufacturer of bingo machines and with the technological advantages was to challenge the dominance of these other companies in years to come. Bally was setting the standard for the future: not only were they using four score reels, but they had incorporated the automatic ball return on all their games.

BULLFIGHT, designed by Ted Zale, was released in January. It featured a target selector on the middle of the playfield that rotated when advances were hit on the playfield. Ted Zale also added seven mushroom bumpers and three pop bumpers, making the game more exciting.

The company released *MAGIC CIRCLE* in June, with a low production run of only 580. This was another clever design by Ted Zale; players enjoyed the variations of gates he used on playfields. The bottom and top gate on this machine returned the ball back to the firing pin.

DISCOTEK was released in September. Bally added a third flipper to this game, on the top left side of the playfield. A player had to use this flipper to shoot the four mushroom bumpers that scored 50 points when lit. The playfield had two gates on it and a ball shooter to the right of the bottom right flipper that shot the ball back up the playfield.

FUN CRUISE, released by Bally in September, had no flippers on the playfield. A player needs to hit the numbered bumpers, with numbers ranging from 1-15. When a number is scored, the corresponding flag in the backglass lights up. The two kickers just above the outhole act as flippers and fire the ball back up the playfield.

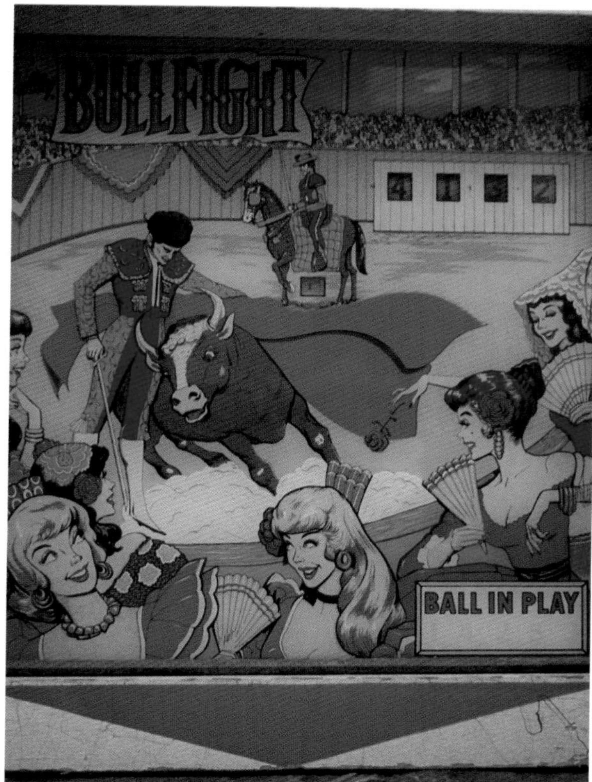

Bullfight. *Jason Douglas collection*. $1500.

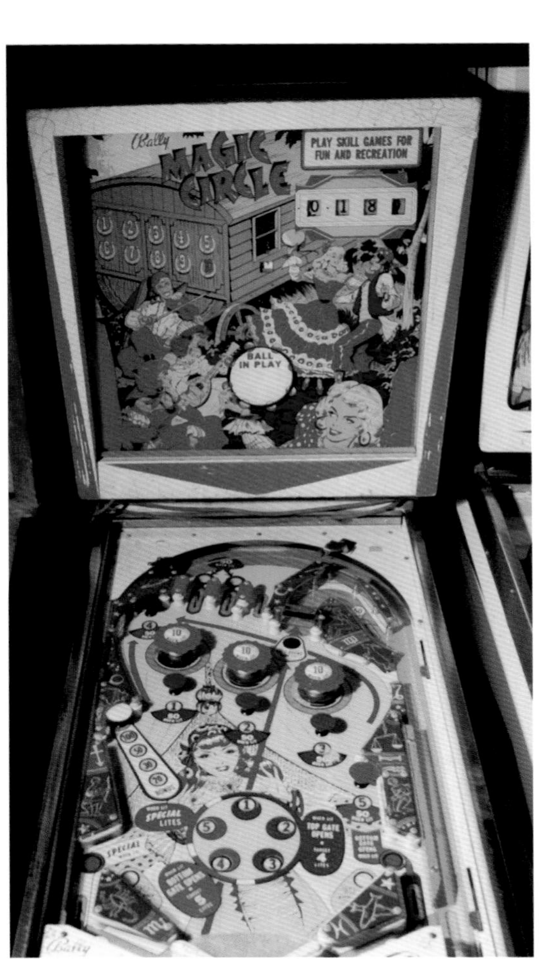

Magic Circle. *Alan Tate collection.* $1600.

Discotek. *Jason Douglas collection.* $1600.

Williams released *PRETTY BABY* in January; this was their last pinball to use the manual ball lift. Steve Kordek designed it. I feel the center beauty on the backglass represents a trait of artist George Molentin; a large majority of his early games featured a beautiful woman in the center, which caught players' attention. By knocking the target and landing the ball in the eject hole, the player can score between 100 and 1000 points. The player's goal is to advance to 1000. Hitting the appropriate colored target or bumper (red or yellow) accumulates scores. What makes the game interesting is that when one color advances the opposing color decreases.

MOULIN ROUGE was released in May. Norm Clark designed it and the artwork was by Art Stenholm. By completing 1-10 on the playfield, a player progressively lights up the backglass to reveal a painting of the famous Parisian night club. When the sequence has been completed, the bottom rollovers light up for special. Completing A-B-C in rotation increases the value of the center eject hole from 200 to 400 points and then special. This game also featured ball shooters on either side of the flippers that would fire the ball back up the playfield.

The Williams company changed the look of their machines. They started using different, more modern bumper caps. The headbox was even a different shape and the customer could even include his or her name on the customized title strip at the bottom of the backglass.

LUCKY STRIKE was released in August. Designed by Norm Clark, it was based on the recreational game of bowling. Ten buttons in the middle of the playfield are lit up at the start of the game; as the ball rolls over them they go out. Once they are all out, they reset and a strike is registered. This game featured animation on the backglass: when a strike is made the female bowler in the center of the backglass bowls the ball. There are ball kickers on either side of the flippers that fire the ball back up the playfield; by making three spares a player gets a replay.

Fun Cruise. *Alan Tate collection.* $1400.

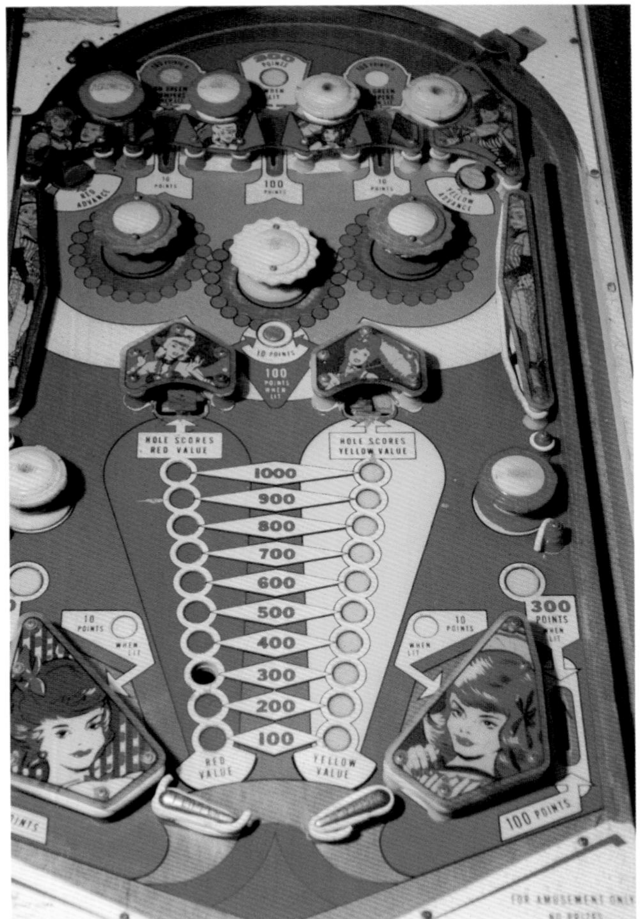

Pretty Baby. *Alan Tate collection.* $1600.

Moulin Rouge. *Jason Douglas collection.* $1500.

Lucky Strike. *Alan Tate collection.* $1300.

Backbox animation was electromechanically activated and was used by companies to attract players to the game – it was essentially a visual gimmick on the backglass. Gottlieb released *SKYLINE* in January with an animated backglass. When the advance targets are hit, the elevator doors open to reveal a crowd squeezed inside it. The objective of the game was to complete the sequence 1-12. Wayne Neyens, who once again created something different, designed this game. It is the first machine to use the multi-bumper, located in the center of the playfield and surrounded by five pop bumpers. When hit, the twelve different contacts around it score the corresponding number. The player could also complete the sequence by going down the lit rollovers. Making all twelve numbers re-lights a rollover at random for special scoring. On this game, the company used a new style of bumper plastics, described by Gottlieb as "Colorful Sunburst pop bumper caps." They continued using the ball lift shaft, though all other companies had advanced to the automatic ball lift.

THOROBRED was released by Gottlieb in February, and again features the multi-bumper. This bumper has six contacts around it; when one is hit, it lights up the corresponding pop bumper and rollover. When all six have been hit, the center rollover lights up, enabling the player to shoot for an extra ball.

Skyline. *Jason Douglas collection.* $2000.

One of the most collectible pinballs was *KINGS & QUEENS*, released in March. The flyer for the machine notes "Gottlieb state Kings & Queens another great creation from the Master-Maker of card games." There are four eject holes on the playfield. A ball landing in any hole is kicked in succession into holes on the right until it is ejected back into play by the extreme right hole. This created a new and novel appeal for players. At the start of a game, all the rollovers are lit. Rolling over them lights the corresponding cards on the playfield. Completing any four of a kind lights a hole for special scoring. When all cards are lit by the player, the top center rollover lights up for special.

Thorobred. *Author's collection.* $1600.

Kings & Queens. *Jason Douglas collection.* $3000.

Gottlieb next released *HI DOLLY* in April, in which artist Roy Parker incorporated many characters from his previous games on the backglass. The characters from Ship-Mates, Square Head, Egg Head, Texan, and Gaucho are talking on the phone to the gorgeous dolly. There are even cut out paper dolls hanging up on the top of the backglass that spell "Hi Dolly." The machine had a dual roto-target in the center of the playfield. By completing A-B-C-D, a player lights the outhole to score 100 points; by hitting the star target the player receives an extra ball.

We are in the classic period again for Gottlieb machines and *BUCKAROO*, another highly collectible machine, was released in May. Designed by Wayne Neyens, this machine had a 3-D animated backglass that featured a bucking horse. Every time 100 points is made by the player, the bucking horse kicks, causing the cowboy bending over on the right to somersault. This feature attracted players and spectators alike to the game; unfortunately, however, players would be so busy playing the game that they wouldn't notice the animation. On the playfield, completing the A-B-C-D on the top rollovers light up the special rollover. This is a hard shot to make as there is a dead bumper just above it. The player had to light up four numbers in a row to score a free game. The number 4 was the most important. The numbers appear on the roto-target; when hit by the ball they register on the playfield. The two center rollovers between the flippers also spot the numbers.

Gottlieb Released *COWPOKE* the same month, which was the Add-A-Ball version of *BUCKAROO*. Instead of winning free games, the player wins extra balls, extending the time of play.

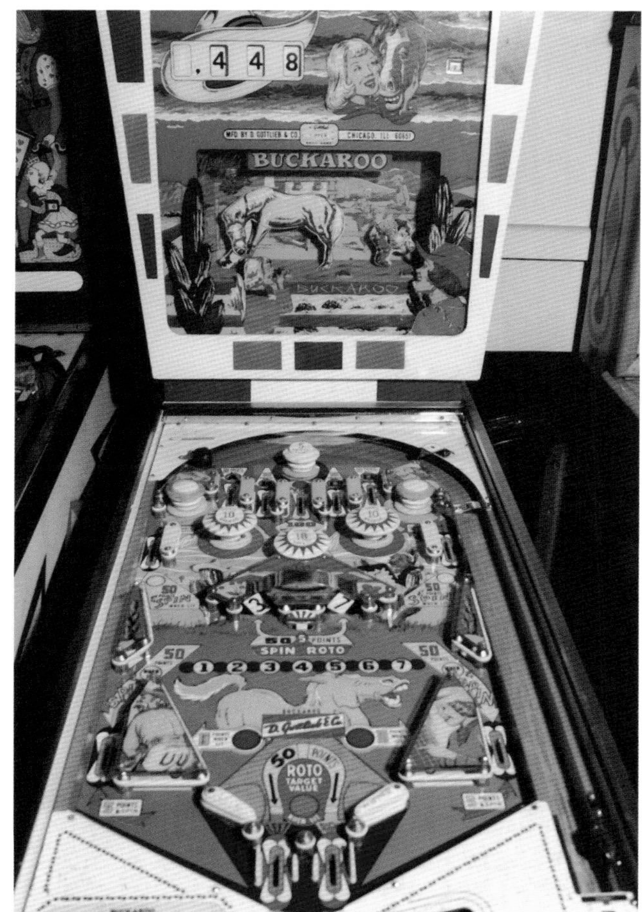

Buckaroo. *Paul Brisbane collection*. $3000.

Hi Dolly. *Author's collection*. $1700.

Cowpoke, the Add-A-Ball version of Buckaroo. The playfields are identical. *Alan Tate collection*. $3000.

In September, Gottlieb released *BANK-A-BALL*, the first machine to come out with a return lane at the bottom of the playfield. The return lanes gave players another chance when the balls went down the sides. The players loved it – now when the ball rolled down the return lane they could time the perfect flipper shot. This machine was designed by Ed Krynski and also featured an animated backglass where miniature pool balls drop as targets are made on the playfield. Gottlieb promoted this game as "A New Idea in Animated Scoring with Exciting Playfield Action." It is based on the popular game of pool. At the start of a game, the fifteen pool balls appear behind the backglass scattered on the pool table. As a player makes a ball, the corresponding light goes out on the playfield and on the backglass and a miniature ball drops into the rack in the backglass. Completing 1 through 7 or 9 through 15 lights the center target to score the 8 ball and a special.

Bank a Ball. *Alan Tate collection.* $2500.

Most of the games I played as a child were designed by Ed Krynski. Little did I realize that many years later I would have the opportunity to contact him and share stories about his work at D. Gottlieb & Co. Krynski was the man who took over from Wayne Neyens in 1964 as chief designer at Gottlieb. He has inspired and influenced millions of people with the innovation in his designs.

Ed was born in February 1927 and grew up in Chicago. His first job after leaving school at the age of fourteen was working in a hardware shop. He was introduced to electronics when he started working at Western Electric Co.; he worked there for three years and became inspector. A friend of Ed's, Otto Dehrens, was the Assistant Chief Engineer at Williams Manufacturing; at the time, the company needed another relay designer and Ed was hired and commenced working there in early 1952. I asked Ed what inspired him in designing games, and he replied "life in general." The first machine that Ed designed at Gottlieb was *DODGE CITY* (1965) and the last was *EL DORADO CITY OF GOLD* (September 1984). I would like to acknowledge and give credit to another one of my "heroes" who has given so much to the pinball industry.

I asked Ed to share a little about his experience in the coin-op industry:

My experience in the game industry began at Williams Manufacturing Co. as a relay designer. The Chief Engineer had me hand wire one of the games in process and was impressed enough to transfer me into his department. I was assigned the job of designing the circuits for and hand wiring the games for Harry Mabs. He designed the playboards and I would do the rest. Working in this section gave me the chance to learn game design from Harry Mabs, Harry Williams, and Sam Stern. I stayed at Williams from early 1952 until early 1954.

I worked in the design department of Sunbeam Corporation for two years, then returned to the games industry at the J.H. Keeney Co., working on various products being developed by that company. These included vending machines, but the main product was gambling machines (electronic slots) being sold to the English market as well as several places in the United States. The laws changed in the early 1960s and it became difficult to continue in this line. After testifying in several court trials involving illegal gambling machines, I decided to change careers and applied for a job at D. Gottlieb & Co.

Pinball designer and legend Ed Krynski. Prior to starting work at Gottlieb in 1964, Ed worked at Keeney. He was sent to Cardiff, Wales UK, to teach operators how to repair games. *Courtesy Ed Krynski.*

This photo was taken at a Bristol, UK hotel, September 1963. *Courtesy Ed Krynski.*

I was interviewed by Bob Smith (Chief Engineer at the time) and Wayne Neyens. They hired me on a trial basis and I started a career, which lasted from February 2, 1964 until the Gottlieb Company (then known as Mylstar Electronics) was closed down by what had become the parent company (Coca-Cola) on September 24, 1984.

When I had proven to Wayne Neyens that I could handle the design phase, I was left alone in my design room (which I called "118 North Tower") to keep building as many games as I could dream up, the only condition being that I had at least four games lined up ready to be chosen as the next production number.

Over the next 20 years and 8 months, I designed and machined the playboards, drew circuits for, and hand wired some 216 games– of which 185 went into production. This included the design of new "gimmicks" to keep the games interesting, such as the Drop Target Bank, the Vary Target, the Carousel Target etc. The idea that gave me the most satisfaction was not visible to the players: I simplified the "Player Unit" on the four player games by eliminating 90% of the disk wiring with cams on an extended shaft. Switch stacks on the stacks eliminated the four relays used to control player-scoring units for each player.

The idea that seemed to solidify my position at Gottlieb was the use of the switch bank in the light box to do double duty by using the motion of the switch actuator to drop pool balls into view in Bank-A-Ball. This game took the 'Best in Show' awards at the 1965 coin machine show.

All in all, it was a satisfying time of my life and I will always be grateful to Judd Wineberg, Alvin Gottlieb, Bob Smith, and Wayne Neyens for giving me the opportunity that I enjoyed.

—Ed Krynski

Ed Krynski on the left with Judd Weinberg, David Gottlieb's son-in-law, in 1965. *Courtesy Ed Krynski.*

Ice Revue. *Jason Douglas collection*. $1700.

Hula-Hula. *Author's collection*. $1600.

ICE REVUE, designed by Ed Krynski, was released by Gottlieb in December. This game is packed with features. By shooting the ball into the top rollovers, the player lights up the corresponding pop bumpers. Once all the bumpers are lit, the special lights up on one of the rollovers – the special light alternates as points are being scored. There are six numbered targets on the playfield; by hitting the six targets, the player lights the bottom rollovers to score 50 points and increases the value of the eject holes from 50 to 100 points. Once completed, the targets reset, and the second time the sequence is completed lights the eject hole for 200 points. The third time lights the eject hole for special. This machine had two rollovers on either side of the flippers, as opposed to the ball return lane that was a hit on *BANK-A-BALL*.

Chicago Coin released *HULA-HULA* in July. This was the only pinball released by the company this year, as they were concentrating more on arcade novelty games. The artwork on the machine, by Roy Parker, is very similar to that on a Gottlieb game called *PLEASURE ISLE* released later in the year. The machine had an animated backglass that showed the hula dancer moving her hips every time 100 points are scored. The machine also featured the "Flash Score Traveling Light" on the playfield; the score would vary from 10 to 100 points. The center rollover and the center target score 100 points, making the hula dancer dance. This machine was designed by Al Schlappa, Jerri Koci, and John Gore and is very popular among collectors.

1966

Bally released *BAZAAR* in August, designed by Ted Zale. George Molentin's artwork on this game had an exotic, middle eastern theme. The Bally company was still making bingo machines, which were far more complicated to build than pinball machines. This was the first pinball to feature the "Zipper Flipper," which means the flippers close and come together to stop the ball draining into the outhole. Hitting the U mushroom bumper closes the flippers and hitting either of the L bumpers re-opens them. Bally produced 2,925 of this model; the year before the company was only averaging 700 per model. This was a huge leap in production.

Bally released *CAPERSVILLE* in November. This was another hit for the company, which produced a record 5,120. Like *BAZAAR*, this machine had "Zipper Flippers." It was also the first to feature three ball multiball play and the first to use angular artwork that appealed to the younger generation.

Bazaar. *Jason Douglas collection*. $1300.

Williams released *8 BALL* in January. This machine was a two player, designed by Norm Clark. A problem with multi-player games was that the machine couldn' t keep track of what targets had been hit. On single player games this wasn't a problem, as the targets hit would carry over to the next ball. *8 BALL* was the first multi-player game to remember what targets had been hit, thanks to Norm Clark's development of the "Split Bank." This game is based on the popular game of pool. Player one shoots solids and player two (if playing) shoots stripes. The first player must complete 1-7 and the second player 9-15 to light the 8 ball. Shooting into the horseshoe gives the player an extra ball.

I asked Norm Clark if he could explain in a few words how the split banked worked:

Michael, about the split relay bank, and why it was developed: back in 1966, when I designed 8 BALL, the nature of the game made it necessary to keep track of the pool balls that each player made and to bring them back each time the player played his ball; in other words, to put memory into an electromechanical game. To do this would have taken two relay banks, adding extra expense to the game. I went to Frank Murphy, the chief mechanical engineer, and suggested using one relay bank with two reset mechanisms and two reset coils. This was far cheaper than using two relay banks and also took up less room in the game, which was already overcrowded.

—*Norm Clark*

8 Ball. *Jason Douglas collection.*
$1200.

The company released *FULL HOUSE* in March, also designed by Norm Clark. The player is dealt a poker hand, which is shown on the three reels in the center of the playfield, and competes with the dealer. The dealer' s hand is shown under the backglass. There are three rollovers on top of the machine and three targets in front of the score reels on the playfield. Hitting the target on the left advances the reel on the left, hitting the target in the center advances the center reel, and hitting the target on the right advances the reel on the right. As the ball hits these targets the player's hand changes so the player must stay alert. Getting the full house lights up special on the two bottom rollovers.

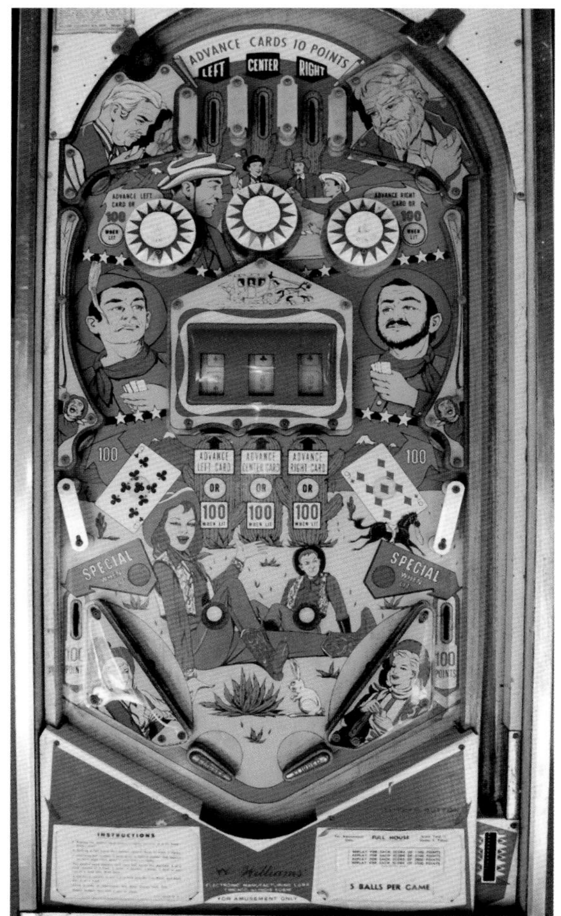

Full House. *Alan Tate collection.* $1400.

This year saw a change in the artwork style on pinball machines by Bally and Williams. The first Williams machine to use this new style was *A-GO-GO*, released in May with a production run of 5,100. The new artwork design was referred to as "angular artwork" and was done by Jerry Kelley. This machine was also the first to

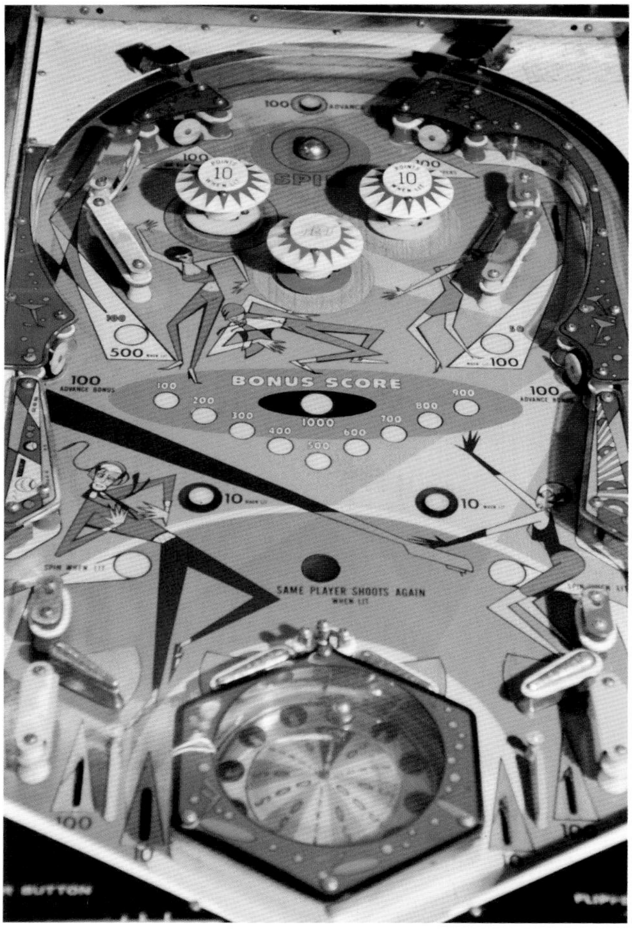

A-Go-Go. *Author's collection.* $800.

use the captive ball spinner, invented by Norm Clark. The spinning roulette wheel at the bottom of the playfield had a miniature ball in it. The player, by landing the ball in the eject hole on top of the playfield, spins the wheel, which awards the player bonus points or an extra ball. The machine had two sets of flippers at the bottom of the playfield just above the captive ball spinner.

HOT LINE was released in September, designed by Steve Kordek. A player, by making the lit rollover buttons in the center of the playfield, lights up the next letter in "Hot Line." Once completed, this lights up the special. Completing A and B opens the free ball gate on the top right side of the playfield. Shooting the ball in the gate when it is open lights the next letter in the sequence.

CASANOVA, also designed by Steve Kordek, was released in November and uses the captive ball scoring feature on the backglass. Every time a player loses a ball the captive ball is propelled in the backglass, giving the player 100 points, 300 points, 500 points or 500 points and an extra ball. This added bonus feature made the game popular with players.

Hot Line. *Jason Douglas collection*. $800.

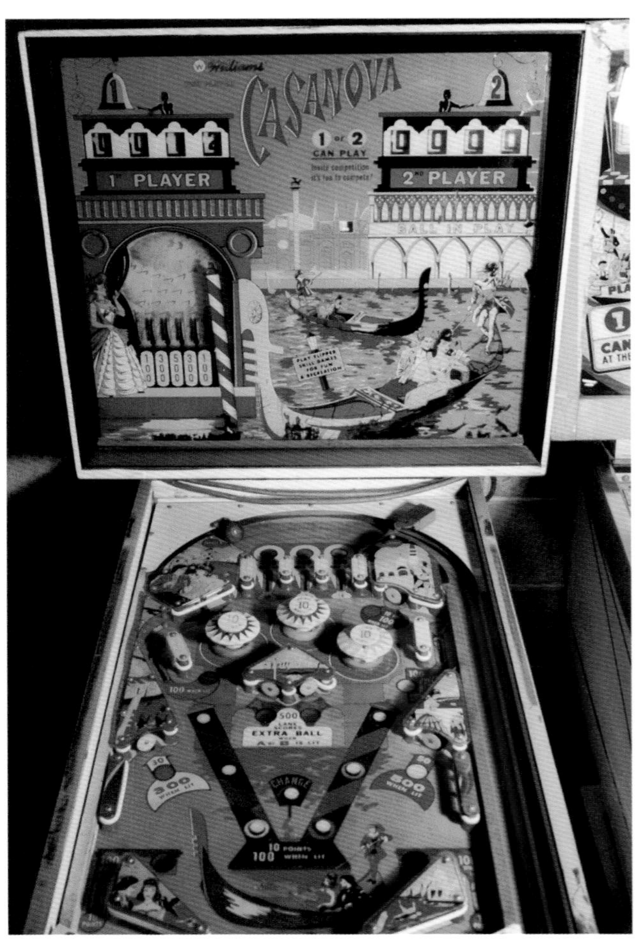

Casanova. *Alan Tate collection*. $1300.

Gottlieb released *MASQUERADE* in February, designed by Ed Krynski with artwork by Art Stenholm. The machine had an animated backglass – the scoring would reveal the lace fan on the face of the "Belle of the Ball." A player had to spell the words "Masked Beauty" on the playfield, which was achieved by going down the rollovers or by hitting the contacts on the multi-bumper in between the four pop bumpers. Completing one word multiplies the target value by 10, completing both words multiplies the target value by 100.

One of the most famous parks in the world is Central Park in New York – a place where New Yorkers and tourists gather for fun and recreation. D. Gottlieb & Co. captured this famous landmark on a pinball machine called *CENTRAL PARK*, released in April. This machine had a 3-D animated backglass – every time 100 points is reached the monkey strikes the bell. By completing 1-5, a player advances the left target value; completing 6-10 advances the right target value. When either sequence is completed, the target value increases by 10 until special is reached.

Masquerade. *Author's collection.* $1500.

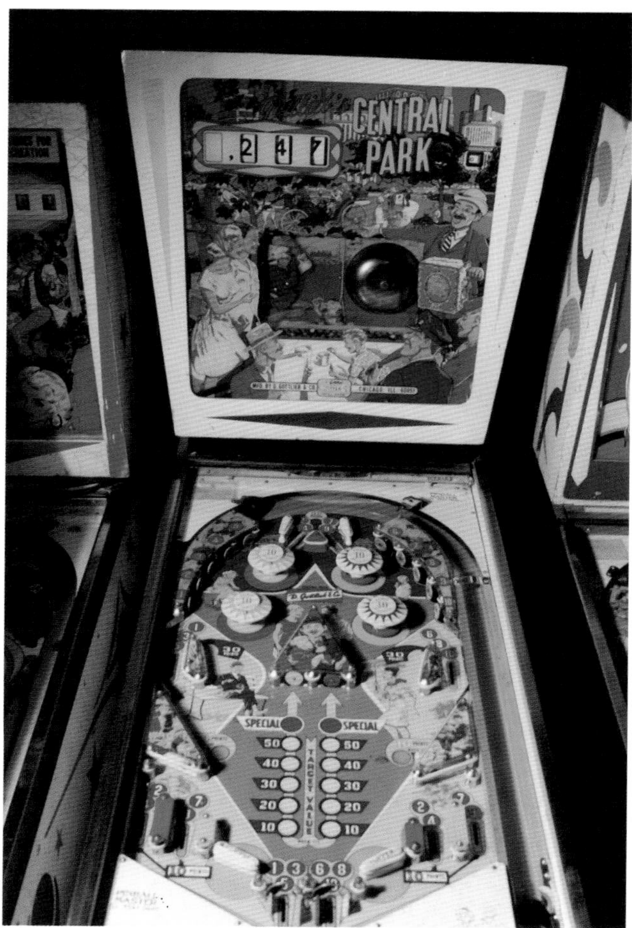

Central Park. *Alan Tate collection.* $2000.

MAYFAIR was released in July, designed by Wayne Neyens with artwork by Roy Parker. It was the first Gottlieb machine to use the swinging target on the playfield. Besides the flippers, there are two auto shooters that fire the ball at the swinging target. The nine rollovers advance the red and yellow bonuses and the four rollovers turn the bumpers on and off. Gottlieb was still using manual push up, while all other companies had automatic ball release. Also in this period, Gottlieb was still using three score reels with the dummy (1) lighting up to indicate that 1000 had been reached.

This was the last machine that artist Roy Parker did for Gottlieb before his sudden death. Roy Parker has attracted more people to the game than anyone in pinball history. His backglasses were bright and colorful, full of humored detail, and contained hidden messages. He was a part of the great team at Gottlieb that had dominated the pinball market in the 1940s, 1950s, and up until his death, painting virtually every Gottlieb pinball backglass from before World War II till this point. His artwork will be remembered forever.

Another classic game was *CROSS TOWN*, released in October. It featured an animated backglass – the elevator doors would open revealing the passengers jammed together when 100 points was scored. The four top rollovers light the corresponding bumpers, while the center target scores 10 points. When the yellow and red values are matched and the player hits the center target, they are awarded the indicated value. The Add-A-Ball version of this game was called *SUBWAY*.

Mayfair. *Author's collection.* $2500.

Cross Town. *Scott Gray collection.* $2500.

Chicago Coin only manufactured two pinballs this year: *FESTIVAL* in June and *KICKER* in August. *KICKER* is a very popular machine as it featured backbox animations. The company also released *POP UP* in June, a combination of a pinball and an amusement game. With this game, we see the return of the turret shooter. The player shoots at targets to make the balls pop up, receiving 10 shots per game. Getting the balls in a vertical line scores 30 points, a diagonal line scores 50 points, a diamond shape scores 100 points, and all corners scores 150 points.

Pop Up. *Alan Tate collection.* $1500.

1967

The artwork of pinballs from the 1950s and early 1960s was going through a change. In the past, the majority of pinball players had been males and the artwork on the backglass portrayed voluptuous beauties. By 1967, the psychedelic age had arrived, youth culture was becoming more advanced, fashion was changing, and the Beatles had hit America and the rest of the world. Pinball manufactures realized there was a vast market that was unexploited. Pinball machines were being played not only by adults, but also by teenagers and school children. To attract the new age group, we see a change in pinball art. Williams Electronics and Bally Manufacturing started using the sharp-angled artwork and were moving into Gottlieb territory. Gottlieb, on the other hand, was reluctant to change and continued with their own style as the older generation didn't take to this new artwork. In 1967, Gottlieb stopped using the manual push up ball. Bally had previously stopped using it in 1964 and Williams in 1965.

Bally released *ROCKET III* in January, designed by Ted Zale. It featured a spinning disk in the top center of the playfield and Zipper Flippers. It could be modified to Add-A-Ball or replay by moving a plug from one socket to the next by the operator. By completing the sequence "ROCKET" on the playfield, the player advances a planet in the solar system shown on the backglass. Once the ninth planet is reached, a free game is awarded. Note that Bally originally released *ROCKET* in October 1933 and again in April 1947; this was their third rocket game.

DOGIES was released in August, also designed by Ted Zale. The artwork was by Jerry Kelley. It featured a double free ball gate and Zipper Flippers. The machine depicted the American West with the new sharp-angled style artwork.

DIXIELAND was released in October. The artwork was by Christian March, who attracts players with the colorful and comical backglass. This machine features the carry-over bonus system. The objective of the game is to light up D-I-X-I-E-L-A-N-D on the backglass; if the sequence hasn't been completed at the end of the game it carries over to the next game. The clarinet eject hole is on the top left side of the playfield. By hitting the two yellow mushroom bumpers, the player scores 100 points and advances the clarinet bonus. This is a great game to play and is full of gimmicks. By entering Basin Street at the top right of the playfield, a player zig zags the ball through pins to score 10, 200 or 500 points.

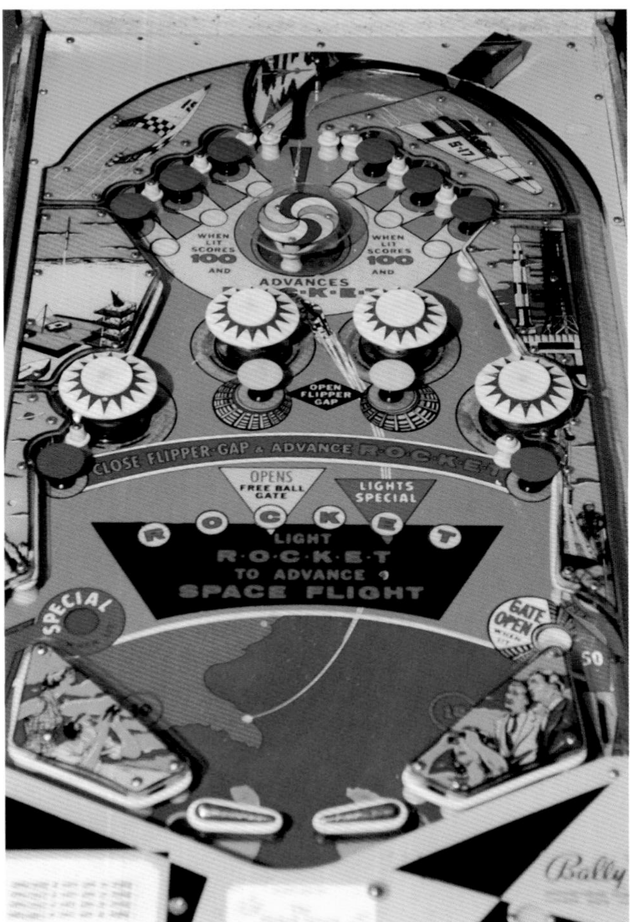

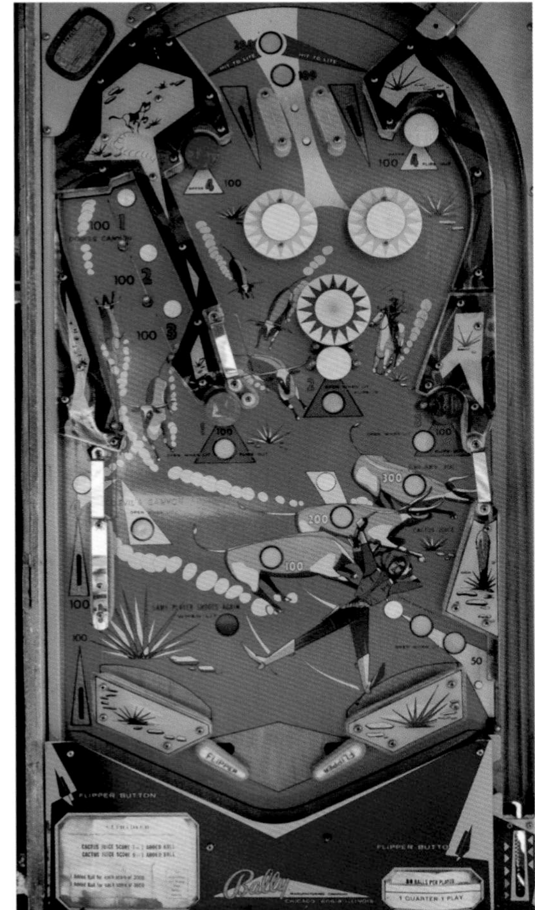

Rocket III. *Author's collection*. $800.

Dogies. *Author's collection*. $1200.

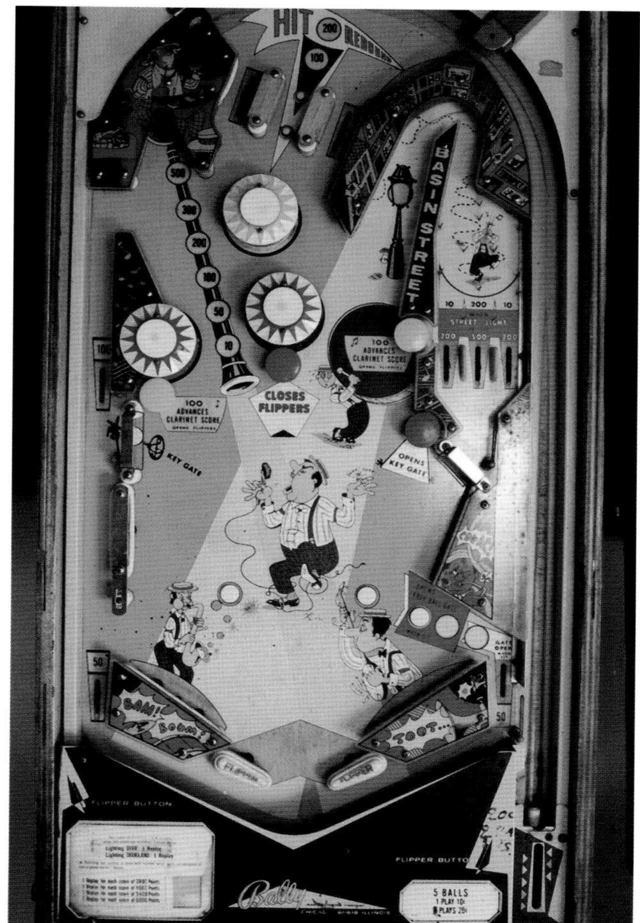

Dixieland. *Jason Douglas collection*. $1000.

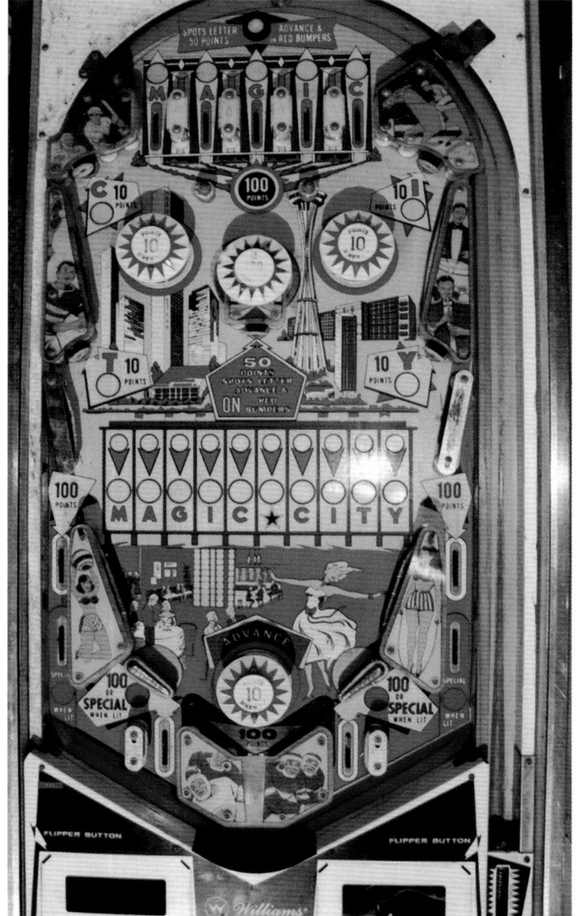

Magic City. *Jason Douglas collection*. $2000.

George Molentin had done the majority of the artwork on Williams's games from when the company was formed in 1946 till now. He had also done the artwork on many Bally, Exhibit, and United games. He added color and humor to pinballs and loved drawing beauties; his artwork was creative and captivating. Molentin become director at Advertising Posters in 1961, supervising other artists; he remained there until his retirement in 1979. The last electromechanical game he did the artwork for was *MAGIC CITY*, designed by Norm Clark and released by Williams in January. It glorified the pinball capital of the world: Chicago. The objective of this game is to light the words "Magic City" on the playfield, which is done by rolling down the top five rollovers to light "Magic" and by hitting the four targets to complete "City." Hitting the center target or crossing over the button on top of the playfield spots the letter indicated. Once the sequence has been made, the outside bottom rollovers light up for special. Between the "Magic" and "City" is a star target; if this is spotted and the player hits the center target or the top rollover button, the two bottom rollovers under the flippers light up for special.

APOLLO was released in June. It was designed by Norm Clark and featured a miniature bagatelle in the backglass. With the Apollo 7 mission launched in October, American history was being written. I can still remember standing outside my classroom looking up into the sky trying to get a glimpse of it. I was in kindergarten and the shuttle was reported to be flying above Australia. This launch was one of the greatest achievements in history and the pinball game associated with it was an instant hit. The objective of the game was to complete the countdown, which was indicated by ten lights set vertically in the center of the playfield. A player advances towards blast off by hitting the targets on the playfield, the lit top bumper, or the lit rollover. When the countdown advances to "1" the center yellow target lights up for 300 points. One more advance brings the countdown back to "10" and lights the launch light indicator between the flippers. As soon as the ball is lost, the rocket is launched in the backglass and the player earns 50 points, 300 points, or wins a free game by going down the special.

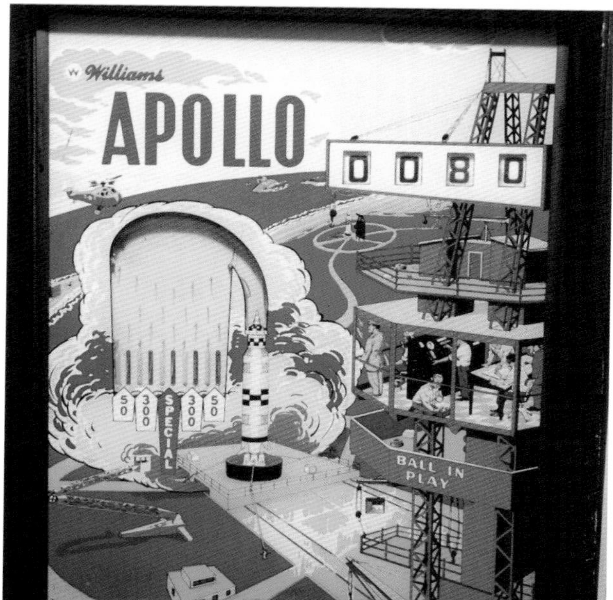

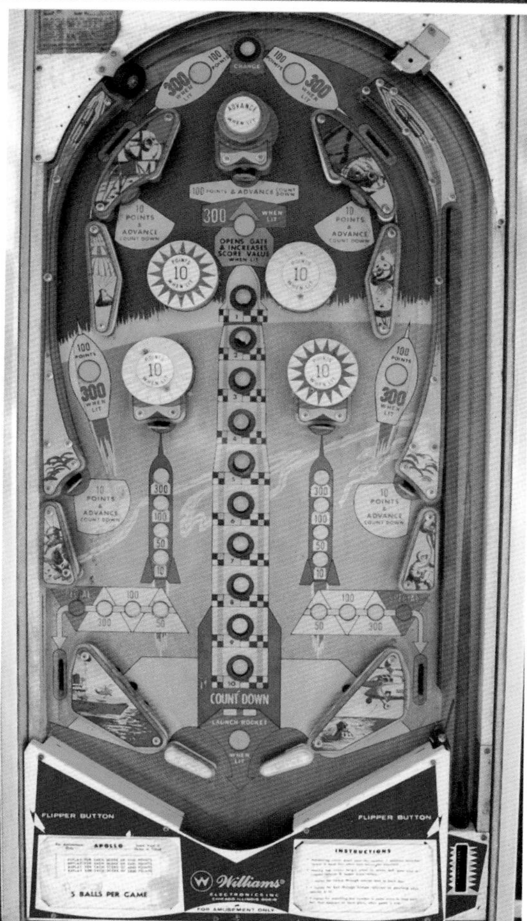

Apollo. *Alan Tate collection.* $2000.

DERBY DAY was released by Williams in October and had an animated backglass; these machines still appeal to players today and are in great demand. This machine uses the turret shooter: the player aims at the targets and fires the ball up the playfield by hitting the shooter button. The machine had four flippers and featured a four position target on either side of the playfield. These targets would rotate: on the left side they were numbered 1, 3, 5, and star; on the right side they were numbered 2, 4, 6, and star. Hitting the number on the target would move that horse on the backglass; hitting the star would move the three horses on that side. The targets on top of the machine move the horse as indicated. This is one of only a few machines made that had no bumpers.

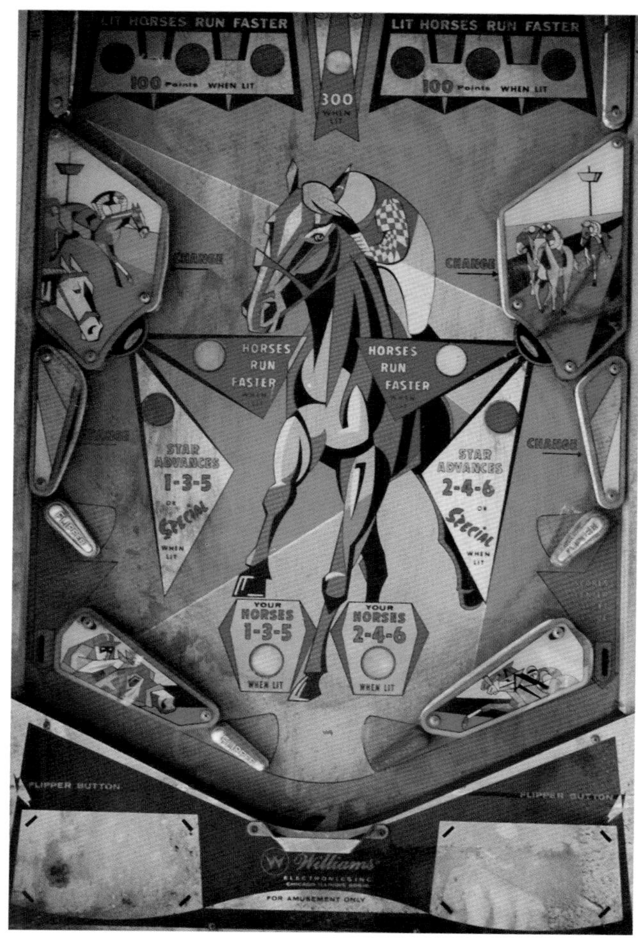

Derby Day. *Alan Tate collection.* $1600.

TOUCHDOWN was released in November. The backglass had gridiron animation on a vertical playfield located on the left side. As scores are made, the ball goes up and down the playing field. The five bumpers in the middle of the playfield give the game plenty of action. Another feature on this game was the two methods of scoring: the scoring on the top part of the glass accumulates your score and the bottom window accumulates your points. The operator sets the replay level on both these scores, giving the player another way of winning a free game.

Touchdown. *Author's collection.* $1200.

KING OF DIAMONDS was released in January and was the first single player Gottlieb pinball to use the automatic ball lift. This machine is very similar to the 1965 game called *BANK-A-BALL*, but instead of pool ball dropping into the backglass, *KING OF DIAMONDS* has cards. It is undoubtedly one of Gottlieb's best card games and was packed with features on the playfield. There is a roto-target in the center of the playfield, giving the player five chances to hit a card. A player can also spot a card by going down the rollovers or by hitting targets. As soon as one has been made, the corresponding card drops in the backbox. Completing cards 2 through 9 lights the bottom two rollovers for special; when all the cards have been completed the player receives a replay and lights one of the corresponding targets on the playfield for special. This machine had the "ball in play" and "game over" shown in the instruction card; still Gottlieb was using the dummy (1) to indicate that 1000 had been reached.

Gottlieb was finally using four score reels on all their games, as they were committed to change. *HI SCORE* was released in May. It had a spinning roulette wheel at the bottom of the playfield with a miniature ball in it; landing the ball in either eject hole on the playfield spins the wheel and gives a player the indicated value of A-B or C. Or, if the ball lands in the star pocket the player receives an extra ball. This machine has two sets of flippers at the bottom of the playfield, just above the captive ball spinner. At first they are awkward to use, as the left flipper button activates the two flippers on the left side and the right flipper button activates the two flippers on the right side.

SING ALONG was released in September and featured the four eject holes in a horizontal line in the center of the playfield that were made famous on *KINGS & QUEENS*. The ball landing in any hole is kicked in succession into holes on the right until it is ejected back into play by the extreme right hole. By completing the four color sequence, a player advances the hole value from 10 points to 50 points and special; the center target scores 100 points. The brochure for this machine advertises it as a 40th anniversary pinball, since D. Gottlieb & Co. had been in business since 1927. Ed Krynski designed the machine and the artwork was by Art Stenholm, who did a brilliant job adding color and humor to it.

King Of Diamonds. *Alan Tate collection.* $1800.

Hi Score. *Author's collection.* $1200.

Sing Along. *Jason Douglas collection*. $1500.

1968

Bally had re-entered the pinball market first; copying Gottlieb's games and marketing approaches, the company was promoting their new style of game that mainly younger players were drawn to and was setting the trend towards the future. America was experiencing a pop culture revolution and Beatlemania was sweeping across the country. Bally released *MINIZAG* in February, with artist Jerry Kelly capturing the youth culture on the backglass. This game had Zipper Flippers, a captive ball in the "Zagger Lane" that can score up to 400 points, and the free ball gate; add mushroom bumpers and the asymmetrical playfield and you have a Ted Zale classic.

Williams released *LADY LUCK* in March, designed by Norm Clark. In this game, the player plays the game "21" against the machine. If the player can beat the dealer and gets "21", a free game is earned; if they beat the dealer's score, 300 points and an extra ball is awarded. The dealer's score is lit up in the bottom right corner of the backglass and is shown on completion of each ball. The trapped bumper on top of the playfield gives the game plenty of action.

Williams released *HAYBURNERS II* in August; designed by Steve Kordek, it was the first pinball machine to use the 3" size flippers. This machine also used a turret shooter: the player would aim at the targets on top of the playfield and hit the shooter button to launch the ball. The bottom flippers were set apart to enable the turret shooter to shoot the ball the full width of the playfield. As soon as a point is scored, the flippers close in but still leave a gap wide enough to lose the ball. When a target is hit on the playfield, the corresponding horse moves in the backglass. As noted previously, machines with this kind of animation are highly sought after today.

Hayburners. *Gary Coleman collection*. $1500.

Lady Luck. *Jason Douglas collection*. $900.

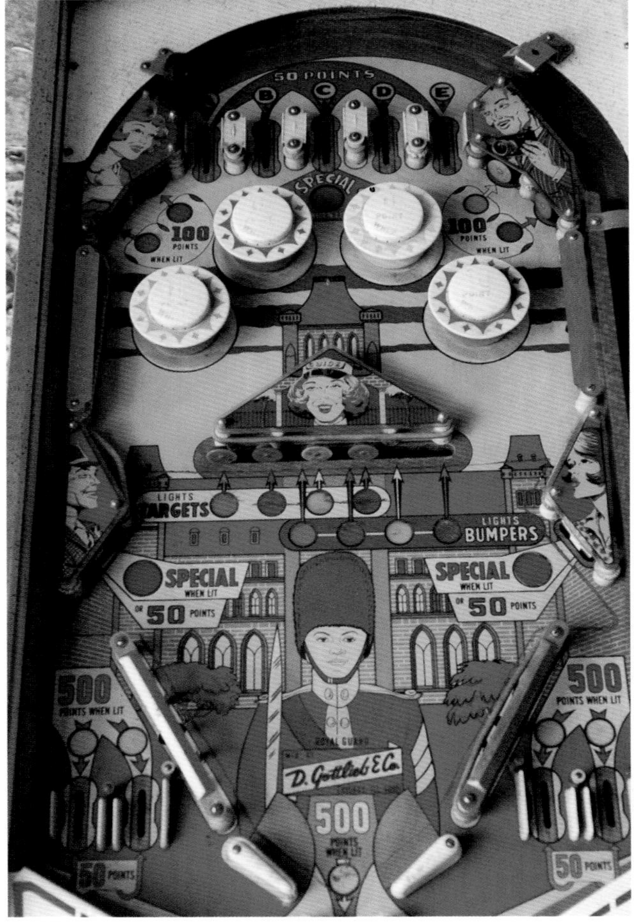

Royal Guard. *Scott Gray collection.* $1200.

Gottlieb released *ROYAL GUARD* in January. This machine featured four shifting "snap targets" in the center of the playfield. By lining up the colors and hitting the target, the player lights the top targets or the bumpers. Completing the A-B-C-D-E rollovers on top of the playfield lights the bottom rollovers to score 500 points and lights the top "C" rollover for special. The backglass shows tourists watching the changing of the guard at Buckingham Palace in London.

Gottlieb started using the newly designed pop bumper cap; it was first used on the game *SURFSIDE*, released in December 1967.

SPIN WHEEL was released in March, featuring a spinning arrow in the backbox that scored 50 to 500 points and also gave the player an extra ball. The arrow is activated by the lit eject hole, the side kickouts, or the bottom rollovers. By lighting the top five eject holes, the player lights the center target alternatively for 500 points, lights the pop bumpers to score 10 points instead of 1, and lights the top targets for 100 points.

FUN LAND was released in May and was a great game to play. The player has to complete the sequence 1-10, which can be done in two different ways. The first is by going down the lit rollovers or by hitting the targets. As soon as a number has been made, the corresponding number lights up on the numbered ducks surrounding the bull's eye target on the playfield. The second way is to spot the numbers by hitting either of the spinners. Hitting the spinner causes the arrow to rotate around the bull's eye target and spots the number it lands on. When all the ducks have been completed, any one of ten numbers lights up for special. Players need skill and luck to land the spinning arrow on these numbers to complete the sequence. This game was appealing to players and was another success for Gottlieb.

DOMINO was released in September. It was designed by Ed Krynski, who was designing the majority of Gottlieb games in this period, and the artwork was by Art Stenholm, who had big shoes to fill following Roy Parker. On the backglass, a couple is playing the relaxing game of dominos and another couple is in the background – the girl is playing the guitar and the boy is singing. The backglass is appealing, but I miss the Roy Parker touch as I see opportunities to create that little extra something missed on this backglass. The machine has a dual roto-target in the center of the playfield and two eject holes on either side of the playfield.

Funland. *Tony Matther collection.* $1200.

Domino. *Alan Tate collection.* $1500.

I asked Wayne Neyens to share a few words about Ed Krynski:

Ed Krynski came to Gottlieb in 1964, just at the time Gottlieb needed another designer. Tony Gerard, the factory superintendent, was retiring and Robert Smith moved up to take his job. I moved into the chief engineering position and Ed Krynski was now the game designer. Ed was not an amusement game designer when he came to Gottlieb but had designed games more in the area of gambling. However, being very bright and capable, he adapted to the Gottlieb style and his designs took off from there. Ed was a very quiet and unassuming sort of person, a real team player.

—*Wayne Neyens*

Ed Krynski and his wife Gilda, celebrating her 75th birthday.

As we have seen, *HUMPTY DUMPTY* – the first flipper game, with six flippers – was released in October 1947. Twenty-one years later, in September 1968, Gottlieb released *PAUL BUNYAN*, which also featured six flippers on the playfield. Wayne Neyens, Ed Krynski, and Steve Kirk designed the game, based on the popular "tall tale" of a giant lumberjack. The captivating artwork on the backglass is by Art Stenholm, who knew how to attract the attention of players. It shows Paul Bunyan sitting on the edge of a lake with beautiful girls pampering him. By completing the A-B-C rotation sequence, a player re-lights the "Running Light" rollover and target for 500 points. Completing the bull's eye targets lights the top roll-under for extra ball. The two eject hole on either side of the playfield are tricky shots to make and light to score 600 points.

Paul Bunyan. *Alan Tate collection*. $1500.

Chicago Coin was still focusing on both pinballs and amusement machines and was making a few pinball machines every year. In February, they released *ALL STARS*, a pitch and bat baseball machine. Baseball theme machines were very popular with players. As a player moved a man to base, a light on the backglass lit up to indicate it; the player could win extra balls on the game by lighting up "ALLSTAR."

The next machine released by the company was *GUN SMOKE*, released in April. This was the first pinball to use the "up-post." When activated, this post closes the opening between the two flippers and keeps the ball on the playfield for more action. The company referred to this as the ball saver. The machine was designed by Ed Sermonti and Alban Peters, who added the "Gun Smoke player control score feature." Trapping the ball in the top hole, side hole, or passing through the bottom Gun Smoke lane when lit starts Gun Smoke scores flashing on the backglass. The player must then press the Gun Smoke button on front of the cabinet to stop the flashing score; it flashes between 50 and 500 points and then resumes play. A player could build up the bonus from 50 to 500 points by rolling over the four rollover buttons on the playfield. The bonus score is collected in the center eject hole; advancing the bonus to 500 opens the gate on the right hand side of the playfield and raises the ball saver. The "ball count" and "game over" are illuminated and are shown next to the plunger. This is a classic machine and players loved it.

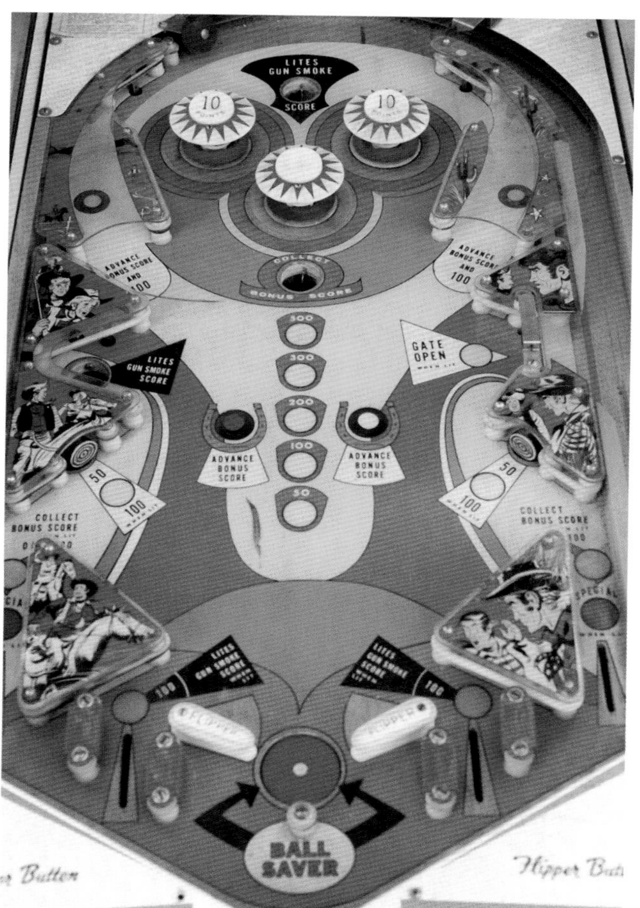

Gun Smoke, the first machine with the up-post. *Alan Tate collection*. $1500.

Playtime. *Paul Brisbane collection.* $700.

PLAYTIME was released in October and also featured the ball saver. On the playfield, there are two eject holes on either side that kick the balls from side to side. The machine also featured the Top Hat score, which appeared in the bottom center on the backglass. Hitting targets on the playfield steps up these scores. When three similar numbers appear and the ball leaves the playfield, the bonus values are scored.

1969

Williams, the kings of baseball machines, released *FASTBALL* in March – another classic game. The scoring on this game is cleverly put into the eyes of the two players. The machine featured an extra wide playfield and had pop-up outfielders as well as backglass animation.

SUSPENSE was released in May and used a captive ball spinner that was at the bottom of the playfield, giving players a chance to win between 50 and 2000 points. The machine used four flippers, two of each size, and had two eject holes on either side of the playfield that spun the captive ball when the ball landed in them. Making the A and B lights the eject hole for extra ball. The machine was designed by Norm Clark and the artwork was by Christian Marche, who captured the psychedelic era on the backglass.

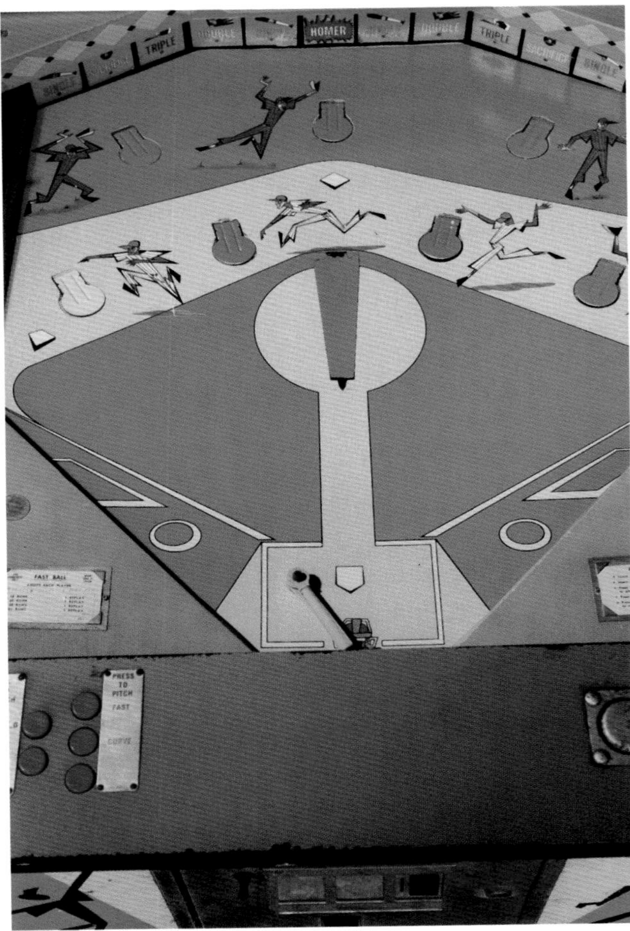

Fast Ball. *Alan Tate collection.* $1200.

GRIDIRON, a unique game based on the popular game of football, was released in October. It had an animated clock on the backglass that counted down the four quarters of the game. The bottom of the backglass also had gridiron animation on a horizontal playfield; as scores are made, the ball goes up and down the playfield, adding to the excitement of the game.

Suspense. *Author's collection*. $1200.

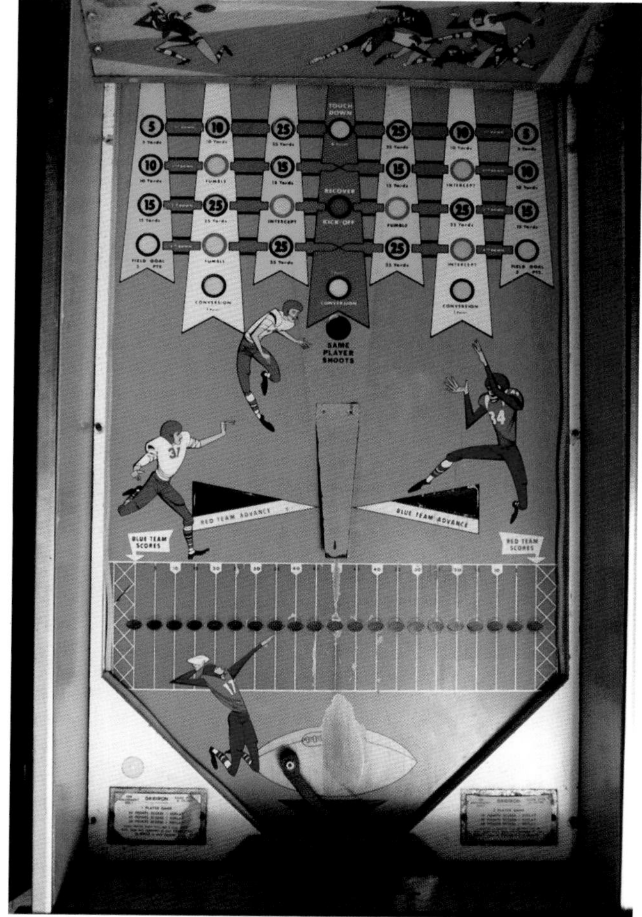

Gridiron. *Jason Douglas collection*. $1000.

Gottlieb released *FOUR SEASONS* in January, with captivating artwork by Art Stenholm that draws the player's attention. The backglass is divided into four sections showing the outdoor activities of the seasons: winter, spring, summer, and autumn. The machine was designed by Ed Krynski, who allows players to control the scoring values by hitting the red or green arrows on the playfield with the ball. The arrows indicate the scoring value of the targets, eject holes, and the rollovers. The headbox looks different, as the company used this new style on only a few machines and then went back to the traditional look.

AIRPORT was released in April, designed by Ed Krynski. It was the first machine to use the "vary-target." There were two of these targets on either side of the playfield; depending on how hard they were hit scored 10 to 50 points. If the 10 times value was lit, a player could score up to 500 points. This machine really challenged a player's skill and coordination.

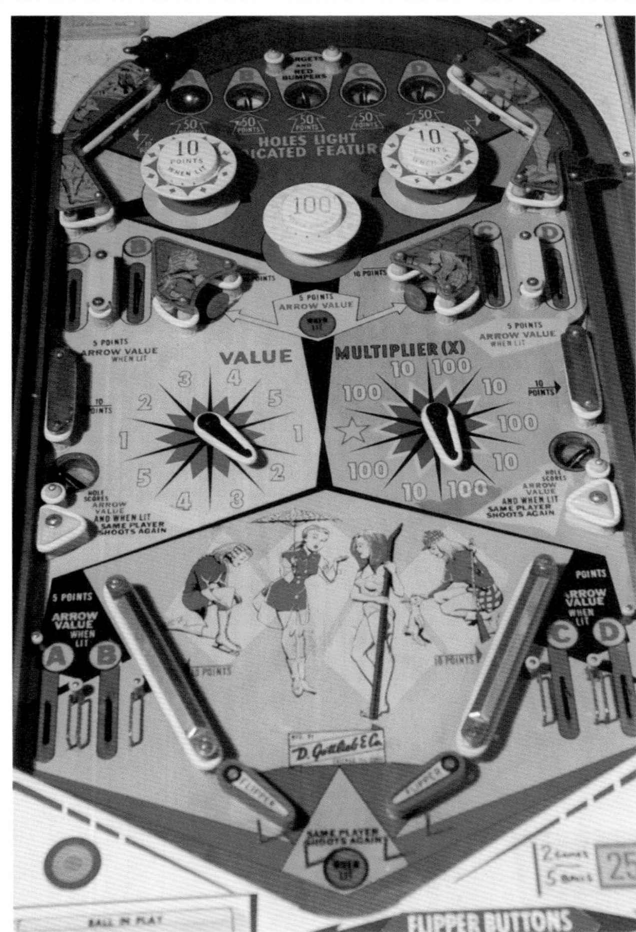

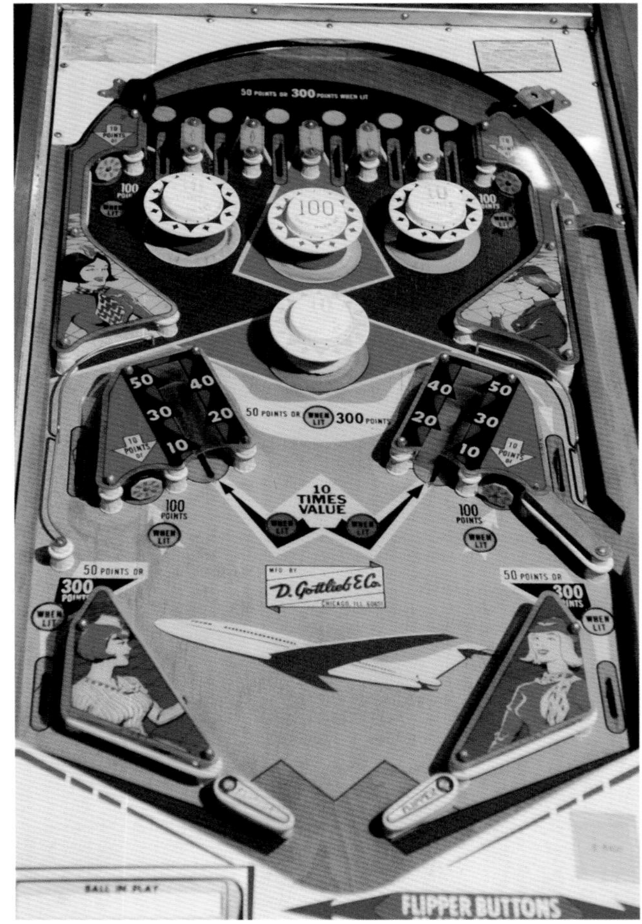

Four Seasons. *Alan Tate collection.* $1500.

Airport. *Alan Tate collection.* $1200.

Ed Krynski (left) and Wayne Neyens (right) have between them designed some of the most collected games in the history of pinball. *Courtesy Wayne Neyens.*

TARGET POOL was released by Gottlieb in June and is a game I spent a lot of money playing. There are twelve pool targets and three rollovers on the playfield; once one has been hit the corresponding number lights up on the lightbox. Completing the sequence lights up the bottom rollovers for special. There are also fifteen blue and red targets that score 50 points unless the arrow is pointing to it; the value then is worth 300 points. This was a hard game to play, as the eight blue and red targets in the center make it difficult to shoot the ball back up the playfield to hit the pool ball targets. These games that really challenged players did well for operators.

MIBS was released in October. This game was previously released as *RACK-A-BALL* in 1962, then as *BOWLING QUEEN* in 1964. It was a very popular game and rather than re-release it, the company came out with a different name and a different theme. The three games are, however, identical to play. At the start of a game, the twelve rollovers are lit up. By scoring any lit rollover, a player racks a ball in the backglass; each rollover only racks one ball. Special is scored when the indicated number of balls is racked up. Hitting the three targets – red, green, and blue – lights up the bumpers and the side kickers to score 10 points and also lights the bottom rollovers for special; the special light would alternate as points are hit.

Target Pool. *Author's collection.* $1300.

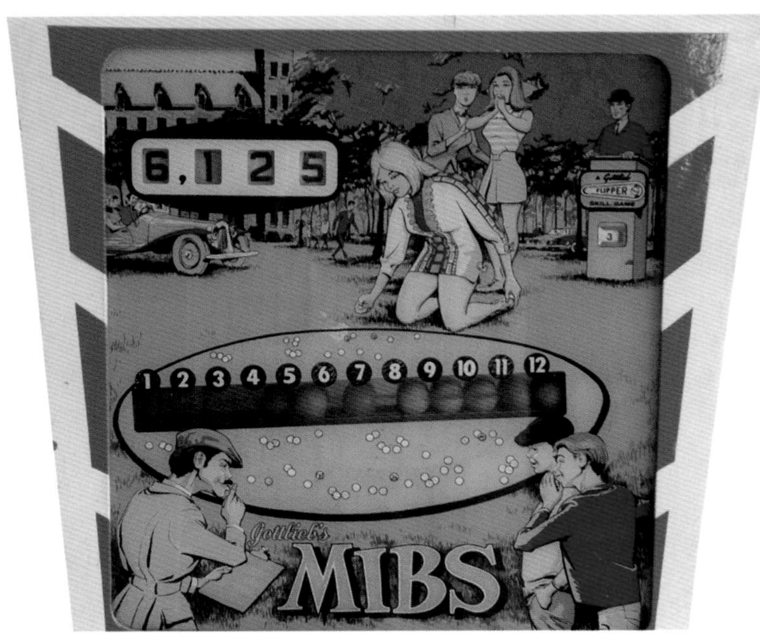

Left & above: Mibs. *Scott Gray collection.* $1200.

By the end of the 1960s, we see pinball machines becoming more challenging to players. The introduction of the 3" flipper gave the player better ball control. Add-A-Ball games had exposed pinball to many areas where they had been previously outlawed. Pinball artwork also changed with the times; the artwork in this period was more angular and symbolized the psychedelic era. By the end of this decade, pinball machines were being exported all over the world on a larger scale and people loved them, as they were another form of American entertainment.

Gottlieb staff meeting, c. late 1960s. Left to right: Wayne Neyens, June Dyla, Robert Smith, Judd Weinberg, Nate Gottlieb (Dave's brother), Alvin Gottlieb, Bill Koehler, Cliff Strain, and Gus Vrettos. *Courtesy Wayne Neyens.*

CHAPTER FIVE
KEEPING THE DREAM ALIVE

There are many collectors, restorers, authors, and other pinball enthusiasts who are keeping the dream alive. I have had the privilege of knowing many of them for years or getting to know them while writing this book and would like to share their stories (and dreams) with you here.

A PINBALL MUSEUM

I mentioned earlier in the book about helping Alan Tate set up a pinball museum on the Gold Coast Australia. I am very good friends with Alan and his family and will be there for him when his dream becomes a reality. I have asked Alan to share his story:

My first memory of pinballs and amusement machines was on holidays in 1960 with my family. It was an early baseball game located at the Chevron Bowl, Surfers Paradise. I can still remember my fascination with the animated backglass and standing there watching other people play, not having enough money to play myself. (Sixpence a game was a lot of money for a ten-year-old back then.)

From that point on my love for pinballs was born and many days were spent trying to make my own games in the back shed.

Eventually, after marriage, children, working, and many years, my interest was rekindled and I purchased my first pinball machine – a 1984 Jacks to Open. While enjoying modern pinballs I still desired to own an early machine and on inquiring around Queensland I was told that "all those old machines had been scrapped and were worthless anyway." I then realized that my dream probably would not eventuate and another period of inaction transpired.

Alan Tate standing in front of a few of his machines, which will be on display in his museum in the future.

The actual commencement of my madness followed my wife's trip back home to Canberra in the early 1990s, returning with a N.S.W. trading post. In it was an ad selling some early machines. I couldn't believe my luck and on phoning the number my friendship with Michael Shalhoub began.

Sheds and garages full of wonderful old amusement machines – it was like being in a sweet shop, so amazing, and a man so enthusiastic and passionate about pinballs that it was contagious.

As the collection grew thoughts of building a working museum (the dream) resurfaced. A place where people could view history and acknowledge the pioneers and escape from reality into a land of fun and wonderment.

At this point in time the land has been purchased on the Gold Coast, Qld. but many more machines need to be acquired and of course the building erected. I am eternally grateful to Michael Shalhoub and his wonderful family for all their assistance in making my dream come true.

—Alan Tate

PINBALL COLLECTORS AND ENTHUSIASTS

Pictured next to a 1940 Genco *METRO* is great historian and collector Russ Jensen. This machine is one of Russ's favorites, mainly because of Roy Parker's "city of the future" artwork, its unusual bell-shaped bumpers, and advanced play features such asthe "build-up bonus." I asked Russ if he would help me by providing some photos of the great men behind the pinballs that have made them what they are today. It was also through Russ that I made contact with Steve Kordek, Wayne Neyens, and Harvey Heiss, three of the greatest designers in the history of the game.

Since making contact with these three legends I have been tremendously encouraged and hope that what I have written about them honors their achievements in the industry. Russ has done a lot of brilliant work – he has written pinball articles and researched pinball history. Before becoming interested in pinball machines, Russ had an interest in electrical things (his father was an electrical engineer in the telephone industry). It was here that his knowledge of electrical circuits started.

When Russ was twelve years old, he was on a quest for electrical parts and this led him to the shop of coin machine operator Glenn Catlin, of Montrose, California. Russ asked if Catlin had any spare electrical parts, but instead of parts he was given two pinball machines, Variety and Vogue, both manufactured by Bally in 1939. After setting up the machines in the garage and using his electrical knowledge, it wasn't long before Russ had both games up and working.

Other kids in the neighborhood played these games and, after asking Russ where he got them, they went and saw Mr. Catlin. He gave them a Chicago Coins Majors of 41 and a Genco Victory. Since they had no electrical knowledge however, Russ was called upon to get these machines going and thus started repairing pinball games.

Russ has been involved with pinball machines ever since. His most memorable moment associated with pinballs was when he met the great pioneer Harry Williams and interviewed him in 1978.

Another friend of Russ's was the great pinball historian, Richard Bueschel, who sadly passed away on the April 18, 1998. His work will never be forgotten, as he was another great man who dedicated so much time to this wonderful game.

If you need troubleshooting help on how to repair electromechanical pinballs, you can email Russ at rusjensen@aol.com, or check out his great site at http://members.aol.com/rusjensen.

Russ Jensen pictured next to his favorite pinball, Metro.

I have met many people from around the world who collect pinball machines. One of these is Barry Gooding, who I met at the Chicago Show in 2000 and who has some great machines in his collection. Here is his story:

I bought my first pinball twenty years ago and it was not long before I was hooked. Owning a great game is satisfying, however the hunt and the people you meet are half the fun. I tell everyone that I collect pins and vintage arcade games, resulting in some great finds. A couple of years ago a neighbor told me that he had found a "Ping Pong Machine" for me. It was a 1952 Gottlieb Happy Days in very good condition that had been in the same home since the 60s. My cousin found my 1952 Gottlieb Coronation in an older gentleman's home. Coronation had been a gift from his brother in 1954 and was in excellent condition.

Not all finds are in nice shape. 10 Strike was a basket case, taking almost two years to restore. A couple of years ago I had a pin for sale on Mr. Pinballs web site. I received a phone call from Michael Shalhoub saying that he would take the game. At this point I thought to ask where he was located...Australia! Unfortunately, shipping was not possible and the game went to the U.S. Michael was not about to be discouraged and I was able to sell him a few games the following year.

Sometimes you are lucky to find that rare and valuable game. I work for Dow Chemical and was meeting once with a technical rep from one of our suppliers. As we completed our business I mentioned that I collected pinballs and gamers items. He had a stunned look then said, "I have an old Coke machine." When I went to look at it, I couldn't believe it – it was a nice working Vendo 44 that was added to my collection.

—Barry Gooding

Barry Gooding in his gamesroom.

Ron Coover resides in Pennsylvania, where he collects United bingo machines. To complete the collection, Ron still requires these seven: Bolero, Circus, Leader, Tahiti, 3-4-5, Touchdown, and Zingo. If you have these machines, please contact me at pinballmaster@ozemail.com. I asked Ron to share his story:

Ron Coover, with part of his United bingo collection.

The game I am standing beside is one of the many I have. I don't really have a favorite game but if it says United bingo, I like it. I started playing bingo machines when I was twelve years old and purchased my first game when I was sixteen – it was a Bally Broadway. That was about the time they outlawed them in Pennsylvania. When I was in my early twenties I decided I wanted to specialize in United bingos only. I have been picking them up ever since. I am now fifty-eight so you can see I have been at it for a long time. I now have twenty-two different games so I only need seven more to have every one. I have lived in south central Pennsylvania since I was five. I graduated in 1960 and started my own business in 1965.

—Ron Coover

There are pinball collectors all around the world, but none like Tim Arnold from Las Vegas. Tim was born in February 1956 and grew up in Minnesota and Michigan; he has one of the largest collections of pinball machines, with over one thousand in his collection. Tim sees himself as an operator with an appreciation for pinballs. He has managed to collect every Gottlieb game – his last being Bone Buster, which he acquired in May 2000. Growing up, Tim didn't play pinballs till junior high and then started playing them on a regular basis in high school. One of the first games he remembers is a Gottlieb Baseball made in 1970. He also prefers the Gottliebs from 1965 till the end of the electromechanicals in 1979.

Tim Arnold, standing in front of part of his collection.

Tim started operating pinballs and gum machines while still at school in 1972 and has managed to keep his first four games that he started with. They were ThoroBred 1965, Mayfair 1966, Royal Guard 1967, and Dixieland 1968. When I asked Tim what he considered to be a great game he replied "Machines that made a lot of money." Tim opens up his collection twice a year for people to come and enjoy; he believes that his machines are there for all to appreciate. At his open house, people from all over the world come to play the pinball machines. He also has a series of videos that all pinball enthusiasts should own; if you would like to purchase these you can write to him at 2620 S. Maryland Parkway 241 Las Vegas, Nevada 89109. Tim is an amazing guy and I hope to meet him one day as we both have the same passion at heart.

Shay Assad has one of the best collections of woodrail and wedge head machines in the world. Shay is a retired Executive Vice President of the Raytheon Company. He held many positions of responsibility with Raytheon including Chairman and CEO of one of its largest subsidiary companies, RE&C. He is presently the President and CEO of his own International Consulting Company and resides in Massachusetts. It was a pleasure making contact with him for this book and I have asked him to write a few words about how he got started collecting these classic games.

My fascination with pinball started back in the mid 1950s. I was born and raised in an inner city section of Fall River, Massachusetts named "The Flint." My parents owned a small restaurant in the neighborhood and, as is necessary for anyone familiar with the restaurant business, they were there seven days a week.

Now, if you are working seven days a week and you have a hyperactive kid (me!), what do you do with him? The answer was easy. Find a milk crate, put him in front of a pinball (the restaurant got a new Gottlieb every two months), give him a bunch of slugs and let him play away! In addition to my parent's restaurant, there were ten other stores and restaurants in my three block neighborhood where pinball could be played. It was pinball heaven in the 1950s and 60s! That's how it all started.

In the early 1990s, I started to get the urge to recreate some of those childhood dreams. I have been on the hunt ever since. My collection focuses on Gottlieb games from 1949 through 1965; Williams games, including baseball pitch and bats, from 1953 through

Shay Assad standing in front of a few of his machines. Notice the woodrail "Flipper" on the left, a very rare game.

1960; and mannequin bowlers (10 strikes). (I must confess that I have a few of the new ones: Adams Family Gold, Medieval Madness, Cactus Canyon, Theatre of Magic and Tales of the Arabian Nights).

As with most of us, I ran out of space and concluded that there was only one answer. Find a place where the games could be displayed. That resulted in the acquisition of a building, which I guess you could call a quasi-museum on Cape Cod, Massachusetts. The showroom floor houses about 125 games from the era (set up and running) at any particular time, and I rotate the displayed games through every so often. Basically, the collection is complete, with over 95% of the games in Class 1 original condition. Now the fun begins!

The jewels of the collection are: Mermaid, Flipper (woodrail cabinet), Gin Rummy, Niagara, Four Belles, Knockout, Mystic Marvel, Jockey Club, Green Pastures, and Williams Army-Navy. I do have duplicates of several games (always need trading material). My favorite player of all time is a 1955 Slugging Champ.

I would like to say that my wife shares my love of the games but that is not exactly true. Don't get me wrong, she enjoys playing them but she rightfully has interests of her own. Actually I am the luckiest guy in the world. I have a beautiful wife and three great daughters. All of whom have learned to tolerate Dad's obsession (OOPS I mean love) with the silverball!

—Shay Assad

I met Jeff Grummel a few years ago when he was on the lookout for a Buckaroo. I tracked one down for him but he had managed to find one in his state of Western Australia. I remember he swapped a 1958 Turf Champ for it. One of his favorite games is Rainbow, with its hippie inspired artwork. This is a one of a kind machine that was repainted at Sydney's famous Luna Park in the late 1960s during the Aussie artwork explosion. If anyone knows the history of this particular machine please contact me. Jeff is another mad collector and here is his story:

I can remember quite clearly my first encounter with the pinball machine. It was in a delicatessen in Pooraka South Australia. There were four machines in a row: Ice Revue, Heat Wave, Central Park, and Buckaroo. The first pinball I ever played was Buckaroo. What I remember though, being a little kid, was how cool it was to see the horse buck and spin the cowboy on the machine – that's where my obsession began. I fell in love with pinballs and like most fellow pinheads played them on the way to school and coming home from school. I have fond memories of those days; I even remember the day one of the locations got a Flash pinball – the sound blew us away – then Gorgar, what a spinout, the machine talked to you. Does life get any better than this?

I must confess when video games came out I found myself playing them and drifting away from pinballs. A few years later the bug hit me and the memories of playing Buckaroo came back. I was re-living my childhood, I was back in John's Deli playing the game. I thought I could make a phone call and would have my choice of ten Buckaroos – how wrong could someone be. At first, this was the only machine I wanted – I never intended to collect pinballs, although I was shocked to find out how scarce a Buckaroo was. I decided to start buying machines until one came up. The first machines I bought were Crosstown and Apollo and I had bought over twenty machines before I found my Buckaroo. You couldn't wipe the smile off my face, I was so happy. Today I have about 130 or so pinballs and arcade games in different stages of repair, including three of the four pinballs that got me hooked. I'm working on an Ice Revue at the moment.

—Jeff Grummel

Pinball collector Jeff Grummel in front of his Rainbow.

One of the greatest delights of being in business has been seeing the joy that pinball machines bring to people. I met Troy Meredith a few years ago and he has since bought a few games from me. When he first saw part of my collection he was totally amazed and bewildered. Here is his story:

Pinball collector Troy Meredith in front of two of his favorite machines.

Growing up, I would visit the local pinball parlor and play games like Spirit of 76 and Volley. I remember older games there as well, but they didn't appeal to me as the flippers were smaller. Those were the days – I only wish I had a time machine. Well, the seventies and the eighties flashed by and I lost interest in pinballs.

In 1992, I was on holidays with my family. We rented a log cabin in the bush and the farmer's back shed had two old pinballs in it – not running of course. One was a Slick Chick and after seeing this machine I contacted the farmer, asking him if he wanted to sell it. He said no, they have been in the family since 1969. It brought back so many memories that I wanted my own pinball machine. Years went by and still in the back of my mind I was thinking, I'd love to get one of those old pinballs.

Finally, in February 1998, I got my first pinball: Sorcerer by Williams. I still wanted an old clunker, however, and found out that a couple of local blokes had some old pinballs. After hassling them both for a while, one finally sold me my first mechanical pinball, Gottlieb's Top Score, in June 1998. The day I brought it home I played all night. I kept admiring the score reels, the 100 pop bumpers, and the chimes. I knew that night I wanted more – I had the bug for more pinball machines, as this was my new hobby. I had the urge by now for a 1960s pinball, so first I traded a Kiss for a Bally Dixieland and a '70s pinball. I finally got my first '60s pinball, buying a Gottlieb's Flying Chariots from an auction in Melbourne. I was on my way. Since the early days (1998) till now, I have built up my collection to a happy medium. I have eleven '50s and '60s pinballs in my bar room and a 1961 Rockola wall jukebox. I also have a 1960s coke vending machine holding my cans of beer and three gun games from the '50s, but being the typical collector that I am there are more pinballs in the shed. Of course I don't have the room to set them up but I couldn't bear to part with them.

Now I'm trying to convince my wife that the bar room is too small (9 meters x 4 meters) and that we may have to extend it – priorities, priorities. I still have my Top Score pinball as I think I could never part with it; it was my first pinball and has much sentimental value. As for the old farmer with the Slick Chick, I chased him up and he had given it to his son. I still visit him asking if he wants to sell it yet ...perhaps one day.

—Troy Meredith

Del Reiss is a pinball enthusiast. He owns Bumper Action Amusements, located in South Melbourne, Australia. Del was born in December 1951 and his love for pinball started at the age of thirteen. He has been in the pinball business for twenty-nine years, helping with the resurgence of the game mainly in the home market. I first met Del in the late 1980s and have been friends with him ever since. He sees pinballs as a lifestyle: "They're about skill, poise, timing, courage under pressure, and of course massive amounts of sex appeal." He has one of the best set-ups in Australia, with over two hundred machines from different eras set up in his showroom. He also sells all types of pinball parts and accessories. Del started "Pinball Faith" in October 2000, where pinball enthusiasts meet on the last Friday of the month to have fun and play pinballs. You can find more information at his website, www.bumper.com.au.

Del Reiss from Bumper Action Amusements with one of his favorite pinballs.

A good friend of mine, John Edwards, has been collecting games for a few years now, I can still remember getting a call from him asking to buy some machines. Every machine that he wanted I had; the day he came to my dad's place I had pulled out Gigi 1964, Central Park 1966, and Queen of Diamonds 1959. I can still remember the expression on his face when I rolled up the garage door. We have become good friends and I asked him to share his story:

It all started when I was in fifth grade during a school trip to a lakeside resort just outside of town. I think it was an excursion to see the "Hume dam spillway" which flows into the "Murray River."

At the end of the tour, we were allowed to visit the resort store and I remember going to the back of the shop where the ice-cream counter was located. I heard some bells ringing. The sound was coming from behind a curtain of streamers to the side of the shop. I had to investigate the source of this noise and made my way through the streamers to find four pinball machines in a dingy little room with no lighting or carpet. I was instantly attracted to the rosy glow of the machines and had to have a game. There were two kids playing the two games which only needed a 10c coin: a Gottlieb Aquarius and King Kool. The others (a Gottlieb Kingpin and a Williams Klondike) required 20c to play. I decided I would wait for one of the 10c games to be vacant. Twenty cents back then was a lot of money.

My parents decided to buy me a pinball machine when I was twelve. It was a King of Diamonds, which had been kept in a storeroom in a seedy pool hall above a shop in the main street of town. There was a Solar City and Bronco operating (current machines at the time) in a corner where the King of Diamonds had stood with a Swing Along pinball some years earlier.

Eventually I tired of playing the game and it was sold for $120. I forgot pinball for a long time and if it weren't for a Solar City that I stumbled upon in an auction room at age 24 in 1992 I may never have bothered about them again. It had been years since I played this game but memories of the fun I had on the game came flooding back.

I thought it would be a novelty to own a pinball again and casually asked about the price. I expected a price of around $200 and was shocked to hear a figure of $450.

I didn't buy the game but a seed was planted and I started wondering what ever happened to all those old games we once played. I went straight to the newsagents and looked in the Sydney trading post under amusements. I found an ad for pinballs for sale. I rang the number and spoke to a guy (the author of this book) who would soon show me some games older than any I had ever played and which were much more attractive. I went mad on these older games (1960s) and bought seven games in one hit.

One game I bought was a Gottlieb Gigi, which I asked for because I remembered it from a book, "Pinball portfolio," which I read as a kid. I traded the game not so long after and have regretted it ever since. I currently own eighteen games, have owned many different games over the years, and have a few ideas on why I prefer some games to others.

Playing games at home now is completely different from playing as a kid in an arcade. To me the thrill

Pinball collector and friend, John Edwards.

is not as intense but I still get a lot of satisfaction from beating a previous high score. For this reason, I much prefer add a ball and multi-player games that favor completing a sequence or knocking down targets to increase a score. I have no need to win a special. I can just trip the coin door micro-switch if I need to play another game. The other thing about home pinball that makes it fun is getting together with friends and competing. I always try to buy games with good scoring features that make for good competition.

Nowadays, beating a machine's hi-score or an opponent is, to me, what pinball is all about. It is different from pinball playing as a kid but I still capture some of that misspent youth every time I play.

—John Edwards

I am indebted to a very good friend of mine Michael Bowden who helped me put this book together. I helped him track down a machine he had played in his teens.

I met the author five years ago as I was in the market to buy a pinball. I finally persuaded my wife that one was needed in our home. The one machine I remember playing was Flying Chariots. It took Michael nearly a year to track it down. It sits in my game room next to the Indiana Jones.

—Michael Bowden

Michael Bowden with one of his favorite toys.

I first met my good friend Jason Douglas in June 1985 when I was on a quest for buying pinball machines. I went to his house and bought all the machines he had for sale: a 1955 Deluxe Slugging Champ, 1960 Lite-A-Card, and 1976 Pioneer. When I first met him we had so many things in common that we clicked straight away. His mother Nora is a great lady whom I am very close to. I don't know how many mothers would put up with pinballs in their bedroom. Jason and I have worked together for many years and between us have sold and repaired more machines in the home market than anyone else in Sydney. I asked Jason, a self-confessed pinball junkie, to share his story with me:

Jason Douglas on the right with Jeff Skews on the left, in one of the many rooms in Jason's house full of pinball machines.

I was born in 1960 and grew up in Newcastle, New South Wales. I remember playing my first machine at the age of seven at Tony's milkbar in Hunter Street. I don't remember the name but I remember my father getting a Coke crate for me to stand on. It was here that I fell in love with pinball machines.

My parents bought me a pinball machine for Christmas when I was 14 years old. It was a Bally Star Jet, which I still own today. I remember riding my pushbike for miles to play these games. When we moved to Sydney my heart was shattered as the removals broke the backglass. If anyone reading this has a backglass to this machine please let Michael know. I have over 300 pinballs in my collection, my favorite being the electromechanical Gottliebs from the 1950s to mid 1960s. I recently had an auction and sold over 120 of my games to make room to set up the classic machines. I have known Michael for a few years now and wish him all the best with the book. I also look forward to Alan Tate opening up the pinball museum on the Gold Coast Queensland.

—*Jason Douglas*

Bruce Thompson is a pinball collector who also sells once in a while. He attends the Pinball Expo and the Chicago Show on a regular basis and here is what he had to say about his hobby:

My earliest memories and first attractions to pinball started in 1971 on a northern Wisconsin camping trip with my family when I was 8 years old. We spent the rainy days at the campground lodge where you could eat pizza, play pool, hear the jukebox, and play pinball.

The first pin I ever played was a 1969 Gottlieb, Mini Pool. All the Wisconsin pins were Add-A-Balls, as state law prohibited replays as awards. I remember the thrill of hearing the "clunk" when completing the sequence and winning a free ball. I recall also playing Playmates, Card Trix, Flipper Pool, and Williams Klondike, BigStrike, Alpine Club, and Doodle Bug back in those early

Bruce Thompson with a North Star he has just purchased.

days. I purchased my first machine back in 1980 when I started my first job at age 17. I called an ad in the local paper and brought home a 1949 Gottlieb College Daze. College Daze was the first woodrail I had ever seen. I spent many hours tinkering with that machine and really had it playing great.

I bought Roger Sharpe's "Pinball" book at a local bookstore at that time. By 1980, Sharpe's book was on the discount rack at $9.99. It is still my favorite pinball book to this day as it showed so many of the EM pinballs I remember in their original environment. My space for collecting pinballs has always been limited but I have bought, sold, traded, and enjoyed several machines over the years. My interest in collecting pinballs tapered off in the early 1990s and I pursued other collectibles for a while, then returned back to the hobby in 1998. I can't say that I have a favorite machine at this point but I really like the machines from the late 1950s through the early 1970s.

—Bruce Thompson

Robert Young was born in 1952 and started playing pinball machines at the age of twelve. He grew up on a farm in a western suburb of Sydney, Liverpool, then his family moved to Newcastle, two hours south of Sydney. He remembers his mother asking him to go the shops to buy some milk. He went, but not after putting up a little protest. As soon as he discovered the shop had a pinball, however, his mother began wondering why he took such a liking for going to the shops. For Christmas 1991, Robert purchased a 1981 Dennis Lillee pinball machine for his children. As soon as he got it home he wanted more, especially the older mechanical ones. It wasn't long before his collection grew; today they are his pride and joy.

I have done business with many Americans in the past few years and have found them to be extremely friendly, trustworthy, and a pleasure to work with. I met B.J. Cunningham this way and found him to be a great man who has helped me out tremendously. Here is his story:

The first time I remember playing pinball was in a small local cafe as a boy in the 1960s and I immediately felt the lure of the silverball. Throughout my teenage years during the '70s I played as often as I got the chance. Although I played the early video games, my true passion is for 60s and 70s mechanical pins. I purchased my first machine in 1977, out of an old pool hall not far from home. It was a Williams Pretty Baby and we have played thousands of games on it; it is still part of my collection.

From my humble beginnings as an owner, I met a retired repairman who taught me to work on games. As I fast became addicted to the satisfaction of bringing games back to life, my collection grew and I have refurbished and sold many games over the past ten years. I enjoy the pleasure of sharing my love of the game by selling and allowing others to play my games. I readily share my knowledge with anyone willing to listen.

My collection now includes many classics – Kings & Queens, Buckaroo, and twenty others. I love them all so would be hard pressed to choose a favorite, but I play the Bowling Queen most often. Although I have plenty to play, I am still searching for the next great find ... perhaps that elusive Midway Whirly Bird that still is not part of my collection that I played as a teenager in the dime store. Hunting for the games is most rewarding, and they often have stories to tell.

This hobby has allowed me to meet many people and travel to many places, and has contributed to many happy hours with my family and friends. With a basement full of pinballs you always know where your children and their friends are, which is what pinballs are made for – to entertain.

My father has often related a story of his youth as a paper boy who spent all his nickels in the pinball machines and I have carried on the family tradition. As I purchased my first game prior to being married, my wife of 23 years has accepted my disease and my children have grown up surrounded by the bells and whistles. I hope that they will always have a pinball machine in their home, to remind them of their dad.

—B.J. Cunningham

Pinball collector B.J. Cunningham with some of his favorite games.

I met Paul Brisbane a few years ago and am good friends with him today. With three rooms full of pinballs in his house and even some stored in the garage, he has run out of room and his dad won't let him collect any more pinballs. Instead, he now collects tin toys and Coke memorabilia. Every time I see Paul he has bought something new. Here is his story:

My love of pinball machines started from early childhood and I had always wanted to own one. In early 1992, I answered an advertisement in a trading post paper and contacted Michael. I couldn't believe what I saw walking into his showroom– my past had come back to life and I wanted to buy all his machines. I eventually settled on a Gottlieb High Hand and bought my sister and her family a Williams Space Mission. As I got to know Michael, my collection grew and I now have over twenty in the collection today. I also collect Coke memorabilia, and tin toys. I have had a few electronic machines in the collection, Playboy, Mata Hari, Flash and Sinbad, but eventually traded them in for the mechanical ones as they were always giving problems.

I remember once Michael delivered a Gottlieb Solar City that I had just bought and it had a few problems. Instead of asking Michael to fix it I thought I could do it myself. I think by the time I finished with it, it was in worse condition than it was when I started. Michael eventually got it working. I love the artwork on the older games and at the moment my favorite game to play is Pioneer. The machine that I love the most is Buckaroo, as it was made the same year as my birth and growing up my nickname was "Buck."

—Paul Brisbane

Paul Brisbane standing next to his favorite game.

In all my years of collecting pinball machines, I have never seen a *HURDY GURDY*, the Add-A-Ball version of *CENTRAL PARK*. Pete Frasciello, who resides in New Jersey and has been collecting pinballs for over ten years, does have one, however. Here is his story:

Just like all pinball collectors, I remember vividly playing pinball at a very young age. It was at the Jersey shore for me. My brothers and I would save our nickels to spend hours in the arcade. I started out collecting jukeboxes in the late eighties but soon became addicted to pinball. I have been hunting down pinballs in the New Jersey area for over ten years and the thrill for me is the great finds like a Marble Queen, Poker Face, Wild West, three Humpty Dumptys or the Hurdy Gurdy pictured next to me here. My favorite game is Gottlieb's El Dorado. I have obtained over 150 pinballs in the last decade from residential homes and have met some very interesting people, as well as many other collectors this hobby would not be the same without!

—Peter Frasciello

Pete Frasciello with his Add-A-Ball version of Central Park, Hurdy Gurdy.

Another person keeping the dream alive is Gene Cunningham, who has one of the largest collections of pinball machines in the world.

Gene was born in Bloomington, Illinois, halfway between Chicago and St Louis. He started playing pinballs at the early age of eight and it wasn't long before he was hooked on the silverball. Gene's collection began some twenty-six years ago, when a pinball machine in his roller rink was taken out of service. Gene asked the operator what they were going to do with the machine. He was told it was going to be reconditioned, then sold to the home market. He bought the machine and has been buying them ever since. That first game was a Williams Strato-Flite; in one year he had bought six pinballs and a jukebox. He soon outgrew the garage and the machines were then kept in the barn.

Pinball artist Dave Christensen (left) with Georgia and Gene Cunningham.

In 1983, Gene broke his hip; it was then that he sold off his gun collection and started buying even more machines. "When the bug hits you, you lose control," he explains. I can definitely relate to this. Gene then built a 21,000 square foot building behind his house to keep his machines in. He bought the pinball company Capcom after it ceased operating in December 1996. He also purchased the remaining inventory from Alvin G when they closed down and the Williams/Bally parts when those businesses ceased trading. He has over seven million parts in stock today. Another business Gene bought was Tag Silkscreen; he hopes to soon reproduce backglasses and plastics on the playfields.

In April 2001, Gene held an amusement auction in Illinois and over 630 games were sold. This created a little space in Gene's shed, but he still owns over 1000 games.

Ron Tyler bought his first pinball in 1954 while he was still at school. He is a pinball enthusiast who attends pinball shows with his good friend, historian and collector Russ Jensen. I have asked Ron to share his story:

Ronald Tyler in his gamesroom.

I began playing pinball in the early 1950s. A friend and I would go to bowling alleys, service stations, malt shops, and other places that had pins. I don't remember the names of any, but they had projection for replays and had flippers. I recall playing Humpty Dumpty in a small café when it first came out. We could play for hours for a few nickels. It was 5 balls for 5 cents then!

I actually purchased my first pinball in 1954 from a classmate for $20. It was a Williams Dew-Wa-Ditty (1948). It worked when I got it but ended up being totally dismantled when it quit (sad). Through friends, Russ Jensen and Richard Conger, I purchased a Dew-Wa-Ditty in 1985 for $200 and it is now in my game room with my other thirteen pinballs. It was missing the projector replay assembly, but I got one from Steve Young.

From about 1960 to 1975, marriage and higher education took all of my time and pinball was essentially forgotten. But in 1975, with my wife's encouragement, I purchased a Stoner Davy Jones (1939). The backglass was shot but two students painted me one, which served well. It was through this game that I became close friends with Russ Jensen. He came to my house and taught me how to get the game up and running. Russ and I have worked on dozens of games since then. We shopped out some for Ed Burton in exchange for a few games to keep for ourselves. Russ has taught me most of what I know about working on pinballs. His book on their repair evolved from much of our troubleshooting various games. We still do some of this for people.

I have had a hundred or so pinballs go through my hands and presently own fourteen. They range from 1948 to 1987. I prefer EM but have two solid state games (Williams Flash and F-14 Tomcat). I have a large game room which my wife "encouraged" me to build. In it reside these fourteen pinballs, jukeboxes, gumball machines, signs, Coca-Cola signs, light up clocks, a penny scale, and a cash register. They afford much fun and relaxation for my friends and me.

—Ronald L. Tyler

When I started collecting pinball machines I met Tony Mather. He had a few machines for sale, and me being the type of guy I am, I bought all of them. I remember looking at his 1960 Rifle Range that he had which he regrettably threw away. Every time I mention it to him he replies "stop talking about it as it makes me sick," for the machine today is worth a lot of money. I have asked him to share a few words about his love for the game:

Tony Mather in his game room.

Writing this was great therapy, as it took me back to my childhood growing up in a seaside town called Bulli, south of Sydney, Australia. I have been actively collecting now for twenty-four years, long before it became a hobby. My dad was the one who turned me on to the silverball, as he played all the classics of the 1950-60 era growing up. Now I have passed that onto my own children, who get a huge buzz playing the same games I played with my dad.

I was longing for my very own pinball arcades. My mum bought my first game in 1977 as a reward for getting good grades at school. That game was a mint non-working Buckaroo for AUS$30 (US$15), not a bad first machine, and how those finds are long gone.

So I started my collection...through High School I built up a great collection of pins ranging from a 1959 Gottlieb Miss Annabelle to a 1977 Gottlieb Centigrade 37. One clear memory I have as a child was when there was a school swimming carnival. A group of us had other ideas: we would sneak up to the beach kiosk and play pinball instead of swimming. We would all take turns watching for a teacher while the rest played. This place always had about twelve really well maintained electromechanical pinballs. As a side note, have you ever noticed the wonderful smell these old games have when you open them up? Or is it just me? Without doubt my favorite place in the world is playing pinball with my children.

—Tony Mather

John Williams was born deaf and cannot speak. He resides in Sydney Australia. His whole life revolves around pinball machines. He is self taught and is a "Pinball Wizard."

Paul Sides with his lovely wife Deanna, the lovely couple who opened their heart and home on my last trip to the States, for which I am forever grateful.

REPAIR AND RESTORATION

Lee Feldwick and Gordon Williams are good friends and have known each other since the early 1990s; they met through pinballs and have formed a close friendship. Together they formed "Pinball Rescue," putting Australia on the map for reproducing playfield plastics and backglasses. If you need a set of plastics or a backglass, they can be reached at www.pinballrescue.com or write PO Box 611, Burleigh Heads, QLD Australia 4220. I have had the pleasure of meeting these two great guys and asked them to share their story:

After adding extensions to our house, the section off our poolroom had enough room for a bar and maybe something else, maybe about a pinball? I had always had a keen interest in things mechanical, especially older cars, and when we added the extensions to the house there was enough room for a few cars. We were not pinball freaks by any stretch of the imagination. My wife Lesley and I had always enjoyed a game of pinball, whether at the pub, the milk bar, or the movie theatre, but did not know anything about the collectability or history. We made some enquiries and ended up at a local business that sold and repaired older machines; after a couple of weeks of umming and arhing we settled on a Bally Kings of Steel. A great first game and although we sold it in less than a year we still have fond memories of it. The first few games we bought were solid state machines, but as I got more involved in the hobby my preferences turned towards the older machines – probably because I could repair this type of pinball – although Lesley still prefers the newer ones like Dr Who and Next Generation.

Over the years we have had varying amounts of machines, at one stage around forty, but we've kicked the habit a little since then and we're down to around twenty (but have branched out into other arcade games and jukeboxes). Since the very first pinball, I have always looked at ways of restoring the artwork, whether it was the backglass, cabinet, or playfield, so when my friend Lee Feldwick suggested that producing playfield plastics might be an interesting project I didn't hesitate at all. I had been doing repro backglasses and plastics for myself and friends for a number of years. As I had a printing business with all the necessary equipment, it seemed like a logical step and so Pinball Rescue was born. The rest as they say is history...As far as pinballs are concerned today, I am gradually replacing my solid state machines with electromechanical and hopefully woodrails. It is amazing how working on artwork from the older machines gives you a greater appreciation for the technical skills of the era; even today with the help of sophisticated computers it is difficult to produce a product of comparable standards.

—Gordon Williams

My story starts as a young boy always fascinated with the games that were in the pinball parlors. My family traveled from Sydney to The Entrance on the New South Wales Central Coast of Australia most weekends when I was young. The main street of The Entrance, which was then a quiet little holiday town, had three amusement parlors: The Esquire, Humphrey's, and Full Of Fun – all busting with fascinating games. Money wasn't plentiful then but I always remember begging my mother to let me have a game on the shooting machine because this was the only machine I could use properly– it had an old milk crate that I could stand on and see the targets. These amusement arcades all had one thing in common: an older machine in the rear of their shops where most of the games were still ten cents; this was especially a good deal. Humphrey's was my favorite. It was an old shop even back then and the block next door had several large trampolines that you could play on for twenty minutes for ten cents. Humphrey's attracted me most for the older machines – they had such a large variety of them. If I had only known then what my future was to behold, I would have probably tried to buy the machines right then as I walked around on those old wooden floor boards.

Gordon Williams and Lee Feldwick, holding a reproduced Nags backglass.

As I grew up around this town, I watched my favorite machines being replaced by electronic solid state pinball machines, then the Space Invader era, and so on, with all these newer machines standing where once my original games of skill took prime place. My enthusiasm was given a large boost when my parents bought me a Lost World pinball machine in 1980, which my friends and I gave a real working over every day for years. I still proudly own the Lost World with its original rubbers from new. Buying and restoring American cars was one of my hobbies. It wasn't long until my interest really took hold and I had to own another pinball, jukebox, and anything else I could put a coin in. I married my wife Jenny in 1993 and we moved interstate to Queensland. We had left the machines behind in Sydney but it wasn't long before we had them sent to us. From that day on our lives have been a huge collecting spree: we have traveled near and far in search of that classic machine, whether it be a jukebox, pinball machine, or any other sort of coin operated amusement machine. I have often said that I could write a book telling the places I have been and the people I have met. The year 2000 saw Jenny and me travel to the U.S.A to experience first hand the Jukebox and GameRoom shows in Chicago. Pinball was not forgotten in this trip, for we traveled across to Las Vegas to Tim Arnold's home to see his large collection and then to the Pinball Wizards Convention; this is where the inspiration behind the idea to reproduce pinball playfield plastics came into play. Travelling home with these great ideas in mind it wasn't long before I was teaming up with long time friends and collectors Gordon and Lesley Williams and "Pinball Rescue" was born.

Gordon and I spend countless hours making our products the best that they can be: checking and rechecking artwork, always trying new methods and new materials. We hope that our contribution to the pinball fraternity is helping to save more and more pinball machines from being parts machines and helping them instead to be part of someone's proud collection.

—Lee Feldwick

Steve Young, from "Pinball Resource" (pbresource@mail.idsi.net) has supplied parts to collectors and restorers of pinball machines all around the world. I asked Steve a few questions about himself and his hobby:

I grew up in Pleasant Valley, New York (about seventy-five miles north of New York City). The first machine that I remember playing was Williams Cabaret; I was at college and the year would have been 1971 or 1972. The following year I bought my first game: a 1952 Williams Palisades. In my collection today I have approximately 340 machines: one from the 1990s, one from the 1980s, about five from the 1970s, about twenty from the 1960s, and the balance from 1947 to 1960.

I asked Steve when he first met Gordon Hasse:

It was about 1978...Gordon answered an ad to purchase some Gottlieb woodrails I had gotten that were duplicates. We hit it off and have been associates since. We did the Pinball Collector's Quarterly in 81-82, a number of reprints, and so far, the first two volumes of The Encyclopedia of Pinball by Dick Bueschel.

I asked Steve when he started Pinball Resource and what inspired him to start it:

It started in 1991 after I had been running the business informally for many years...It just kind of happened...I needed parts to do refurbishing of games that I was buying and selling, had difficulty in buying parts, and wanted to keep some inventory so that each machine didn't create a need to order parts...soon others found that I had parts and things grew. When I retired from IBM in 1992, it was still my intention that the business remain a part-time "hobby" but it wasn' t to be...with the closure of Gottlieb. We acquired production machinery, parts, and rights and needed a space bigger than my house (which was housing over a million parts). We moved into commercial space, hired two more people, and then the hobby kicked into high gear...Now we have over ten million parts in stock, five people working here, and constant eighty hour weeks. With the closure of Electrical Windings, we have begun to set up a coil winding department, so the saga continues.

I asked Steve what was his favorite machine and what era of pinballs did he favor:

We never answer this question...haven't played them all! Favorites include Queen of Hearts, Happy Days, Coronation, Twin Bill, Comet, Whitewater. The era of games that I prefer: 1952-1957 Gottliebs.

I asked Steve to add a little about Richard Bueschel, who was a very good friend of his:

Richard is very much missed...he was a remarkable person, probably the preeminent industrial historian who related developments in industry to the popular culture in a unique manner. A big void that Gordon is working at filling (and doing a good job!).

—Steve Young

Herb Silver, owner of Fabulous Fantasies Inc. (www.fabfan.com), has operated his business since 1988 and has been incorporated since 1992. Today, collectors from all over the world contact him when they are restoring their classic games. Herb's company carries a large selection of reproduction pinball and arcade game backglasses and is working on playfield Mylars that will bring more pinball games back to life.

Born in Los Angeles California, Herb has been a pinball collector since 1972, when pinball machines became legal to operate in California. That year, he bought his first brand new pinball game, a Bally Fireball, which he operated at a local college. One game turned into two and continued on until a hobby turned into a collection. The collection theme has changed many times over the years, ranging from Bally pinball games of the 1970s to low production and prototype games. At one time, Herb's collection of prototype games numbered over eighty and was one of the finest in the world. Some were one of a kind. The games were featured at the four Pinball Fantasy Shows in Las Vegas and California, which Herb also created and ran.

Besides running Fabulous Fantasies, Herb has written articles and columns for various magazines and newspapers, such as *Pingame Journal*, *Pinball Trader*, *GameRoom Magazine*, *Buzz Magazine*, *TWA Flight Magazine*, and the *Los Angeles Times*. He has also contributed to many of the pinball books available today, as well as helped and supported The Pinathon in Sacramento and Pinball Show in Phoenix.

Herb Silver, Slash (Guns N Roses) and Dino Danielli. *Courtesy Herb Silver.*

I have purchased backglasses and parts to restore my machines from Steve Engel at Mayfair Amusement (www.mayfairamusement.com), another individual helping to keep the flame alive in the pinball world. I have asked Steve to share his story:

I first got involved in pinball while I was in college, I bought my first machine, a Centigrade 37, for $150 and set it up in my dorm. From that moment on I was hooked on pinball. When I graduated, I started operating machines during the video game boom of the early 80s but my real interest was with the silverball.

It was in 1986, during the Pinball Expo, that I started getting involved in parts. Gottlieb set up a booth and was selling off their backglass inventory. At the end of the show, they had sold a total of 48 glasses and 33 were bought by me. I made a comment that they should make me an offer on all their glasses and they took me seriously and said OK. Three months later I was the proud owner of 1,300 pinball backglasses and the rest is history. During the next few years, the stock grew to over 5,000 pieces, most of which were brand new. By the early 90s there was an increased demand for Gottlieb glasses from the early 60s, yet even I had few of those in stock. We decided to look into the possibility of reproducing glasses faithful to the way they were originally made.

Mayfair Amusement was the first company to offer reproduction glasses to the hobby and we showed collectors that if they supported us we would supply them with quality reproduction parts. We have gone on to include schematics, paperwork, circuit boards, and a host of hard to find pinball parts for both the collector and pinball enthusiast.

—Steve Engel

Pinball collector Mark Jackson with his wife, Kerry.

I met Mark Jackson a few years ago when he was on his quest for buying pinball machines; it didn't take long before his house was full of them. I have never met anyone who restores games like Mark – every single contact is cleaned. The man is a fanatic, one of the best pinball restorers in Australia. We are good friends today and here is his story:

When Mike Shalhoub told me he was doing a pinball book, I was very happy. Mike has a real love of pinball and as the Australian story is yet to be told who better to do it? He also asked me if I would write my own story down. Here goes.

I was nine, going on ten years of age before I saw and played my first machine. It was a Gottlieb "Sweethearts." I was immediately mesmerized by the lights, the ringing of the bell, and above all by the way the ball seemed to fly around everywhere. Nowadays, a few lights and one bell seem tame, but in 1963 it was like a magical symphony.

There were other places and other machines that I played from 1963 to 1970. I played after this time through to the electronic age as well, but in my mind there is a cut-off point around 1969-1970 in pinball. There was a turning point back then for me. The three-inch flipper came along and so did drop targets and lots of other stuff but to me something had changed. The games just weren't the same.

In my collecting life I have learned about the phenomenal combination of Wayne Neyen's designs with the quintessential and unequalled artwork of Roy Parker. I loved Roy's art when I was a kid and I love it more now. To me, Roy Parker art is pinball.

Now we're in the year 2001 and I've been collecting and restoring machines for over ten years. The places I have mentioned are mostly not around now. I'm glad to play a small part in the preservation of these wonderful machines. In a world of division, politics and strife I take comfort from the words stamped so clearly on so many machines…"For Amusement Only."

—Mark Jackson

Since 1960, Bob and Eileen Borden have owned and operated Borden' s Home Amusements (www.bordens.com), which is located in Morrisville, Pennsylvania and specializes in the restoration of pinball machines and juke boxes. Over the years, Borden's has sold and reconditioned thousands of pinball machines, juke boxes, shuffle bowling alleys, video games, foosball, air hockey, and pool tables, and their showroom always has two hundred or more items from the 1930s to the present day in stock. This company is a great resource for pinball collectors and enthusiasts.

Rob Carruthers with two of his favorite pinball machines.

I first met Rob Carruthers in 1988 as I was trying to sell a pinball machine to him. We are very good friends today and love the occasional pinball and snooker challenge. He is a "Pinball Master" and here is his story:

I am forty-five years old and for the first twenty years of my life I lived at Allawah, a southern suburb of Sydney. The first pinball I ever saw was in the local fish & chip shop when I was five years old. I can't remember the name of the machine, but I know it had light up scoring. At first I would watch other people play. The owner of the shop had a fruit box for kids like me to stand on and play the game. Every day after school, I would go to the shop and see if anyone was playing or, if I had any spare money, I would play myself. This became a ritual and I was hooked on these games. I left school at the age of seventeen and started working as a trainee electronics technician.

My parents sold the house at Allawah and moved to the adjoining suburb of Hurstville. This did not stop me from going to Allawah and playing my favorite machines. The first pinball I bought was a Gottlieb Big Shot, made in 1973. The original plan was to change the playfield and create my own design, but this never eventuated. I finally got the machine going but decided to sell it, using the money to buy two more machines. With these two I ended up with four. I was now in the pinball business.

I advertised in papers, wanting to buy games. I would repair and clean them and eventually sell them. In early 1988, I got a call from Michael Shalhoub wanting to sell me a game. We met shortly after, and when he came over to my house he walked in and bought all the games I had for sale. Mike was buying pinballs all around Australia; he would bring them over to my house to be stored and then repaired. It was from this point in time that I concentrated on just repairing machines. I am still repairing machines to this day.

—Rob Carruthers

PINBALL EXPO

Rob Berk has been playing pinball machines since the age of five and has a passion more for the older ones. In 1985, he staged the first Pinball Expo and since then has continued holding them annually in the pinball capital of the world, Chicago. Rob had four of the greatest pinball designers attend the Expo at one time; they were Norm Clark, Harvey Heiss, Wayne Neyens, and Steve Kordek. I asked him what inspired him to hold this event and he replied "I wanted to honor my heroes." I asked Rob to share his story:

It began as a dream. As a member of the pinball club of Akron Ohio, it was enjoyable to play pinballs with other members. But what about a convention where we could meet other players throughout the United States who shared our enthusiasm for this sport? I proposed the idea many times at our monthly meetings, but not until I joined forces with Bill Kurtz did the Expo begin to take shape.

It was 1984, and the results began to pour in from a questionnaire Bill and I had worked up. These results, which were gathered from subscribers of Steve Young & Gordon Hasse's "Pinball Collectors Quarterly," confirmed that there was indeed an interest in a national gathering of pinball enthusiasts. With this fact confirmed, Bill, Mike Pacak and I put our heads together and Pinball Expo was born, held in Chicago on November 22-24, 1985. The dream continues...

—Rob Berk

Rob Berk, host of Pinball Expo, and Roger Sharpe. *Courtesy Russ Jensen.*

A photo of some of the pinball legends who attend the Expo. This is the only place in the world where so many come together.

John Osborne, Wayne Neyens, Alvin Gottlieb, and Michael Gottlieb (Alvin' s son), answering questions from the audience at Pinball Expo. *Courtesy Russ Jensen.*

Alvin Gottlieb giving a speech at Pinball Expo. *Courtesy Jim Schelberg PinGame Journal.*

Wayne Neyens, Steve Kordek, Alvin Gottlieb, and Norm Clark having their photo taken at Pinball Expo. *Courtesy Wayne Neyens.*

Pinball Expo recognizes the great work of all the artists and designers in the industry. I will quote what pinball historian and collector Russ Jensen wrote about his experience at the first Pinball Expo back in 1985 (he has also attended every one since then): "One of the thrills for me was to finally meet, in person, many people I had only 'met' by phone or correspondence over the years. The opportunity to finally associate names and faces; I loved it! The other great thrill was to meet so many of the industry greats I had only heard or read about. I had known the late Harry Williams and he was great! I discovered, while meeting with and talking to the other industry greats at this show, that they were all so friendly, and just all-round good people, just like Harry. To me it was like having the 'multiple' Harry Williams' all in one room. I loved that too!" I can relate to this I too have spoken with the majority of designers and artists who have worked in the industry and who attend the Pinball Expo.

Two great artists, Jerry Kelly and George Molentin. *Courtesy Russ Jensen.*

One of the past guests who sadly won't be there any longer is George Molentin. I asked a friend of his, Roger Sharpe, to write a little tribute to this great man:

He was an artisan who plied his craft with a subtle flair. At a time when pinball was becoming more firmly entrenched in the public's consciousness, George Molentin was at the forefront of bringing themes to life and providing personality to mechanical wonderments. He was a man for his times, with a deliberate artistry that spanned decades. And, when all was said and done in looking at his body of work – those who celebrate the marvel of pinball, celebrate George Molentin, whose passion and talent remain timeless and inspired.

—Roger Sharpe

Rob Berk has many guest speakers attending, so a Pinball Expo could be your chance to meet and shake hands with some of the greatest designers and artists who have worked in the industry. The show is educational, entertaining, and enlightening for all who attend. For more information on Pinball Expo, please write to Rob Berk at 2671 Youngstown Road, Warren Ohio 44484, or call him at (in the United States) 1-800-323-3547 or 330-369-1192. For those wishing to exhibit, call exhibitor chairman Mike Pacak at 330-549-2596.

Steve Kordek and Harvey Heiss at the Pinball Expo 1986. Rob Berk surprised everyone when he presented a Triple Action pinball machine, designed in 1948, to Steve Kordek. This was to honor his great work in the industry. *Courtesy Harvey Heiss and Steve Kordek.*

Chronicling Pinball: Authors and Publishers

I had the pleasure making contact with Roger Sharpe, author of the 1977 book, *Pinball*. He has inspired so many people with his work, and continues to do so today. I asked Roger to share his story:

I grew up pinball deprived. Although Chicago was, and still remains, the pinball capital of the world, the machines were actually outlawed and so my exposure to the delights of the silverball had to come later in life. In fact, it was probably because of this that my life was inexorably altered as was the ultimate fate of the machines themselves.

I began playing while away at college at the University of Wisconsin and truly fell in love with the machines. Although I was terrible at the start, I did manage to devote enough time to improve my skills and to begin what has been a lifelong fascination with the games.

Ironically, once enchanted by pinball I found myself embarking on a professional career in New York City, where, amazingly, pinball machines were banned. And so it was famine to feast to famine for my pinball affliction. But due to this void in my life, there was also a desire to own a machine and it is this fundamental fact that has had its greatest impact.

I was in a position to write a feature story for Gentlemen's Quarterly where I was Managing Editor and, hence, the fable unfolds. I began a quest to learn all that I could of the pinball industry and attended the MOA trade show back in 1975. I began to meet the notables who had actually helped to shape the fortunes of pinball – Harry Williams, Sam Stern, Steve Kordek, Gordon Horlick, George Molentin, Bill O'Donnell, Herb Jones, Bill Gersh, and the list goes on and on.

The result was a feature story on pinball for the New York Times and suddenly the opportunity to chronicle everything in a book. With the able assistance of a remarkable photographer, James Hamilton, and the desire to leave no stone unturned, we began what would be a three year odyssey to gather information, undertake extensive interviews, travel throughout the United States as well as Europe to capture all that we could.

The events that followed – actually prior to the release of PINBALL! (E.P. Dutton) in 1977 – was my testifying in New York City, before the City Council, to help get restrictions overturned after more than three decades to allow pinball machines to be operated legally in Manhattan. I was the expert witness in 1976, but more so, I was the expert player who would be called upon to demonstrate why pinball was a game of skill and not chance.

The outcome, as they say, is history. New York City opened its doors to pinball thanks, in no small part, to my efforts. There were other court cases where I lent my support and, finally, also in 1976, Chicago as well left behind a drought of over 35 years to legalize pinball machines.

My good fortune was such that I could count an entire industry as my friends and also to savor the opportunities bestowed upon me which allowed me to design machines – one of which, SHARPSHOOTER II, is one permanent display in the Smithsonian Institute.

I never would have imagined that my life and pinball would have become so entwined, but truly, I would not change any of it except to have seen the industry not abandon something that I feel so passionate about and an attraction that is so unique. But, I remain the optimist, and know that no matter what else may come or go, there will always be pinball machines somewhere for intrepid players to challenge and enjoy.

—Roger Sharpe

The team that made the *Encyclopedia of Pinball* series possible are Gordon Hasse, Jr., the late Dick Bueschel, and Steve Young. Author of the books Richard M. Bueschel sadly is not with us today; he has inspired me in so many ways with his passion for the game. He first started assembling materials in the early 1970s to write a multiple volume of pinball books. He was a major historical resource, contributor, and consultant to a number of books that have been written about pinballs. I never had the opportunity to speak with this legend, whose credentials for writing about pinballs are unmatched. He has inspired so many people with his devotion to a game that he remembers playing in 1932 when he was six years old.

I asked Gordon Hasse to share his story regarding his passion for the game and to pay tribute to the great work of Richard Bueschel:

Gordon Hasse at Pinball Expo. *Courtesy Jim Schelberg PinGame Journal.*

I'm not sure when I first recognized there was such a thing as pinball on this earth, but it was very early on. My first clear recollection of seeing a pinball machine must have been sometime during 1953 or 1954 while I was still in grammar school. The game was Williams 1952 Twenty Grand, which sat next to a Williams 1953 Deluxe Baseball in a greasy spoon called Sperl's that catered to trolley car drivers at the end of the #26 trolley line in the community called Fox Chase where I grew up in Philadelphia.

I still remember the day when I first screwed up all the courage a seven-year-old can muster and walked timorously through the rough adult crowd to put my buffalo nickel into Twenty Grand. It was love at first sight. I was bitten. Smitten. Fell completely under pinball's mesmerizing spell. And, once captivated by her alluring and promissory glow, never looked back.

But at such a tender age, there weren't many opportunities to be out and about alone. And on those few occasions when I was, the available pinball venues of the day were either too rough or forbidden entirely.

So my early progress into addiction proceeded in fits and starts. Until two family vacations in 1953 and 1955 took me to Florida. And opened the door to prolonged pinball play for the first time in the arcades of Miami's miniature golf courses and the now defunct Fun Fair (immortalized as a pin game by Genco in May, 1957 – possibly their very last pinball machine). While my memory of the individual machines is vague, I distinctly remember playing some of Gottlieb's 1947 and 1948 six-flipper "Fairy Tale" games as well as being confounded by Roy Parker's Finan Hattie (Haddie) pun on Barnacle Bill's 1948 playfield and backglass.

During the mid-50s, my family also spent several weeks each summer visiting with my aunt, uncle, and cousin at their vacation house in Beach Haven on New Jersey's Long Beach Island. In those days, visiting Long Beach Island was like stepping back into time. And much to my delight, the backwater character of the island and its attractions gave me a chance to play many pinball machines that had long ago disappeared from the larger world beyond.

At the Beacon Arcade (which still stands) I first met and fell in love with Gottlieb's 1952 Queen of Hearts, still one of my favorites. In the same arcade, sharing space with a long row of PTC (Philadelphia Toboggan Company) Skee Balls, I also encountered on location, for the first and only time, Gottlieb's 1950 Joker, 1954 Hawaiian Beauty, 1953 Marble Queen and United's 1951 Proto-bingo ABC. At a little hamburger stand across the road from my aunt's house, my brother Pete, my cousin Kathy, and I were privileged to make the acquaintance of Gottlieb's greats. A 1952 game, Coronation, Crossroads and Chinatown, their 1953 Flying High, 1954 Lady Luck, and Williams 1953 4-Corners – as one terrific "old" game after another passed through the tiny store.

There was also a good-sized arcade at one of the local miniature golf courses that fed our growing addiction. It was there that I first played Gottlieb's Arabian Knights and Guys and Dolls from 1953 and their earlier 1951 Watch My Line. It's also where I came face to face with a 1948 United Manhattan that had been retrofit with flippers. How could such a swell looking game feel so awkward to play, I remember asking myself at the time. Now, of course, I know.

Sporadic forays in other places quickly followed. A 1955 Gypsy Queen and a 1954 Diamond Lill, discovered one behind the other in a narrow candy store near my cousin Kathy's house in Philly. A 1955 Frontiersman in another candy store close by. Gottlieb's superb 1954 Mystic Marvel – the only one I was ever to play on location – found in a luncheonette across the street from Olney High School. A brand new 1956 Gottlieb Rainbow encountered completely by chance in an obscure, now forgotten location. A 1953 Gottlieb Shindig found languishing in a shoemaker's shop. So help me God! Furtive games, played on a 1954 Dragonette in defiance of my grandmother's wishes. A tired Williams Paratrooper, tucked into the darkened corner of a sub shop on Ogontz Avenue. But never enough to sate my appetite.

Then came the summer of 1956, when my pinball passions came completely out of the closet! It was a glorious time. A time consumed entirely by the pursuit and play of pinball machines. There was Gottlieb's 1955 Wishing Well and, later, their 1955 Twin Bill at Rita's Hoagie ("Philly" for hero or sub) shop. A brand new 1955 Easy Aces at Hoffnagle's Ice Cream store. Williams's first multi-player, 1955 Race the Clock, at Shaw's News emporium. A spanking new 1956 Classy Bowler, later replaced by an equally new 1956 Auto Race at Danny's Den. And three games in operation at all times in Buechner's candy store (most notably, my old friend Frontiersman with its 10 game specials) across the street from Woodrow Wilson Junior High School where I was to begin school in September.

That whole long summer of my 12th year was spent logging hundreds of miles on my bike. Pedaling to places with my pals in search of "new" machines and the friendly faces of old ones that had been snatched away prematurely from our favorite locations. We rode the ten miles or so to the now defunct Willow Grove Amusement Park. Once the proud summer host to the great John Phillip Souza's Band, the old trolley-park was in serious decline– its arcade reflecting the sorry state of affairs. But we loved it because we got to play some really "ancient" machines like Gottlieb's Madison Square Gardens and Rockettes, both from 1950, and their 1951 Minstrel Man. Games like those I had played on Long Beach Island. Games that had virtually vanished from the street and traditional locations. Games that were, in fact, even older than most of those I had discovered during previous summers in Beach Haven.

We even made the long bike trek across the Tacony-Palmyra Bridge, which separated Pennsylvania from New Jersey, to play pinball at a bowling alley just across the Jersey Line. Such was the hold that these clever and engaging machines had on our adolescent minds.

That winter, in a vain attempt to curb my growing habit, my parents bought me an old but very playable 1953 Williams Army Navy for Christmas 1956. Followed by a Gottlieb 1952 Happy Days the next Christmas and a Williams 1949 Star Series pitch & bat the Christmas after that.

Somewhere along the line, I added a non-working Gottlieb 1950 Just 21 to my growing collection. A gift from a school friend, I hauled it home in my wagon over the old trolley tracks before they were paved over.

As a result, by the beginning of 1959 I was personally awash in what I viewed, even then, as "ancient" pinballs. But watched with growing alarm the pinball world outside as the woodrail era I so loved ground steadily but inexorably to an end.

First came the metal legs, metal cigarette holders, and waffle-pressed metal flipper button surround plates. Then the banality of score reels replaced the time honored bulb scoring. And, finally, cold metal rails appeared in place of the warm, familiar, sweat-burnished wood ones. So that by the time I left for college in September 1962, my pinball affliction was in total remission. New games no longer held any interest for me, and the few old ones still on location were now buried in the deepest recesses of decaying inner city and seaside amusement arcades.

But the flame never died completely. For during the summer of 1963, while running an ocean front hot dog stand, my buddy John Blakely and I happened upon two tarpaulin covered pinball machines that were being stored on the second floor balcony of the Rio Grande motel in Wildwood, New Jersey. The treasures we uncovered were an aging pair of Gottlieb "woodies" which we purchased for the princely total of $50. We then made two, 150 mile round trips in my MG-A convertible to transport Gottlieb's 1950 Madison Square Gardens and 1954 Green Pastures to their new homes in Philadelphia.

I restored my Green Pastures, took it back to college with me in the fall of 1963, and placed it next to the bar in my fraternity house. Sadly, it was stolen from storage in the fraternity house basement the following summer. John kept his restored Madison Square Gardens in the attic of his parents' home while he was away at college and it went to neighbors when the house was sold. Having resurfaced briefly, the pinball monster lay dormant for more than a decade: through college, through graduate school, and seven years into an advertising career on New York's Madison Avenue.

About 1977, I became aware of a homegrown tabloid called the National Pinball Wizzard (News) which was being published by a guy named Pete Bilarczyk, the owner of Novel Amusements in Linden, New Jersey. Pete's pioneering effort had become a lightning rod for closet pinball collectors and players all over North America. And it was from the pages of the National Pinball Wizzard (News) that I learned of Steve Young and John Fetterman, two engineering graduate students and pinball collectors, who financed their hobby by placing their machines in the dormitories and fraternity houses of Bethlehem, Pennsylvania's Lehigh University. I also learned about Canadian pop-culture curator Wayne Morgan from the pages of the "Wizzard". During the mid 70s, Young and Fetterman contributed some of the earliest critical writing on the subject of pinball to the Coin Slot, a hobbyist publication that, at the time, was geared almost exclusively to slot machine collectors. And just a year or so earlier, Wayne Morgan, working closely with Canadian collector Pat McCarthy, had launched the first exhibition of pinball machines as kinetic art. The exhibit premiered at the Dunlap Art Gallery, the host museum in Regina, Saskatchewan, and then traveled to four more venues across Canada in late 1974 and early 1975 garnering record breaking gates and attracting worldwide attention.

While Young and Fetterman's woodrail articles were informed and highly informative, Morgan and McCarthy's nostalgic portrait of pinball's "Golden Age" of innocence in their exhibit catalog TILT! Pinball Machines 1931-1958 was absolutely explosive! Nothing short of a high voltage cattle-prod to my pinball pleasure center. In an instant, all the old passions were jolted into focus. And it was a short step from learning that woodrails still survived in the hands of private collectors to building a collection of my own. Ironically, the game that began my current collection proved to be one of the woodrail era's finest: a 1954 Gottlieb Dragonette, acquired from pioneer coin-op dealer Ira Warren at Antique Amusements when he was still doing business at 3007 Avenue K in Brooklyn. The next two games I purchased were from future friend and business partner Steve Young: a 1956 Gottlieb Harbor Lites and a 1957 Gottlieb Ace High.

Shortly thereafter, I decided I had to learn how to restore and maintain these complex machines. For if I intended to own them in significant numbers, which I surely did, then I had to become self-sufficient. Enter Cal Clifford: friend, mentor, owner, and sole instructor at Cal's Coin College in Nicoma Park, Oklahoma, where I graduated with a degree in "flipper game repair." As a result, I take pride in having the distinction of being the only living soul who holds degrees from both Cal's Coin College and the Wharton School of Finance and Commerce.

As of this writing, more than three hundred woodrails and nearly thirty years later, my most recent acquisition was a 1952 Gottlieb All Star Basketball, purchased from pinball collector and fellow Duke University graduate Orin Day in Durham, North Carolina. As my collection grew, so did my involvement in the hobby. During most of 1982, Steve Young and I published The Pinball Collectors' Quarterly. Though it lasted just four regular issues and two newsletters, it was the first dedicated magazine exclusively for pinball collectors.

I wrote and Steve delivered admirably (in my unavoidable absence) the very first Pinball Expo seminar on the opening morning of Expo #1 in November, 1985. The subject was pinball art and it focused on Roy Parker's backglass art for Gottlieb during the "Golden Age." Steve and I then went on to collaborate on several additional presentations at later Expos. At about this time, Steve began devoting full time to becoming the pinball parts vendor of choice for most of the world's collectors and many operators as well.

Meantime, in partnership with my friend, pop-culture guru Alex Shear, our company, The Nostalgia Brokers, staged New York City's first pinball exhibit in the lobby of Olympia & York's prestigious Park Avenue Atrium building. Our "Remember Pinball" tribute to the woodrails filled more than a dozen floor to ceiling showcases in the building's lobby and ran for three months during the 1993-1994 holiday season.

Somewhere along the way, Wayne Morgan and I addressed a joint gathering in Toronto of North America's two largest academic organizations for the study of popular culture on the subject of pinball art and design evolution. During the last several years I've written many articles on woodrails for my friend Tim Ferrante's excellent publication GameRoom, as well as serving as a contributing editor. And when the legendary Dick Bueschel encountered barriers with his publisher relating to additional volumes of his definitive history of pinball, Steve Young and I agreed to publish the six-volume Encyclopedia of Pinball for him under our Silverball Amusements marquee. Starting all over again from the very beginning.

At the time of Dick's tragic and untimely death, he has just completed two of the six planned volumes of the Encyclopedia of Pinball. In accord with Dick's wishes, I took on the added responsibility of completing the remaining four. An obligation I intend to discharge, however long it may take.

As I come to the end of my story, I would like to take a moment to pay tribute to Dick. For he was truly the most passionate pinball collector who ever lived. His collection of actual games was rather small. But the pinball knowledge he accumulated and shared so generously was vast indeed. Dick collected the history of the game, both factual and anecdotal, then wove it seamlessly into the rich tapestry that, today, is the fabric that holds the hobby together.

Let me close with the tribute to Dick Bueschel that I delivered during the banquet on the closing night of Pinball Expo 14 in 1998:

Gordon Hasse, Richard Bueschel, and Steve Young. *Courtesy Gloria Pullar.*

> I'd like to say a few words in behalf of a good friend who couldn't be with us here tonight. That good friend, of course, is Dick Bueschel. And the words I'd like to say in his behalf are that he loved this industry and this hobby and all the people in it. Especially those who are gathered here in this room. He found you open. And generous. And honorable. And a wealth of fascinating information. For once everyone understood what he was up to…you were supportive of his every effort.
>
> If Dick had had his way, he would have expired at a gathering just like this. In fact, I'm told, he had asked to be taken to the last Chicagoland Show on the very evening of his death. It didn't surprise me. That was Dick Bueschel. To say that he was bigger than life would have upset him. For he failed to see the distinction between whatever engaged his vast energies and talents and life itself.
>
> He was the consummate family man. Fiercely devoted to his beloved wife Helen, his two daughters Stacy and Megan, and their respective spouses. He was the consummate advertising man. One of the last of the great copy/contact giants who once dominated industrial advertising. An intrepid cold caller, fearless presenter, persuasive closer, and creative firebrand.
>
> He was also the consummate author. The inevitable result of being a voracious accumulator of things, people, and ideas. He was a tireless researcher. An incisive interviewer. A profound thinker. A highly disciplined and prolific writer. A man gifted with the talent to transform whatever touched him deeply into something incandescent. Whatever his subject. From World War II Chinese aircraft to ragtime composers to coin operated amusement machines.
>
> Though he avowed atheism, Dick had an unwavering faith in the goodness and worth of his fellow man. He was trusting almost to a fault. Routinely concluding important business and financial arrangements with a simple handshake. And though he spent most of his successful career in a business that has traditionally been stained by moral cowardice and personal compromise, Dick managed to emerge unmarked.
>
> Unjaded by the cynicism. Uncorrupted by the cynics. Someone less worldly, astute or centered might have been labeled a Pollyanna. But it was part of Dick's vast and engaging charm that he raced headlong into everything he did with rose colored glasses.
>
> His generosity was legend. And all you had to do to lay claim to huge amounts of Dick's time, knowledge, or experience was to be genuinely interested. The same was true of the things he owned. For if you loved something of Dick's, as much or more than he did…it was yours. In many cases as an outright gift. But always for far less than it would take for him to replace it.
>
> And that is the final irony and sadness of Dick's passing. That so many of the gifts he had intended to give us will never be conferred. We've lost an important advocate and a good friend at a time when the industry is struggling to redefine itself. Ultimately, there will be a turnaround. A new kind of pinball will be born out of vision, talent, and just plain guts that will take this great game and industry into the new millennium and beyond. That success will be the finest tribute you could pay to Dick's courage and to the great confidence that he had in all of you.
>
> —Gordon Hasse

Jim Schelberg publishes the internationally famous pinball magazine *Pingame Journal*. As he was growing up he never played pinball machines, but he was always interested in getting old things that were dirty and junky, cleaning them up, and getting them to work. Jim is a qualified podiatrist and runs his practice in Farmington Hills, Michigan. His wife Marilyn bought him his first pinball machine on his fortieth birthday; it was a 1959 Straight Shooter from Gottlieb. Jim found great pleasure in restoring this game and it led to a collection that now numbers more than fifty games. In his collection today are many classics from different decades, including Slick Chick, SkyLine, Gold Star and FireBall. Jim's favorite machine is Triple Action, made by Genco in 1948, because this was the first pinball to have two flippers at the bottom of the playfield. It was also the first machine designed by pinball icon Steve Kordek.

It didn't take long for Jim to make a name for himself collecting and restoring pinball machines. He had an ambition to reach out to other pinball collectors and did so when he began publishing *Pingame Journal*, which celebrated its tenth anniversary in May 2001. The magazine, which covers new games as well as classics, provides information on repair and restoration techniques, pinball events, and other subjects related to the hobby. Jim hopes that via his magazine he will contribute to the revival of pinball. Those interested in more information can contact him at 31937 Olde Franklin Drive, Farmington Hills, Michigan 48334-1731 or online at www.pingamejournal.com.

Jim Schelberg, editor/publisher of *PinGame Journal*, with one of his favorite machines.

I recently caught up with Chris Soulidis (lilkris@arcom.com.au) at a pinball auction. He is the only editor/publisher of an Australian pinball collector' s magazine. I have traded and bought pinballs from Chris over the years and asked him to share his story for this book:

Growing up a kid in the 1960s was an experience and an adventure. I'm sure other decades had special memories for everyone, but there was a change in society and the cultural shift from a predominantly British way of life in Australia was happening. Up till then it seemed every phrase that was spoken contained "God save the Queen."

But change was on the way. Amongst the Australian cars on the road there was always a good serving of Austin, Morris and Hillman's, but the GM cars are being assembled right here in right hand drive! What was to follow was an influx of the American Pop culture, as where my older sister still paid homage to her British upbringing I was reveling in the onslaught of U.S. television – like Leave it to Beaver, Gilligan's Island, Twilight Zone, Monkees, Banana Splits, Batman, and all those great Saturday morning cartoons.

I played pinballs every chance I could. In 1986 I married Lily and a few years later we had our first child, Evelyn. It was around this time that I caught up with an old work friend who mentioned that his uncle had just purchased a poker machine and a Williams "Lucky Seven" pinball from an arcade technician. He also mentioned that this guy had a real old machine that was in poor shape and that I would probably remember playing. I asked him if he recalled the name of the pinball and he said it was either "Sing a Song" or "Sing Along"! I jumped up as Gottlieb's "Sing Along" is one of my all time favorites, I played it when it was new at my friend's grandparents' Fish Shop in Chester Hill in Sydney and I absolutely loved it!

Now I must at least get to see this game, so I went around to talk to this guy and there it was – how great to see it again after twenty odd years, and really it was just the cabinet which was a little worse for wear. I had never considered owning my own pinball machine. How would I maintain it? Where would I keep *it? O.K., how much? $200 – I think to myself, is that a lot of money? Would you take $150? Deal done!*

Then one day whilst working from home I realized I had fifteen minutes to get to the bank before it closed. On my way I noticed I hadn't checked out that antique store in a while. So I pulled over and thought if I run over there quickly I can still make it. I opened the door, looked to the right, and there was an object that resembled a pinball machine, with an unusual amount of wood. It looked old and the name on the backglass was "Grand Slam," but no manufacturer. Incredible how something told me to go and check out the shop; weird forces at work here!

I made it to the bank, then went back to buy the game, I did some research and found out it was a Gottlieb 1953 woodrail pinball. I fell in love with it, but wondered why there was no identification – and to top it off, inside the head was stamped "Made in West Germany."

Totally perplexed by all this, I gave Gottlieb a call to shed light on the question surrounding this machine. They put me through to someone who had knowledge of the history of their games; I don't remember the gentleman's name, but what he said was most interesting. He explained that the Europeans, especially the Germans, were not happy with the games they were producing during the early days, so they would buy the American pinballs and remove any obvious trademarks and make them their own. This would explain how the game ended up in Adelaide because of the large German population especially in the Barossa Valley.

I began to appreciate the 50's games and started looking for them. I was lucky to find a few that weren' t snapped up as yet – it would be almost impossible to find them just anywhere now.

I haven't really looked for pinballs in the last five years or so; I guess I am happy with what I have. The other great thing to come out of this hobby is the circle of friends I have gotten to know around Australia and around the world. These people would always bring up the fact that the hobby is growing and what we are lacking is our own collector's magazine, so we can bring everyone together. Well I decided to embark on this challenge and started the "Arcade & Flipper Pinball Review" about a year ago, thinking that a quarterly publication would be often enough for Australia. The magazine has been very well received, even selling overseas which is unbelievable. I have attended two pinball auctions and I can feel the energy that this hobby is generating. It will continue to grow, with more and more remanufactured parts becoming available. It makes it easier to refurbish your favorite games.

Chris Soulidis, with copies of *Arcade & Flipper Pinball Review*.

I see the new guys starting out with the same "fire in the belly" I had, only there isn't the availability and the prices are much higher. Pinball may have changed with technology but still remains fundamentally a basic game of skill. It isn't generated on a video screen, it actually happens before your eyes and every game is different. Whether it was a game you enjoyed in your youth, or the game play itself, or the artwork that draws you, one thing for sure is that they were an integral part of my childhood – I can play my machines today and think back to a time that I cherish.

—Christopher P. Soulidis,
Editor/Publisher, Arcade
& Flipper Pinball Review

I asked Tim Ferrante, publisher and editor of *GameRoom Magazine* to share his passion for the pinball with me. Tim is a self confessed pinball addict and his passion for the game has made the magazine a huge success. He is one of many who keep the flame burning. Tim grew up in New Jersey and here is what he had to say:

Tim Ferrante, Publisher/Editor of *GameRoom Magazine*. *Photo courtesy of Jacq Ferrante.*

Michael Shalhoub, you amaze me! Taking on a project of this scope is certainly due high praise. So from one writer to another, you have my deep admiration. You also have my gratitude. In these silverball-filled pages, you've surrounded me with the top games and luminaries of the pinball universe. It's an honor to be in their company. It's an honor that's rarely bestowed. I thank you.

We all share an unusual passion, drawn to it like bass to a fisherman's lure. Spotting it, chasing it, and after taking a mouthful, the fisherman sets his hook. From then on, there will be no escape! In our case, the fishermen performed their angling from Chicago pinball factories, casting their lines wide and often. Placing their lures in taverns, bowling alleys, sweet shops, pizza parlors and arcades throughout the land. And in the year 1966 AD, at the age of 11, I swallowed a lure. It was Bally's BAZAAR, a wondrous single player featuring the world's first appearance of Zipper Flippers. I surrendered my free will there and then, permitting that beautiful piece of machinery to set its hook. It was a life changing moment. I just didn't know it at the time.

By 1969, my parents agreed to buy me my very own machine. I chose a Williams RIVER BOAT (1964) with its five pop bumpers and an exciting feature where you could score unlimited Specials during all five balls! That is, of course, if you had the skill. I still own RIVER BOAT to this very day. Needless to say, it sent me even deeper (and willingly) into the pinball abyss.

So, for the past 35 years I've been an unabashed admirer of the folks who created and built them. To put it a little more bluntly, I'm a pinball slob. An apostle preaching the word. A collector, a fixer, a restorer, a hunter and a writer.

Since 1996, I've had the delightful pleasure of supplying the world with a dose of pinball and other coin-op information via the pages of GameRoom, a monthly hobby magazine I publish and edit. GameRoom began in 1989 and the sudden passing of its owner resulted in me and my wife, Jacqueline, purchasing the magazine in September 1996. The topic of pinball is enormously popular and we've had the proud and esteemed pleasure to bring to the hobby some of the most fascinating silverball articles ever written. Many of which are authored by the great writers, designers and historians who lived and breathed them. I'm humbled by their presence and grateful for their friendship.

One such friend and author, Richard "Dick" Bueschel, was instrumental in steering the sale of GameRoom in my direction. His help was incalculable, his friendship unwavering. He passed away in 1998, but his influence on me and on GameRoom is long lasting. With every monthly issue, there is a part of Dick within it. It's subtle things, nuances and touches that few would recognize. Dick had bottomless enthusiasm and a warm spirit, and deeply respected the people within the hobby regardless of their place in the pecking order. There is no one out there that could replace him. He was unique.

GameRoom is light years beyond what it had been in 1996. It didn't have an e-mail address in those days even though it was simple to get one. Today, we have a feature-filled website with our own online coin-op book and merchandise store. We offer a show and auction calendar, an article archive, a photo gallery, a back issue department, online classified ads and hundreds of links with other pinball and coin-op websites. We're also the domestic distributor for two overseas magazines, Pinball Player (published in England) and Arcade & Flipper

Review (published in Australia). Both are fine publications that we're privileged to import and represent. Most notably, we published the world's first arcade video game price guide in 2001 in conjunction with ArcadeCentral.org. We've come a long way since 1996, so please pay us a visit online (www.gameroommagazine.com) or drop me an email: timf@gameroommagazine.com.

There is an old saying of which I'm quite fond. It applies to many other pursuits, but it happens to describe the passion for pinball so beautifully. It goes: "For those who understand it, no explanation is necessary. For those who don't understand it, no explanation is possible."

—Tim Ferrante,
Publisher/Editor,
GameRoom Magazine

STERN PINBALL

The decision by Midway, who had taken over Williams and Bally, to cease manufacturing pinball on October 25, 2000 marks the end of an era. Today, Stern Pinball is the only company manufacturing pinballs; the future of pinballs is in their hands. Good luck to Gary and his team as we all hope he can revive this pastime that has brought so much joy to many.

Gary Stern was born in 1945. He started working in the Williams stockroom when he was sixteen years old and has a lot of cherished memories. Under the tutelage of his father, Sam Stern, and Harry Williams he learned endless lessons about what makes flipper games profitable and fun. I asked Gary to write a little tribute to his father:

Working with Sam Stern caused me to know my father differently than his friends and differently than children normally know their parents. I knew Sam's weaknesses that others did not know, but more important I knew strengths normally unrevealed. Sure I saw some egocentric reactions like we all have, but I learned Sam's generosity of which others could have no idea. I knew truths of Sam where others sometimes knew only images he projected. Friends and children could not know a person the same as I knew Sam.

Likewise, Sam knew me for real. There is a limit to what can be hidden every day. It is a special and wonderful thing, to know a father or a son like that. Parents strive to teach their children, through example and through experience. Often the opportunity becomes very limited as one's children grow up and go out on their own. Spread their wings, they must. Because I worked with Sam every day, Sam's helping, teaching, and guiding continued as I grew older, yet without clipping my wings. Just knowing Sam as I knew him turns out to be an education about myself still cropping up today.

As you pointed out, sons are often more aggressive and fathers more conservative. Some of my youthful exuberance rubbed off on Sam, guiding and challenging him. This education of each other is special for a father and son that work together – it expands their lives. A fantastic and unusual example comes to mind. In my youthful, single days I was not an early riser. Knowing this and desiring to aid my acceptance of responsibility, Sam called me each morning. He could not call to wake me up. Sam arose at 6 each morning and thought of a new idea about our business; then he called me at 7 a.m. to tell me. We both knew the call was to wake me up, and some of the ideas were pretty harebrained. But some were exceptional. Imagine as I started the tasks of my day having a new idea about the day's work handed to me. Imagine the interesting exercise Sam had each day thinking of those ideas. Imagine how exciting our interaction – on some of those days with some of those ideas – must have been.

Parents have pride in their children. The pride of a parent working with their child is different - I don't mean better or greater, but more knowing. A businessman father is proud of the accomplishments of his son the doctor, the writer, the master mechanic, or even the businessman in another field. The pride is different when the father is there, in the same business, knowing the challenges and participating in his son's accomplishments. In recent years, when I hear a father talking of his son in the business, it brings Sam back to me. And the pride becomes a reciprocal, knowing pride.

My father has been gone since 1984. I continue to learn Sam as others could not know him. We all get more conservative as we get older. I appreciate Sam more each day, as I become more conservative with age and as each day in the pinball business I go through some experience that Sam had. While as a young brash son I might not have accepted something then of Sam, age and experience have often brought me the understanding to see strength in what I used to think was a weakness of Sam. You mentioned the business transition, its planning and the parent letting go. The father will worry what will fill his life. As I get older, I realize that Sam was thinking more of whether he prepared me, made education available and taught

Sam Stern in his office. *Courtesy Norm Clark.*

me himself. Sam, as any father, hoped he had left an adequate base and business, knowing a child will have to guide in his own direction. On reflection, that transition period gives me the highest level of respect for Sam.

The father-son working relationship often has difficulties, as you pointed out in your column. Sam and I avoided the mention of Midas, where the father became active again in the company and threw the son out. Once when I was a student working in the summer for Sam, I explained to my mother trying to wake me that Sam had fired me. She said she just rehired me and I should get myself out of bed and get to work. I guess Sam and I knew thereafter that we had to make our relationship work and rewarding. I would advise those fathers and sons going through any difficulty with each other in the business to try – if it works, there is no better ride.

I am a lawyer, not a doctor/psychiatrist. Yet I have to think that my special relationship with Sam must explain many things about me. What I learned of my father and from my father did not relate only to pinball machines. However, I know I will remain committed to making pinball machines not just as a business but as an expression to Sam.

I have said much of this to others in the years since Sam died. I never said it to Sam. Maybe I didn't realize until later the depth of that special father-son relationship that grows from working together. I want to express now, how much I loved Sam Stern, who I was lucky to know so specially. For those others who work together in family businesses, let me be presumptuous and say it about their families for them here too.

—Gary Stern

Gary Stern – the future is in your hands. *Courtesy Shelly Sax.*

CONCLUSION

Pinball machines are a unique form of entertainment. Writing this book I have had the chance to share my story and my experiences with you. Growing up and playing pinballs, I would always imagine who and what the designer was like. I wanted to know their stories. This experience has enabled me to contact some of the greatest designers and artists, people who I never, in my wildest dreams, thought I would speak to. I have written this book to revamp the interest in pinball machines and to honor my heroes. I would like to thank God for giving me the strength when I have needed it, and for the opportunity to meet so many wonderful people. And for the chance to write this book.

Let the pinball dream continue.

—Michael Shalhoub

My daughter Ashley, helping with the photos for this book. It took a week to sort them out.

BIBLIOGRAPHY

Bueschel, Richard M. *Pinball One: Illustrated Historical Guide To Pinball Machines Volume 1*. Wheat Ridge, Colorado: Hoflin Publishing Ltd., 1988.

Bueschel, Richard M. *Encyclopedia of Pinball Volume 1 and Volume 2.* New York: Silverball Amusements, distributed by The Pinball Resource, Volume 1, 1996; Volume 2, 1997.

Bueschel, Richard M. *Collector's Guide To Vintage Coin Machines.* Atglen, PA: Schiffer Publishing Ltd., 1995.

Colmer, Michael. *Pinball.* London: Pierrot Publishing Limited, 1976.

Flower, Gary, and Bill Kurtz. *The Lure of the Silver Ball.* Secaucus, New Jersey: Chartwell Books Inc., 1988.

Kurtz, Bill. *Arcade Treasures*. Atglen, PA: Schiffer Publishing Ltd., 1994.

Rossignoli, Marco. *The Complete Pinball Book.* Atglen, PA: Schiffer Publishing Ltd., 2000.

Sharp, Roger C. *Pinball.* New York: E.P Dutton, a division of Sequoia-Elsevier Publishing Company, 1977.